Anar,

I hope you enjoy this as much as I have! Chapter 4 is all about C100!

Thank you for helping us build Planet Canada!

Laura + the C100 team

PLANET CANADA

PLANET CANADA

How Our Expats Are Shaping the Future

JOHN STACKHOUSE

RANDOM HOUSE CANADA

PUBLISHED BY RANDOM HOUSE CANADA

 Published in 2020 by Random House Canada, a division of Penguin Random House Canada Limited, Toronto. Distributed in Canada and the United States of America by Penguin Random House Canada Limited, Toronto.

www.penguinrandomhouse.ca

Library and Archives Canada Cataloguing in Publication

Title: Planet Canada : why our expats are the key to our future—and the world's / John Stackhouse.
Names: Stackhouse, John, 1962- author.
Description: Includes bibliographical references.
Identifiers: Canadiana (print) 20190232889 | Canadiana (ebook) 20190232897 | ISBN 9780345815804 (hardcover) | ISBN 9780345815828 (HTML)
Subjects: LCSH: Canadians—Foreign countries. | LCSH: Cultural diplomacy—Canada. | LCSH: Canada—Relations.
Classification: LCC FC104 .S73 2020 | DDC 303.48/271—dc23

Text design by Lisa Jager
Cover design by Five Seventeen
Image credits: (Canada goose) © Justin Lo / Getty

Printed and bound in Canada

10 9 8 7 6 5 4 3 2 1

For Matthew and Lauren

CONTENTS

Introduction | The Eleventh Province

As I neared the end of a sweeping tour of modern Canadian history, I was met by a lone display meant to sum up our country's place in the world. It was a backpack. A rumpled one, from the 1980s, emblazoned with a maple leaf. Next to it, encased in Plexiglas, was a Canadian passport, and with it a heartwarming, if slightly syrupy, message about the maple leaf and how it's become, to the world, "a symbol that reflects positively and warmly on the Canadian wearing it."

The Canadian Museum of History in Gatineau, Quebec, across the Ottawa River from Parliament Hill, had placed the display at the end of an interactive tour of domestic events and achievements, as a way of showcasing some of the personal tethers we have beyond our borders. It struck me as a kind of gentle ode to the Canadian globetrotter—not the heroic peacekeepers, or celebrated astronauts, or movie stars on Hollywood's Walk of Fame, but the ordinary Canadians who set out to attempt some extraordinary things. There are plenty of them, certainly, who can be spotted almost anywhere by the Roots hat, Lulu sweatshirt and MEC bag embroidered with a little red flag. But after 150 years as a nation, I had to wonder, is this really how we see ourselves in the world? A nation of loveable backpackers?

Like Sean Mannion, the owner of the two items on display, I had travelled through Asia in the 1980s, as proud of the maple leaf on my backpack as I was protective of my Canadian passport. So I was struck by a photograph within the display that showed Mannion, in 1983, standing with two Americans he had met in Fiordland National Park, New Zealand. It projected that boundless, rugged affability the world sees in us, and we seem to assume is our national trait. But I figured there had to be more to him—a bit like Canada's place in the world—and decided to track him down. Mannion still lived in the Ottawa region, not far from the museum or where he was raised. He had grown up by the river, becoming a whitewater guide, a skill that would take him to New Zealand and then Nepal, India, Guatemala, Mexico and the western United States. In those days, when he was hitchhiking between rivers, he learned the maple leaf was his best ticket. People everywhere, he discovered, loved Canadians. They loved our sense of community, our respect for other cultures and our collective humility, which you can hear in Mannion's voice when he says "son of a gun" and "where the heck."[1] They open their doors to us because, as a country, we've opened our doors to them. As the museum display states, in an uncharacteristic burst of immodesty, "Canada is one of the world's most admired countries. Its reputation and public image reflect stability and compassion, natural beauty and political freedom. It is an extraordinary work in progress."

Unfortunately, in the decades since Mannion traipsed around Asia, a lot has changed. Our middle power status has eroded, leaving us to feel a bit like those kids in the middle row of a class picture. Necessary, nice and unnoticed. We're no longer the go-to nation for peacekeeping, or the reliable friend of foreign aid. On trade, we've been pushed around by the big kids in the back row of that class picture, while in business we've lost far more global head offices than we've built. But in that same period, something equally remarkable has happened. While Canada's share of global everything—GDP, defence, aid, R&D—has declined, our share of expat influence has grown. They've traded backpacks for briefcases and have started to shape the world and our place in it. In an age of communities and networks, powered by individuals more than states, they've become Planet Canada. These are the Canadians who aren't just visiting. They're living, working, studying and connecting abroad, increasingly as a diaspora. Some are well-known, like Mark Carney, formerly of the Bank of England and now leading the fight against climate change, or Lorne Michaels of *Saturday Night Live*, or Rachel McAdams of Hollywood fame. But most of Canada's two million or so expatriates are known only in their own circles.[2] They're Canadians, usually by birth, always by passport and often by association, but they're forgotten to Canada in terms of spirit and impact.

When I first went overseas in the 1980s, Canada was the model of abundance in a world shaped by scarcity. Like Australia, and a few others, we were the land of plenty, with educated people and prolific resources, along with the peace and prosperity that were so lacking elsewhere.[3] We were one of the only middle powers with connections to East and West, North and South. When the world opened its doors, we entered. But today, with abundance everywhere, the internet has given everyone access to everything. And there are a lot of everyones. The global population is adding a new Canada every six months, and on average, each generation is better nourished, educated and connected than when Mannion and our generation went abroad. That means that in the 2020s, there will be more countries brokering peace, building sustainable businesses, pursuing justice and human rights—in short, doing what Canada once considered its special role. Which means Canada and Canadians will need to imagine ourselves in the spirit of an Israel or Singapore, thinking less like a middle power and more like an entrepreneurial people, harnessing our global population to build our place in a more crowded and connected world.[4]

Sadly, we may be the only major country—or minor one, for that matter—that doesn't think strategically about its diaspora. We should start by recognizing that we have one, and reaching out to them, which is what our closest allies and rivals are doing with theirs. From Ireland to India, nations with global populations are increasingly turning to their diasporas for help, recognizing the decades ahead will be influenced by people networks more than power centres.[5] In a world of smart machines, stateless corporations and economic forces beyond the control of any government, those nations seem to realize such networks will be to the twenty-first century what naval fleets were to the nineteenth and multinational corporations to the century in between.[6]

I first began to appreciate our global population in the 1990s, when I became part of it as an overseas correspondent for the *Globe and Mail*, based in New Delhi. Over nearly eight years living and working abroad, pretty much everywhere I went there were Canadians forging interesting and important paths. Some were civic builders, designing a university course in Nairobi or engineering a pipeline across central Asia. Some were lone wolves, running trading operations in Jaffna or Kinshasa. Some were up to no good, like the Bre-X geologists in Indonesia or the Khadr family, whom I traced across northern Pakistan before 9/11. I knew most Canadians had always been seen, and welcomed, as good global citizens. But in that brief window between the Cold War and the War on Terror, as every corner of the world opened up, some peacefully, some through violence, it was evident that many Canadians—Louise Arbour, Stephen Lewis, Sergio Marchionne—were doing more than just going along. They were stepping to the forefront, to lead in ways that perhaps our country no longer could.

At the dawn of this new global age, the internet remade global commerce while cheap, easy air travel put more strangers in more strange places than humanity had ever experienced. Cheap, easy telecommunications kept them more connected, too, in ways we'd never imagined. As borders softened, and cultures melded, a new great migration took form. Immigrants headed west, and refugees headed north. At the same time, a new global class of migrants moved east and south, with a small clutch of Canadians in the vanguard. The academic and former diplomat Jennifer Welsh was among them, keeping one foot in Florence and the other in Oxford as she tracked the political upheaval caused by these movements, and the progress they could unleash. Entering the new millennium, and a new digital age, Canadians, Welsh felt, needed to reimagine ourselves, "to conceive of our country not just as Canada with a capital *C*—the corporate entity represented by the flag or by government officials—but also as *Canadians*."[7] This new Canada was one that could outgrow geography and transcend borders, projecting itself through its diaspora as a voice for principles and values, and an approach to community that the rest of the world was starting to lose in its tribal retreat to a smaller, older age of identity.

Historically, diasporas have been rooted in negative events—expulsions, pogroms, wars, any of the horrors that cause people to leave their homelands en masse. Their existence was captured in a simple word drawn from the Greek *diaspeirein*, to scatter. Once scattered to the winds, a diaspora had to find ways to come back together, through language, culture and a shared narrative, and to preserve a common identity that was often the only thing its members had brought with them. Increasingly, diasporas the world over have needed those strengths to absorb the shocks of nationalism and growing resistance, in places, to the very idea of newcomers. For most of our existence as a country, Canada was spared those conflicts by an orderly approach to immigration, a reasonable view of accommodation and a convenient distance from the world's troubles.[8] This combination has allowed Canada to attract diasporas from every corner of the world, stitching them together in an ever-growing mosaic. Ironically, we entered this century not appreciating we also had a diaspora of our own—a large mass of Canadians who had scattered, driven not by hardship, scarcity or fear but rather compelled by hope, choice and ambition.

Of all the Canadian expats who could make sense of this changing dynamic, Stephen Toope was among the most knowledgeable—as a student of humanity on the move and someone who had been on the move himself since the 1970s. Toope was born and raised in Montreal, an anglophone in the depths of Quebec's identity wars. He studied history and then international law at Harvard and Cambridge, developing in both places a more acute sense of Canadianness beyond language, province and hockey. He came to appreciate our instincts for mutual accommodation, and our ability to find strength in difference. He later became dean of McGill University's law school, president of the University of British Columbia (UBC) and head of the University of Toronto's Munk School of Global Affairs, where he encouraged me, as a senior fellow at the school, to research our diaspora. In 2017, he was appointed vice-chancellor of Cambridge University, the first foreigner in eight hundred years to hold the top position there, which put him among the most influential people in academia.[9] [10]

I went to see Toope at Cambridge in early 2019, to share some of the stories that follow and test some of my ideas against his own experience as a global Canadian in an age of pointed nationalism. To see the contrast, he only had to look outside his medieval campus, where Britain was tearing itself apart. The Conservative government was on the precipice of collapse, as was its plan to leave the European Union. Brexit wasn't just a shambles for Westminster; it had thrown Cambridge, like all British universities, into upheaval. Toope had barely unpacked when he found himself in emergency planning meetings to determine how the campus might cope with border chaos. Where would they get fresh fruit for the dining halls? Or water purification chemicals? Would European staff, be they professors or groundskeepers, be allowed to stay? And the research money that Cambridge received every year from the European Union, as it centralized academic funding to compete with the United States—what would be its fate?

A Canadian might not be able to stop Brexit, but a Canadian might help a place like Cambridge cope with the transition, and in so doing place Canada at the forefront of change. I put this idea to Toope, who deftly deflected it and turned instead to a story of his own return to campus, where he saw the value of Canada's amorphous global identity. He began the story by recounting what a colleague told him early in his tenure: "You couldn't do this job if you were American." Americans tend not to listen, the colleague explained, due to their deeply felt sense of national exceptionalism. Britons, Toope realized, were not much better, due to their deeply felt sense of class entitlement. Cambridge had produced some of history's great figures—among them Isaac Newton, Florence Nightingale, Charles Darwin and Jane Goodall—as well as Canadian leaders like future governor general David Johnston and business magnate David Thomson. But as the world around it changed, Cambridge was also deeply challenged, which was one reason it had turned to a Canadian. The university had spotted Toope's ability to mediate, and to bring together faculty, students and benefactors on an eight-hundred-year-old campus that functioned as a federation of colleges, each behaving at times like the baronies that once controlled them. "Devolved power structures is what we do," he explained. "Canadians have a tenor of mutual accommodation, of making conflicts or differences work. We're comfortable with a devolved structure of authority."[11]

The irony was not lost on him. Earlier in his career, Toope had helped create the Pierre Elliott Trudeau Foundation, a non-partisan organization to advance Canadian academia. He quickly became accustomed to connecting Canada with the world, and with Canadians around the world. But at Cambridge, with its students, professors and researchers from every continent, he saw less and less of Canada. At 160 or so, the number of Canadian students hadn't grown in years, while there were a lot more people from everywhere else. And for the most part, those other countries were keen to stay connected with their students and expat faculty. Even after his own celebrated appointment and a burst of initial excitement, Toope said he had little contact with the Canadian government, other than the occasional function at Canada House in London.

This is where Toope's story, and his thinking about our diaspora, turned positive, reflecting the opportunity for Canada that he sees from his global perch. As head of one of the world's great universities, he has sway over hundreds of millions of research dollars and, critically, in an age of networks, the choice of institutions Cambridge might work with. Enter Edwin Leong.[12] In 2018, during an outreach trip to Hong Kong, Toope met with the Hong Kong billionaire who had studied computer science at UBC in the 1970s and completed his masters at the University of Toronto (U of T).

After building a financial fortune through real estate, Leong had spent much of his time giving it away, largely through education, including scholarships for Chinese students to attend Cambridge, Toronto and UBC. His dream project was a massive medical research effort focused on the quality of human life. Leong felt medical research had failed to stitch together the phases of life, to understand the connections between pediatrics and geriatrics, and everything in between. He dreamed of the project through its proposed name, "100 Healthy Years," believing a century-long human life needed to be seen as one journey. The same collective thinking would be needed by researchers, he felt, which was why he wanted to include his Canadian alma maters, if he could get them to co-operate. Toope reached out to his former colleagues, Meric Gertler at U of T and Santa Ono at UBC, to explore how they could collaborate on the unprecedented research project Leong wanted to fund. None of them could do 100 Healthy Years on their own. It was remarkable that Canada was even in the conversation. If the Hong Kong billionaire hadn't studied in Canada, and if a Canadian wasn't running one of the world's top universities, the call probably would have gone elsewhere. Instead, the three Canadian academic leaders agreed to take on Leong's dream. Toronto would lead on pediatrics research, examining how early childhood development affects our health through life. UBC signed up to examine old age, and what influences our condition in our final decades. Cambridge researchers would bridge the two. The $90 million Leong volunteered for the project stands to place Canada, and Canadians, at the cutting edge of global research on human longevity, and it almost certainly wouldn't have been discussed without a global Canadian determined to make it happen.

As I left Cambridge, I realized this is what a diaspora could do for Canada. We just need to do our part to help them. We can start by acknowledging their strengths and numbers, and ensuring they have what they need to represent Canada in a very different time. In a digital century with fuzzy borders, influenced as it is by networks without official sanction, these expats can articulate a new global purpose for Canada. Many already are, through what they do as Canadians abroad. Detached from Canada the place, they're showing the world what it means to be Canada the people, without the backpack and maple leaf. An undeclared eleventh province, they're quietly shaping our global identity, and can do much more if we let them.

1

Outliers

WHAT IT MEANS TO BE CANADIAN IN THE TWENTY-FIRST CENTURY

Look for a pediatric surgeon in Boston or an international lawyer in Brussels, a deep-shaft miner in Mauritania or an oil rig operator in Malaysia, a country music writer in Nashville or a video producer in Mumbai—if they're foreign, they're more likely to be Canadian than any other nationality. At one point in the 2010s, the universities Princeton, Berkeley and Johns Hopkins were all run by Canadians, as was the Royal Mail, the Bank of England and Médecins Sans Frontières (MSF). Chris Cooter has spent most of his diplomatic career representing Canada on the edges of the global economy, serving in South Asia, West Africa and, most recently, as ambassador in Ankara, where he was always surprised to find Canadians in the unlikeliest of places, like a gold mine in central Turkey. "Per capita, I think there are more Canadians out there in the world than [people] from any other country," he told me. "Everywhere I've been, there's always a Canadian."[1]

Because the federal government doesn't track emigration the way it does immigration, we don't really know how many Canadians live and work abroad. There is no census of expats, or even regular surveys. Their whereabouts are known only if they volunteer their information, or their new home countries share data about the origins of residents. The United Nations (UN) Department of Economic and Social Affairs, which studies global population growth, once put the number of Canadian expatriates at 1.3 million, but that estimate did not include data from the hundred or so countries—among them, Ukraine, Bangladesh and most of Africa—where official statistics are unavailable.[2] The UN also counted only Canadian-born individuals, missing the large number of dual citizens from Canada in places like Lebanon and Hong Kong. In 2004, Alison Loat,[3] a public policy expert who splits her time between Boston and Toronto, produced a report for the Privy Council Office that estimated the expat population to be about two million, or 6.4 percent of our total population. That would put us on par, proportionately, with Italy and Australia, and well ahead of France, which says its global population is about 3 percent of its domestic population.[4] India's diaspora, which is among the world's largest and most influential, puts its international population at about twenty million, which is still only about 2 percent of the country's total number. In 2011, the Vancouver-based Asia Pacific Foundation of Canada commissioned the first major study of overseas Canadians and estimated there to be 2.8 million, with two-thirds of them in the U.S. and another 20 percent spread across Britain and Australia.[5]

To better understand Canada's global population, I led a research group at the Munk School of Global Affairs, which pulled together census data to estimate how many Canadians had left over the decades. We used median age and survival rates to figure out how many likely were still alive. The group's conclusion: between 2.98 million and 3.5 million. We then asked Facebook to screen how many of its users living outside Canada listed themselves as Canadian. The social network's number: 1.9 million. Given that many people do not list themselves on the platform by country of origin, and Canadians in restrictive places like China would probably mask their data or avoid social media altogether, the estimate seems to support the other studies that put the number in the two to three million range.[6] (While expats are traditionally defined as people living outside the country of their birth, the term increasingly includes "naturalized" citizens who immigrated to and then emigrated from a chosen country. For this book, "expat" refers to any Canadian citizen living outside Canada.)

Clearly there are enough Canadian expats to become a force. Trouble is, not enough make themselves known. Among the exceptions is Tyler Brûlé, the writer, editor and entrepreneur who in 1989 left Toronto for London to join the BBC, just as the Berlin Wall was falling, and then discovered in the years after the Cold War he was as much a citizen of the world as of Canada. Three decades later, Brûlé's company, Monocle, presents itself as a kind of troubadour of transnationalism, with an eponymous magazine, luxury guidebooks and podcasts designed for citizens without borders. He's added cafés and retail shops to sell clothing, books and other travel items to this aspiring global class in some of the biggest cities where expats congregate: London, Singapore, Hong Kong and Tokyo, and most recently Toronto to capture the growth of Canadians in his tribe. Brûlé calls them "a globally minded audience of readers hungry for opportunities and experiences beyond their national borders."[7] As he circles the world, advising global companies on their branding while he also builds Monocle's, Brûlé wonders why so many Canadians out there can't do more to make a collective statement, the way he sees the Japanese in Sao Paolo or French and Germans in Los Angeles projecting themselves. Even in his new home of Zurich, he's found an emerging international population—Australians, Americans, Britons, Swedes, Danes—who are rejecting the insularity of so many other global centres for a more confident global community in the digital age. All that's missing, he's noticed, is Canadians. "We tend to go out and scurry back home," Brûlé has found, wondering why his compatriots lack the boldness he injected into Air Canada's rebranding in 2017, when the airline ditched some of its maple leaf clichés for a more stylish, and sleek, black-and-white design that says to the world, "We've arrived."[8]

A better map of Canadians in the world would help. A better sense of collective identity—of Canada's place in the world—would help, too. Beyond wanderlust, what's the common thread of our eleventh province, the one characteristic that defines Canadians as Canadian long after they've left home? I put the question to every expat I could meet.

"It's caring and being interested in the rest of the world, which is what took me out of Canada," said Atlee Clark, an Ottawa-born digital specialist who helped launch the C100, a network of expat techies in San Francisco.

"Exotic but not threatening—like a panda bear," added Joe Medjuck, the Fredericton-born producer of *Ghostbusters*, *Space Jam* and *Trailer Park Boys*.

"We're quite open to other cultures," stressed Martina Stawski, a Pickering, Ontario, teacher who with her husband, Simon, became YouTube stars in the 2010s in South Korea and Japan. "We don't think of things as weird. If people say take your shoes off at the door, we take our shoes off at the door."

Lisa Tedeschini, a corporate lawyer in London, found that her ability to blend in—her non-identity, as she calls it—helped her succeed both with British colleagues and as a counsellor to European companies. She finds in Canadians an optimism and openness, and "a sort of innocence that is charming and not defensive." "I can get away with things because I am not British and so I am not expected to behave in a certain way. I quite like being incognito."

Tim Evans, a global health expert who spent much of his career in Washington, D.C., found inclusion to be the one value most Canadians carry with them abroad. "It isn't my way or the highway. It's 'What's our way? What can we do together that we couldn't do on our own?' We're not interested in imposing our design on others. We're not big enough to impose."

"We're boring," added Margaret MacMillan, the Canadian historian who moved in 2007 to Oxford University, where she became a leading voice on the dangers of nationalism. "We're not nationalistic. We don't beat our chests. Look around this campus. You don't see us wearing maple leaves."

Like most Canadians of his generation, Steve "Spaz" Williams grew up watching American television and movies, which the celebrated computer graphics animator feels made him an authority on the American way of life. "We knew the Americans better than they knew themselves, because we watched them all day on TV. They didn't watch us. We watched them," he said decades later. The 1973 film *American Graffiti* awakened his appreciation, as an 11-year-old in Toronto, for the alien land next door,[9] preparing him to become the perfect "participant observer," as sociologists would call it, when he moved to California in the 1990s and was able to blend in with Americans and yet challenge their methods. This natural state of Canadian expats—the polite dissidents—helped Williams transform filmmaking, with the *T. rex* in *Jurassic Park* and the digitally contorted face of Jim Carrey in *The Mask*, along with computer-generated creatures in *The Abyss* and *Terminator 2: Judgment Day*. "Canadians grow up with eight colours whereas Americans grow up with sixteen colours," he observed.[10] "Our brain is forced to fill in the blank with the most powerful weapon it has: imagination. As children, we turn the chesterfield into a fort, a bowl into a boat, pine cones into cottage art. That's Canadian."

Matt Wyndowe would add the component of Canadian niceness, which he came to appreciate only when he left Toronto for Silicon Valley in 2000 to work at a startup ("before working at a startup was cool"). After then studying business at Stanford University, he joined Facebook in 2007, and in 2014 went to Uber to run product partnerships, integrating the ride-hailing app with Google Maps and payment platforms. Along the way, he discovered, "Canadians are beloved. You just mention where you're from and people smile."

Marc Tessier-Lavigne was reminded of his knack for being Canadian when he interviewed in 2016 to be president of Stanford. The campus had been rocked by rape allegations against a member of its swim team, and the #MeToo brush fires were just beginning to scorch the Valley culture that Stanford had planted. Tessier-Lavigne, a respected neuroscientist and former president of Rockefeller University, had the academic credentials to make the Stanford short list, but it was his Canadian manner and outlook that helped put him over the top. He brought to his final interview a quiet moral purpose, which the university, despite its rack of Nobel Prizes and billion-dollar endowments, had been struggling to identify. Moreover, he put people at ease, regardless of their background. "How do you spot a Canadian on the street?" he told the search committee, hoping to show a more human side. "It's the person saying please and thank you to an ATM." The committee loved the line, but its members were more interested in his thinking about "arrogance and entitlement" and how they had become the Valley's, and perhaps Stanford's, Achilles heel. They felt Stanford needed a "humble champion" and decided a Canadian could be that.[11]

Lylan Masterman, a venture capital investor in New York,

learned something else about his Canadian identity when he took an MBA at Chicago's Northwestern University. He signed up for improv classes to get out of his comfort zone, and was told the secret to the art form was to listen. Improv is based on the rhetorical idea of "yes, and," in contrast to traditional American business school classes that thrive on "no, but." In improv, the device keeps a gag going, just as in business it can draw in a diversity of speakers and ideas. Masterman discovered he was good at it because "I listened in order to understand, not to defend or respond." His classmates told him it must be a Canadian thing.[12]

According to research by the Asia Pacific Foundation,[13] most of our expats go abroad in their early twenties, often starting with a study term or grad school. Men are more likely than women to leave Canada. New Canadians are more likely to move, too. The biggest driver, though, is economic opportunity, which is common among expats from other nations as well. According to the 2018 edition of an annual survey[14] of global expats by the multinational bank HSBC, 38 percent had moved abroad for better job prospects, while 31 percent had gone for a better quality of life. The Asia Pacific Foundation's research revealed that slightly more than half of Canadian expats returned home at least once a year, and 69 percent expressed an intention to return to Canada and establish permanent residency. Their main reasons: "enjoying the quality of life and culture in Canada" and "being closer to family members and friends." But here's what's key: even those who were gone for good continued to see themselves as Canadian. It almost didn't matter how long they had been abroad. In fact, for many, the longer they had been away, the stronger the psychological sinews were to home. Driven by nostalgia, or guilt, they were more Canadian than ever.

In late 2017, while visiting England, I was invited to a lunch at a country home near Oxford where I was seated next to an American finance executive. Upon learning my nationality, she asked why pretty much every Canadian she had met while living overseas was both, in her words, nice and excellent. "Not like Americans," she stressed. I suggested it might be because most Canadian expats leave home on their own. Americans, like Germans, Japanese and Koreans, often ride on the wings of multinational corporations or large government agencies. Canadians, by contrast, typically aren't dropped into a foreign subsidiary where they can move onward and upward simply by making the boss back home happy. They have to swim on their own or sink, using a blend of charm, global awareness and what limited Canadian networks they can find. Combined, these forces tend to lead Canadians to assimilate faster than most expats. Another Canadian at our table took issue with my argument, saying most Canadians go abroad as professionals and then develop skills on the global stage to qualify for the main event. They succeed by showing up and fitting in, he argued, referring somewhat cynically to "the convenient Canadian." "We don't have global leaders," he found. "We have global experts." Our sardonic tablemate had just visited the Japanese office of a leading U.S. research agency, where he learned the director was a Canadian who, like most of his compatriots, had no formal connection anymore with Canada. He was in a category of one, pursuing his passion rather than representing the interests of his country. He had been shaped by Canada, educated by Canada, raised by Canada, but he hadn't taken Canada with him.

Go anywhere in the world and you can find expats through their language or culture, or perhaps spot them in groups watching a hometown sports team. With the rise of a global professional class, however, those associations are giving way to an affinity based less on nationality and more on education and employment. For those seeking a post-national world, one's alma mater and place of work are the new source code of identity. Angelique Mannella saw this after she graduated from McGill and went abroad to work for a series of tech companies and international organizations: Nokia in Helsinki, Cisco in the Valley, the World Bank in Washington and INSEAD, the Swiss business school, at its office in Singapore. In 2019, she moved again, to Munich, to help Amazon build its Uber-style delivery business.[15] In each place, Mannella found herself identifying as, say, a Cisco veteran or McGill alum more than as a Canadian. Is that a particularly Canadian thing? She tends to think so, because "we like to blend in. We don't promote our nationality the way the Lebanese or Finns or Italians do."

Before he died of cancer in 2012, David Rakoff's voice was known to millions of Americans as a regular contributor to NPR's *This American Life*—a title which, among foreigners, only a Canadian could lay claim to. Like a lot of expats, Rakoff's life was unrooted and beholden to no country or land. His family fled South Africa because of apartheid, and then left Quebec because of the Quiet Revolution. After high school, he left Toronto for New York, where he masked himself with "a certain kind of world-weary, jaded, anxious neuroticism"—a not uncommon mantle among Canadians trying to blend into Manhattan. Settling down as a writer and broadcaster, Rakoff finally fessed up to being Canadian in 1997, in his third stint on *This American Life*. He tried to explain his Canadian sheepishness, telling the audience that we define ourselves by hiding from ourselves, self-declaring only in those Trivial Pursuit moments when we rattle off a list of celebrity expats. Identity through association is not unique to the Canadian diaspora. It's just more acute. For Canadians, Rakoff felt,[16] to be famous in America was part of our identity. Why else would we be there? No Canadian moves to the U.S. to drive a taxi or dig ditches or take on another stereotype in the great American immigrant saga. We're there to make a mark.

That tends to be the pull force for expats. There's a push force, too, which Canadians are less inclined to discuss. It's the push of cast-offs and misfits, who see themselves as exiles in Oz, the ones who can never quite get back to Kansas, even when Kansas is Canada. Chamath Palihapitiya feels he understands the powerful force of exile for those who have chosen to live elsewhere. The son of a Sri Lankan diplomat who declared refugee status in Canada when Chamath was five, he grew up with his family in a two-bedroom apartment in Ottawa, much of the time on welfare. He won a scholarship to the University of Waterloo, to study engineering, and used its co-op system to work his way to Silicon Valley, where in 2007 he landed one of the first executive jobs at Facebook, in charge of growing its user base. He took the social network from fifty million users to seven hundred and fifty million. Four years later, he left the company with enough money—several hundred million—to launch his own purpose-driven fund, Social Capital, to invest in technology companies out to change the world. (He also bought a share of the NBA's Golden State Warriors.) His quiet Canadian conviction helped him land an all-star list of investors, including Peter Thiel (PayPal), John Doerr (Netscape) and Reid Hoffman (LinkedIn), as well as global billionaires such as Hong Kong's Li Ka-shing and Brazil's Jorge Paulo Lemann. Through his meteoric rise, though, he remained cautious about waving the Canadian flag, in part because of the reasons he had left Canada.[17]

I went to see Chamath, as he's universally known in the Valley, at the Social Capital office he built in a converted auto garage in central Palo Alto. Even though he had, by that point, spent most of his life outside Canada, he felt "I owe everything to Canada"—not just for the head start of public schooling and a social safety net but for the quiet values he carried with him. "I'm viewed so much more constructively when people know I'm Canadian," he told me[18] as we sat down in his glass-walled boardroom. "It's a positive brand value. People assume you have a certain moral code." Despite the positive reception that he enjoys around the world, Chamath continued to feel skeptical glances back home, just as he felt as a teen at Lisgar Collegiate Institute in Ottawa. He knew Canadians wanted him to succeed—"refugee kid makes good" plays well to our narrative—but felt we were missing the point of why people like him leave. He referred to it as our "narrative fallacy," the image that many people create for their diasporas and then project back on themselves. Canadians like the idea of a successful diaspora because it makes us all feel successful. And yet, as Chamath explained, "the reason I'm here is not because Canada sent me. I'm here because I didn't belong. I was an outlier." Many immigrant kids feel that way, although the views are not exclusive to newcomers. Toronto-born Spaz Williams said he left because he was a "heretic." In Chamath's case, he felt it was his "shit disturber" mentality that forced him, the iconoclast, to leave. "I owe Canada everything, but the elephant in the room is that it's very hard to be an outlier in Canada," he said. "There isn't an infrastructure for outliers. Expats are people who wake up one day and say, 'It's not happening here.'"

Chamath rattled off a roster of Canadian outliers who, like him, are what he calls "free radicals": Elon Musk; David Foster; Uber's first coder, Garrett Camp; even the author of *Outliers*, Malcolm Gladwell. Canada has so much conformity in our public conversation, he believes, that these misfits and malcontents had to go away to be heard, especially back home. This echoes what the great Canadian diplomat Lionel Gelber discovered about our country in the 1930s, a national trait he called "an intolerance of individuality."[19] We lose the outliers because we eschew them. Yes, diversity may be our strength, at least on the outside. But in Chamath's experience, conformity, at least on the inside, is our nature.[20]

Does that make our diaspora a global population of nonconformists and misfits? A scattering of outliers? It may not be how many expats see themselves, but it's a valuable insight for those wanting to work with them. They've chosen to leave and will continue to follow the beat of their own drummer. This is not uncommon among expat populations. In 2018, five U.S. business professors banded together to study the impact of expatriation, as it's called, on identity and confidence.[21] Led by Hajo Adam of Rice University, the group proposed a hypothesis that living abroad would increase one's sense of self. To test it, they conducted six studies involving 1,874 participants. "When people live in their home country," they found, "they are often surrounded by others who mostly behave in similar ways, so they are not compelled to question whether their own behaviours reflect their core values or the values of the culture in which they are embedded. In contrast, when living abroad, our data found that people's exposure to novel cultural values and norms prompts them to repeatedly engage with their own values and beliefs, which are then either discarded or strengthened." In other words, one's sense of self, and with it self-confidence, tend to explode the moment one leaves home, giving expats, and groups of expats, a strength of will and independence of mind that can be both powerful and disruptive.

That independent streak is not always for the good, especially among those expats who don't carry with them their country's values and beliefs. Consider the case of Alexandre Cazes, a twenty-five-year-old Quebec computer hacker who was found dead in a Thai jail cell in July 2017, after he was arrested at the request of

American authorities for building an illicit cyber empire. The Canadian expat, whose lavish lifestyle was well-known in Bangkok, had amassed a $23 million fortune, including a Lamborghini, a Porsche and vacation homes in Antigua, Phuket and Cyprus by the time the U.S. identified him as the mastermind behind AlphaBay, an illicit online trading forum for narcotics, weapons and stolen personal information.[22] As Cazes showed, Canadians are not inherently virtuous, nor does every Canadian take on the world solely in the pursuit of good. Shane Smith and Suroosh Alvi were celebrated expats until their venture, Vice Media, was exposed for sexual abuse. Smith had built his Canadian magazine property into a global media empire worth close to $6 billion by specializing in coverage of sex, drugs and scandal. Turns out the company did more than write about vice. According to a *New York Times* investigation, "its boundary-pushing culture created a workplace that was degrading and uncomfortable for women."[23] Confronted with these truths, the Canadian duo issued a statement saying "from the top down, we have failed as a company to create a safe and inclusive workplace where everyone, especially women, can feel respected and thrive."[24]

In the age of Donald Trump, many Canadian expats may see themselves even more as defenders of the values Smith and Alvi abandoned. That may be good for the world, but is it enough to sustain an eleventh province, a diaspora the world can call Canadian? Historically, through the nineteenth and twentieth centuries, when diasporas gained influence, they were rooted in the culture of their homelands more than in the work they did in their new land. Language, food, culture, music, sport, even slang—those were the bonds of overseas communities. A century or more after Italians poured into New York, there's still a sense of diaspora among them, four, five, six generations later. Sikhs in London, Turks in Berlin,

Greeks in Toronto—many communities remain stitched together by culture long after their native language has faded from use. In his studies of migration, the Montreal-based demographer Jack Jedwab has found identity to be most commonly rooted in stories, what each generation tells the next. Except, he said, among Canadians.[25] The Canadian story is not commonly told around the world, nor are there cultural touchstones or talismans for Canadians to carry with them. There's no mandatory Pierre Berton or Margaret Atwood, or folklore beyond Olympic hockey. The comedian Mike Myers spoke to this cultural vacuum in his book *Canada*, marking the country's 150th birthday. After Team Canada won gold in 2002 at the Salt Lake City Olympics, defeating Team USA 5–2, Myers wanted to celebrate with other Canadians. So he and Rob Cohen, a writer-director friend who had moved to Los Angeles from Calgary, went to the only Canadian place they knew would be open: a Roots retail outlet in Beverly Hills.[26]

It's one of those unthreatening stories that expose a vulnerability for all Canadians abroad. Our relative place in the world is fading, and not just because other countries are growing and prospering. When we had the chance, we didn't capitalize on our diaspora or use our expats to secure our standing, which as a challenge will only continue to grow. Even in the United States, the old idea of Canadians hiding in plain sight is in retreat. We're just not essential anymore to America, as a country or as a people. In the 1960s, Canada was behind only Mexico as a source of immigrants to the United States.[27] We gave way to Cuba and Vietnam in the 1970s, and then China, the Philippines and Russia. By 2000, the share of Canadians among the thirty-one million foreign-born residents in the U.S. was down to about 2 percent. Mexico alone accounted for roughly a third, and its influence grew proportionately.[28] Increasingly, the influence of our expats, and by extension

Canada, will need to be measured by collective values and principles, not numbers, and our ability to build networks around them.

In 1968, in an essay in *Canadian Forum*, which from 1920 until it ceased publishing in 2000 was a bastion of left-wing literary, cultural and political criticism, the pioneering British development economist Barbara Ward[29] called Canada the first "international nation" due to our approach to bilingualism and the world's "finest web of contacts."[30] Her contemporary, the author George Woodcock, who was born in Winnipeg, raised in Britain and spent most of his adult life in Vancouver, called us a "hybrid nation" in which "it is difficult to determine what is distinctively Canadian, until one realizes that the synthesis, after all, is the point of originality."[31] In a postcolonial world, that ability to synthesize became our calling card, and a kind of signal of the attributes others would need as social complexity grew and the nature of conflict changed. For a time, of course, those hybrid attributes were also mocked, especially by Canadians, as a symbol of milquetoast ambitions and a national adherence to the middle of the road. But in this century, as countries struggle to both define nationalism and shape globalism in a digital age, Canadians such as Ron Daniels are finding purpose anew.

A law professor and university leader, Daniels moved to the U.S. in the early 2000s, just as America was coming to grips with the limits of triumphalism and the West's long march of progress was running up against the War on Terror, the financial crisis and, later, its seeming inability to manage the vast migration underway from the global south. Daniels had run the University of Toronto's law school in the 1990s, moved to the University of Pennsylvania in 2005 as vice president and provost, and in 2009 took over as president of Johns Hopkins University in Baltimore, where he hoped to quietly inject a bit of a Canadian ethos. Instead he was confronted by a new home that was racially divided and civically charged, encased in a nation that was, politically, at war with itself. Even though the university was among the world's best academically, it seemed to many to be insensitive to the city's harsher realities of crime, poverty and urban blight. When the celebrated Johns Hopkins Hospital expanded its operations over the years, it had displaced hundreds of African American families. If that weren't enough, the university cautioned employees and students from wandering past its security perimeter. Into the social morass, Daniels felt he could bring a Canadian sense of balance and belonging. In Toronto, he had watched his family of prominent builders redevelop the city's Regent Park neighbourhood, which was once plagued by crime but had become a model for social integration and public safety. He remembered the power of hope playing a key role. "In truth," he said, "coming from Toronto and a city that works remarkably well in integrating immigrants and addressing poverty, while we're not perfect, it gives you a sense of what's possible for a city."[32]

Under Daniels's direction, the Johns Hopkins University School of Education built a K–8 school in East Baltimore, which is one of the city's toughest neighbourhoods and hadn't seen a new public school in more than twenty years. He then encouraged faculty and staff (through voucher programs and other inducements) to live in the neighbourhoods around campus, and persuaded developers to add a hotel to generate more foot traffic among those visitors who retreated downtown or to the airport rather than stay in the area. These efforts were part of an eighty-eight acre urban redevelopment project that Daniels spearheaded in the communities surrounding the hospital. His most significant act for the city, though, may have been the creation of a coalition of businesses and nonprofits that committed to buy more from local and minority-owned businesses. In the first three years of the effort, the twenty-eight members of BLocal spent more than $280 million in the city and hired seventeen hundred Baltimore residents from underserved neighbourhoods. A prominent Baptist bishop, Douglas Miles, himself an African American alumnus of the university, called it "the most significant economic and jobs initiative in the life of the city." Miles was quoted in a glowing profile of the university in the September 2016 edition of the *Economist* magazine, which singled out Daniels for exhibiting the kind of civic leadership "more often associated with a government than with a private institution."[33]

The spirit of community building was not the only Canadian value Daniels had brought with him. He also maintained a respect for international human rights that was soon challenged in ways he had never imagined, as he watched America's rising sea of populism. Not far from Baltimore, Donald Trump had, from the moment he moved into the White House, mocked every legal right and process Daniels had come to respect as a student, lawyer and professor. At first, Daniels bit his tongue, not wanting to engage his university in a firestorm with the new president. But when Trump signed an executive order barring entry to people from seven largely Muslim countries, Daniels knew he had to take a public stand. The executive order was a violation of the very oath he had sworn the previous year to become an American citizen (to comply with national security requirements for work Johns Hopkins would continue to undertake, under his leadership, with the government). After consulting with colleagues and his Canadian wife, Joanne Rosen, a human rights lawyer who is also on faculty at Johns Hopkins, he wrote an open letter[34] to their university community, and asked the *Washington Post* to publish it, hoping Trump, or at least some of his advisers, might read it.

The letter was among the first counterpunches to Trump, and was deeply personal. Daniels wrote of his own upbringing in

Canada, the son of a Jew who fled Poland in 1939, at age seven, and how he had to come to grips with Canada's strict limits on Jewish refugees during Hitler's time in power, when his extended family, and Joanne's, were decimated in the Holocaust. He also wrote of the jubilation he felt, a year earlier in Baltimore, when he became American. Identity is powerful, he had found, in so many ways. He then made the point, emphatically, "when universities such as ours find our fundamental mission imperiled by an executive order that erodes our core values and the founding principles of the nation, we cannot stand by."[35] Daniels took the stand because he felt the president was violating American norms. But there was more. He felt a quiet Canadian spirit nudging him on.

In the summer of 2019, Daniels found himself at it again, responding publicly to Trump over the president's incendiary comments about Baltimore. In an attack on one of the city's Democrat congressional representatives, Elijah Cummings, Trump had called Baltimore "very dangerous," "filthy" and "rat infested" and said its residents were "living in hell."[36] Daniels and Kevin Plank, the founder and then-CEO of Under Armour, the sportswear giant based in Baltimore, fired back with an op-ed in the *Baltimore Sun* that defended the city's creative and entrepreneurial spirit while accepting its social and economic challenges. They concluded, "We never move forward as a community—or indeed, a nation—by denigrating each other."[37]

The view was held by many, perhaps most, Americans, but Daniels knew it also stemmed from his Canadian upbringing. As he demonstrated, we are more than the easy-going synthesizers of George Woodcock's worldview. Canadian expats, for the most part, are neither collaborators nor moralizers but go places to make a mark, and make it constructively. After Trump's victory in 2016, the Montreal-raised, McGill-educated writer Adam Gopnik tried to explain some of this Canadianness in a *New Yorker* article, "We Could Have All Been Canadian," in which he argued the American Revolution would have been better in the long run had it been Canadian in spirit. He echoed Daniels's sentiment, arguing Canada had been forged on "uneasy compromises" and "the constant search for temporary nonviolent solutions to intractable divides."[38]

That ability to strike an uneasy compromise was among the traits I found in Canadian expats pretty much everywhere, and it was not a recent phenomenon. The history of Canada's diaspora was one of diligence through consensus building and coalition forming. Through the twentieth century, our ability to negotiate and empathize helped secure Canada plenty of nominations for Best Supporting Actor—the fight against AIDS, the International Space Station, the climate challenge—while the superpowers stuck to their leading roles. In the emerging age of hyper-connectivity, more and more of those leading roles will go to individuals who can work with ever-smarter technologies and network with ever-more diverse groups of people. Fortunately, those are among the strengths that can be traced back to our earliest expats, the ones who ventured abroad not to make the world more like us but rather, in subtle ways, make us more like the world.

2

Missionaries, Mathematicians and Misfits

HOW CANADIANS REINVENTED THE MODERN WORLD

By the sunny spring of 2001, a half century of globalization seemed unstoppable. The internet, despite the dot-com bust, was an undisputed global platform of technology and commerce. Europe's embrace of a common currency was nudging others to consider the idea of open monetary borders. And with China part of the World Trade Organization (WTO), capitalism had finally replaced military might as the world's kingmaker. On every front, the role of government was in decline, while transnational organizations, and transnational citizens, were in the ascendant. Earlier that year, before terror attacks and the Iraq War, and later the financial crisis, chased the world back into the thickets of nationalism, a bestselling book tried to capture the spirit of individual triumph in another era of transnationalism. *How the Scots Invented the Modern World* was more than the story of a people and their global flight in the 1700s. It was a profile of a new age of migration, founded on the pursuit of knowledge and export of ideas, which laid a foundation stone for the United States, Canada and Australia, and became the root of twentieth-century globalization.[1]

In the book, Arthur Herman traces the ambitions of Andrew Carnegie and Lachlan Macquarie, the ideas of Adam Smith and David Hume, the inventions of James Watt, and the writings of Sir Walter Scott and Robert Louis Stevenson, using them to show how no diaspora has ever been as influential as the Scots, at least on a per capita basis. He may have added, there was no country shaped more by the Scots than Canada. The Great Eviction, caused by parallel reforms in agriculture and public schooling, led to an exodus of Scots from the countryside to towns and cities, and from there to London and across the Atlantic to Halifax, Montreal and New York.[2] In Canada, those Scots became early leaders of the North West Company and Hudson's Bay Company, and built universities—Dalhousie, McGill, Queen's—in the image of the best Glasgow and Edinburgh schools.[3] At Confederation, eight of Canada's ten "founding fathers" were Scottish. While only three million Scots emigrated during the early exodus, a trickle compared to the flood of Irish, Italians or Germans, their influence far outweighed their numbers as they brought a common sense, civic duty and cultural awareness to the New World, and to an increasingly urban society.[4] Scotland's export of "modernizing humanism," according to Herman, bent the arc of modernism—not only with what Scots took to their new homes but with the spirit and purpose of migration.[5] From then on, you no longer needed to be poor, disenfranchised or endangered to move abroad. You could do it for work, discovery or simply a change of scene. It was the beginning of enlightened emigration.

The Scottish Presbyterian sense of internationalism fuelled a New World rivalry with French Catholic traditions, as Canadians started to look beyond their own borders for both influence and opportunity. In the decades after Confederation, millions of uneducated youth left Canada to pursue physical labour in the more prosperous post–Civil War United States. At the turn of the century, as the new country found its footing, a second wave of emigration took shape, with a growing number of university graduates also going overseas as missionaries to impress upon the world, for the first time, Canadian values. Then, after the First World War, a third wave began, cresting in the middle of the century with highly educated professionals moving to the emerging centres of science, technology and creativity. In each of these three waves, driven by body, soul and mind, there was no game plan to send Canadians abroad, nor was there any sense of how these emigrants could advance their young country's interests, although at each stage there was a simmering tension between nationalists and internationalists that continues to inform our ambivalence toward expats and the idea of a Canadian diaspora. Our population abroad, uncounted and amorphous, was becoming part of the unfinished business of Confederation.[6]

Canada's history of emigration began almost accidentally, as a unified America came to grips with a massive labour shortage in the 1860s and '70s. The National Policy had succeeded in settling the Prairies and connecting the new country with British Columbia, while its signature piece of infrastructure, a rail line, enabled the rapid growth of western agriculture. But America's economic magnet was too great for people to resist. By the end of the nineteenth century, nearly one-quarter of all Canadians lived in the United States, including droves of entrepreneurs. A small-town Ontario pharmacist named John J. McLaughlin—son of the carmaker Robert McLaughlin—moved to Brooklyn in 1890 to begin producing soda pop, under the name Canada Dry Pale Ginger Ale. James Kraft left Fort Erie to start a food company. James Naismith took his notion of basketball south. Alexander Graham Bell followed the same path with his iconic creation.[7] But the biggest and most consequential move in those decades may have been among rural Quebec youth, who through the 1800s formed an exodus. They were the Scots of their age, leaving in droves for work in New England's textile mills and the squalor that accompanied it. An 1886 diphtheria outbreak in Brunswick, Maine, killed seventy-four French Canadians, mostly children. The Québécois were so derided, and isolated, that one Massachusetts official called them "the Chinese of the Eastern States." (Ironically, *pâté chinois*, or shepherd's pie, became a popular dish in Quebec, named for China, Maine.)

The Quebec government finally realized the emigrants weren't coming home, and reluctantly launched what became Canada's first unofficial diaspora program. Led by the Catholic Church, the effort dispatched hundreds of priests to New England, where, by the late 1800s, two hundred thousand Québécois lived in communities known as *petits Canadas*. Soon, there were twenty-one French-speaking priests in Lowell, Massachusetts. Woonsocket, Rhode Island, had twenty-two. Fall River, Massachusetts, home to thirty-three thousand francophones in 1900, boasted eight French-speaking lawyers, twenty-one doctors, eleven dentists and sixteen pharmacists. By one count, there were 195 French newspapers serving the early Canadian diaspora in New England.[8]

Quebec felt it best to fight fire with fire, and developed its own industrial policy to absorb the rural population fleeing the farm. Louis-Alexandre Taschereau, a fervent free enterpriser who served as premier from 1920 to 1936 and transformed the province's economy, was fond of saying he preferred to import capital than export French Canadians.[9] It worked, at least in the short term. Quebec emigration peaked in 1900 and even began to decline after the U.S. imposed a literacy test in 1917.[10] But the earlier outflow could not be reversed. By the 1920s, close to a million Québécois had left the province. (In the most recent American Community Survey,[11] roughly two million Americans identified their origins as French Canadian—far greater than the seven hundred thousand who listed Canada.)[12]

Even as millions of Canadian labourers and entrepreneurs were drawn to America's economic boom, the next generation of emigrants, the missionaries, began to make their way farther afield. In the early 1800s, several thousand Quebec youth had gone abroad as Catholic missionaries, to Haiti, South America and Africa, which the British allowed as a gesture of thanks to Rome for its support during the War of 1812.[13] They were followed by Scottish Presbyterians—the ones behind Canada's first universities—who began to dispatch their youth in a more strategic manner. Their charges became known as the Maple Leaf Imperialists, going overseas to launch social and religious programs alongside Canada's growing business interests in outposts like Bolivia and Cuba. Canada's first recorded foreign mission left from Nova Scotia in 1844, bound for New Hebrides. But on the whole Canadians were late to the missionary movement, and had to settle for far-flung places or subaltern roles, like the Nova Scotians who were sent to Burma in 1844 to support an American mission.[14]

George Mackay, a missionary educated at Queen's University, was a frontrunner for this second wave of expats, moving to Formosa (now Taiwan) in the late 1800s to build Canada's first significant overseas project. Mackay's parents, George and Helen, had been part of the Great Eviction, leaving the Scottish Highlands in 1830 for Canada, where they settled on a farm in southwestern Ontario and raised six children, including George Jr., who was born in 1844.[15] Young George wanted to be among the "sent ones."[16] He worked his way through school so he could study theology at Queen's and

Princeton University (both Scottish Presbyterian creations) and then spent a winter in Edinburgh, where he waited for his assignment as Canada's first Presbyterian missionary. He passed his time studying Hindi, realizing he was at risk of going nowhere in the "ice age" of Canadian internationalism.[17] The Canadian church, he later wrote, "was divided and weak,"[18] and there was little enthusiasm for the world beyond small-town Canada.

Mackay won the Formosa assignment after the Canadians discovered their American and British counterparts had claimed every desirable spot on the Chinese mainland. The isolation was a gift, allowing him to break with tradition. Rather than proselytize, Mackay turned his attention to health care and built clinics across the countryside. He also raised enough money back home, in Oxford county, to build a college that would be based on what he called "Canadian liberality"[19]; the school was open to both boys and girls, taught science as well as Western history and religion, and stuck to the local dialect. Mackay became a vocal proponent for women's education on the island, launching another program to train women to teach women. And while it irritated other foreign missions, he quickly abandoned foreign staff for locals, not least because it was "the plan that is least expensive, most effective and that succeeds."[20] Soon, the Canadian mission was known for a culture that was conciliatory, respectful, professional and focused on outcomes. When Mackay finally departed in 1893, the foreign community of North Formosa wrote a glowing tribute, calling his mission the most successful in China and remarking that "suspicion has given place to confidence."[21] He had developed Canada's first foreign aid project, and planted the seeds for a new kind of overseas community.

Mackay returned to a Canada that, having abandoned the ice age of internationalism, was suddenly alive to the world. Young Canadians were looking beyond the textile mills of New England to the new boomtowns of New York, Chicago and Los Angeles. Everywhere Mackay went he encountered crowds wanting to hear tales from far-flung lands where Canadians could make a difference.[22] Whether they knew it or not, whether they liked it or not, those Canadians would soon be part of the last burst of colonial land grabs, as fading European powers and a rising America sought to control the destinies of Asia, Africa and Latin America. Nowhere was the pursuit of power more pronounced than mainland China, where generations of foreign intervention had stoked a deep-seated sense of nationalism.[23] Tensions between China and the West mounted when the Qing dynasty, having met defeat at the hands of Japan in 1895, ceded coastal outposts to the British and Americans and, in a smaller gesture, allowed a growing number of Canadian missionaries to take charge in the isolated Chengdu Plain in central Sichuan.[24] The Canadians brought a sensibility that was not seen elsewhere in China. Omar Kilborn, a Toronto doctor, was sent to build the first hospital in Chengdu, and drew on Mackay's work in Formosa to help the local Chinese develop their own health system. Kilborn told local authorities his team would train local youth to be the next generation of doctors and nurses. In 1910, as the Qing dynasty was collapsing, Kilborn[25] persuaded missionary doctors to teach in Chinese.[26] He also convinced supporters back at the University of Toronto to raise $1.3 million for a new school, to be called the West China Union University, and to send close to two hundred missionaries to instruct local teachers in basic health care. In 1914, the Canadians added a School of Medicine, and in 1917 a Department of Dentistry.[27] Today we would call it "capacity building," an essential element of any overseas development project. As Kilborn declared, "the day of small things is over."[28]

Following the First World War, the missionaries were gradually replaced by university-educated professionals who planted the idea of Canada as an independent middle power, and Canadian expats as more than understudies for Britons and Americans. Edward Wilson Wallace was among the first, following Kilborn to Chengdu to build a local education system, from kindergarten up, that would be run and staffed by locals, and to focus on the rural poor, especially girls. Wallace was eventually plucked by the Rockefeller Foundation to lead a national commission on education in the 1920s that advocated the rapid spread of rural schools.[29] China's war with Japan in the 1930s put Canadians in the middle of the fighting, and turned the second wave of Canadian expats into a new breed of professional advisers. Robert McClure was their torch-bearer, helping Canadians abroad to stop seeing themselves as missionaries or officials representing the British Empire and to start seeing themselves as global citizens representing Canada.[30]

McClure was born in 1900 in Portland, Oregon, where his mother had fled to escape the Boxer Rebellion while his father, a Canadian missionary, stayed behind in west China.[31] McClure and his mother returned to China, where he stayed until he was fifteen and old enough to enrol in the University of Toronto for medical school. When he finally got back to Chengdu as a doctor, he joined the expanding Canadian medical missions, but McClure was not content with traditional missionary life. A new century was racing ahead too quickly. He worked for a time at the Mackay hospital in Taiwan, where he built a leprosy wing, and during the 1930s was the first Westerner to drive from the Indian Ocean to China, proving to the U.S. military it could use the Burma Road as a supply route for Chinese Nationalists trapped inland by the invading Japanese military.[32] During the war with Japan, McClure stayed with the U.S.-backed Nationalists, creating something of a legend when he inoculated twelve hundred people in one day, using a single needle that he sharpened on a razor belt.[33] McClure's clinics later became combat hospitals, as he bicycled from village to village to identify civilians in need of aid, speaking to communities in the Chinese he had learned as a child. Across the countryside, he became known as Loa Tai-fu, or Dr. Clear.[34]

In 1936, as China's rival Communist and Nationalist forces settled into an uneasy alliance against the Japanese, McClure developed the Hwaiking Rural Medical System, in Henan province, which comprised a base hospital, branch hospital, clinics and local outreach workers (essentially barefoot quacks).[35] Serving 1.5 million people, the system was based on a strategy that no civilian be more than thirteen kilometres from a trained health practitioner. McClure called the strategy "adopt and adapt," writing in his diary that he hoped his design would keep China going until state medicine could take form. In 1937, as the war with Japan intensified, McClure took over as field director for the International Red Cross in north and central China, eventually teaming up with Dick Brown, another Canadian medical missionary who was also fluent in Chinese.[36] The pair travelled largely by bicycle to aid the war-ravaged Chinese interior, moving between Nationalist and Communist territory and occasionally venturing into Japanese-held districts where they learned the occupiers had a policy of executing wounded soldiers. As the Japanese advanced, in early 1938, McClure began to retreat with the Nationalists by train. At one stop, Tungkwan, he heard on the platform of a Canadian who had gone missing. It was Norman Bethune, another battlefield doctor and international adventurer who appeared to be on one of his notorious drinking binges. Bethune had come to China after a stint of medical mission work in the Spanish Civil War, a conflict that had redefined the role of expats in the 1930s.[37] (There were enough Canadians to warrant their own battalion, called the Mackenzie-Papineau Battalion, which quickly lost most of its members to death or injury—a result that shocked Canadians and led Ottawa to pass the Foreign Enlistment Act of 1937, outlawing participation by Canadians in foreign wars.)[38] Taking his bike off the train, McClure rode around the countryside in search of the missing Canadian, whom he found lying incapacitated in a nearby village, drunk on hand rinse.[39] Because Bethune spoke little Chinese, the villagers didn't know what to do with him. So McClure, then thirty-seven, took Bethune, then forty-eight, to the station and sent him in the other direction, to the Communists he was determined to join, and what would become his celebrated meeting with Mao Zedong that remains a centrepiece of Chinese popular history. McClure's rescue of Bethune was the only known encounter between the two Canadian expats, and set in motion a new chapter for Canadians abroad.[40]

A month later, McClure met the British writers W.H. Auden and Christopher Isherwood, who were on assignment for a British publication. The writers were mesmerized by the Canadian, calling him "one of the great apostles of the bicycle."[41] (They would eventually write about the Sino-Japanese conflict in *Journey to a War*.)[42] [43] McClure impressed the British with his approach to development, which he boiled down to a formula: A = R+P. Adventure equals Risk plus Purpose. The Canadian spirit made for good Fleet Street copy, but as war began to envelop the world, McClure realized there was a crying need for more than adventure. He saw the imperative for a global approach to human rights and humanitarian assistance, built on the early Canadian work at Chengdu, which following the war would be replicated by international aid agencies across the global south. Drawing on this Canadian model, McClure established a Quaker outfit called the Friends' Ambulance Unit,[44] and then helped develop the United Nations Rural Rehabilitation Association[45] (UNRRA), an American-launched group that used donations from the United States, Britain and Canada to rebuild bombarded war zones. Even though the United Nations did not yet formally exist, UNRRA was the first attempt by governments to band together to aid the poor and distressed in another land—brought together by Canadians, notably McClure and two other missionary kids he had grown up with: Newton Bowles, a cousin of future prime minister Lester Bowles Pearson, and James Grant, whose Canadian father John had built the rural health system of northeast China. (The younger Grant was born and educated in China, and therefore not entitled to return to Canada, which until Ottawa enacted its own immigration policy in 1947 did not recognize foreign-born children of expats. Grant opted instead for the U.S., which welcomed many dispossessed Canadians as they were expelled from China and would later nominate him to become head of the United Nations Children's Fund, or UNICEF, and leader of the global vaccination movement. Grant fought for the U.S. in the Second World War, and worked with every president from Truman to Clinton. But in the early 1990s, at the end of his celebrated career, he told me in an interview he still considered himself part Canadian—and saw the birth of international development as partly the creation of Canadian expats.)[46]

The missionary movement in China was the first big expression of an outward-bound Canadian spirit. Diffused though it was through a scattering of expats—many of them not even citizens, at least not officially—it laid the foundation for a Canadian ethos abroad. Whether it was Bethune with Mao's Communists, or Grant and Bowles with the UN's precursor agencies, or McClure with his hospital networks, which in the decades following the Second World War he took to northern India, central Africa and what we now call the Palestinian Territories—in each case the Canadians in China had demonstrated what modern expats could do. Despite this enthusiasm, this second wave of Canadian expats felt their home country was not behind them. Even McClure, the master bridge-builder, later complained he could not convince Ottawa to use his informal network of Canadians to help advance Canada's emerging interests in the Far East. In the late 1930s, as the Japanese strafed villages across northern China, he couldn't even convince the prime minister, Mackenzie King, to block nickel shipments to Japan. (It wasn't really King's decision anyway, as Canada's foreign policy, like its citizenship laws, was controlled by Britain.)[47]

These early international Canadians, like George Mackay before them, proved to the world—and their country—that there could be a third way in international affairs. They moved easily through conflicting cultures, navigated warring politics, and could have made the postwar years a Canadian moment. Newly independent states such as Israel and India had started to promote their diasporas to help build and assert their global presence. We relegated ours to UN agencies, foreign universities, American multinationals and other creations of postwar globalism. Even as a new generation of Canadian expats, during those early postwar years, began to make a mark through science and technology, they didn't take their country with them to reimagine, rewire and recode the planet.

During the Second World War, Canada had become a hub for physics and mathematics, not least because it offered a safe haven for British scientists and their American counterparts. McGill, in particular, gained renown, and began churning out hundreds of bright young things who saw the postwar world as an age of opportunity rising from the ashes of wartime destruction. Arthur Kerman was one of them. He had grown up in Montreal, attending Strathcona Academy, which was one of three English-speaking Protestant schools in the city that were part of McGill's feeder network. When Kerman graduated from the university in 1946, winning the Molson Gold Medal for math, one of his professors suggested he continue his studies at the Massachusetts Institute of Technology (MIT). Even though he had never heard of the renowned school, it had built a recruiting pipeline to McGill and offered fellowships worth $200 a month, plus free tuition, to convince young Canadians to move to Boston. That was enough for Kerman, who like many young Canadians coming out of the war years was also mesmerized by America's scientific ambition. Vannevar Bush, a leading voice in Washington, had just written his seminal "As We May Think" essay in the *Atlantic*, laying the foundations for a postwar military industrial complex that would remake the American economy and plant the seeds of Silicon Valley. It would open a door for Canadians, too, creating a pipeline that for the next fifty years freely distributed talent among the new American stables of technology.

Inspired by Bush's vision, Kerman enrolled in graduate physics, and studied under the creators of the Manhattan Project, finally joining their ranks as a faculty member in 1960. A year later, he was recruited by another Canadian, Carson Mark, to Los Alamos, the nerve centre of nuclear research where he eventually would become a right-hand figure to Edward Teller, father of the H-bomb. Over the ensuing decades, Kerman helped write Ronald Reagan's nuclear science policy, teaming up with another McGill grad, Sol Buchsbaum, and used his network across the United States, from MIT to Caltech, to land coveted research positions for Canadians. He estimated that from the early 1960s to the late 1980s, he recruited as many as twenty post-doc students *every year* from Canada. Among his Canadian quarries: Bob Birgeneau, who later served as president of both U of T and Berkeley, and Bob Dynes, who eventually ran California's university system. Kerman was able to do all this for the U.S. on one condition: Washington required him to renounce his Canadian citizenship. When I spoke with him in 2016, a year before he died at age eighty-seven, Kerman recalled typing a letter to the Canadian government, forfeiting his birthright. It still pained him. "I still view myself as Canadian. I consider myself both," he said.[48]

While Canadians had long worried about losing citizens in big numbers to the U.S., the loss of intellectual talent in the early years after the war had taken national anxieties to new levels. Fears of a brain drain reached a fever pitch in the late 1950s, as U.S. campuses took every scientist they could find. In 1958, NASA hired thirty-seven Canadian engineers and another eight computer operators. They were joined a year later by thirty-two Canadian engineers from the abolished Avro Arrow fighter-jet program. In 1963, the journalist Christina McCall Newman wrote a *Maclean's* cover story that sounded more alarm bells. In "The Canadian Americans,"[49] Newman reported that Canada had lost twelve hundred scientists and engineers that year and four thousand more professionals of other kinds. Emigration was no longer about cheap labour for New England textile mills. This was our best and brightest, educated at Canadian universities, taking their brainpower elsewhere.

Even in his final years, Kerman didn't see his departure—or the hundreds he had facilitated—as a brain drain. He saw his network of Canadian scientists more as a brain trust, still at their country's service should someone ask. He could have been a strategic asset through the Cold War, perhaps acting as an adviser to Ottawa or a go-between with Reagan's Washington. University of Toronto tried twice to recruit him, but could not offer the kind of labs he enjoyed at MIT and Los Alamos. He offered to help Canada regardless, and yet said he was never approached by government. He regretted that more than having to renounce his citizenship.

Like Kerman's career through MIT, Los Alamos and the White House, the journey of Canadian expats through the twentieth century was recognized as little more than a saga of individual journeys. At home, we saw emigration as a series of losses for the country, rather than as opportunities to add to our global networks. The Quebec factory workers of New England were lost congregants who needed to be reconnected with their homeland; the missionaries were lost pawns in the last burst of colonial power grabs; the scientists were lost brainiacs, even ingrates, who had gone to another team. If there was a loss, it was our collective failure to see what those three waves of expats could have done for Canada, particularly through a simple mathematical model that Kerman would have appreciated. It was Bob McClure's formula for Adventure: Risk + Purpose.

That Canadian-like spirit is increasingly at play in communities everywhere, through digital technology and social networks. Those are everyone's purview, of course, but they're especially powerful among newcomers, and essential to a fourth wave of Canadian emigrants—the techies—whose quiet purpose in Silicon Valley, the very launch pad of risk in the 2000s, has started to transform our world. They may yet change Canada, too, with a new approach to communities and connectivity.

In their 2016 book, *The Smartest Places on Earth*, the Dutch economist Antoine van Agtmael and journalist Fred Bakker studied rustbelt centres like Youngstown, Ohio, and found an economic renaissance built with this very ingredient of social connectivity—the sort of informal networks that often define diasporas. When properly connected, people from different backgrounds have been able to turn around economically depressed communities. It shouldn't be surprising. Social connectivity is the Valley's secret sauce, and it's seminal to other innovation hubs, too. As van Agtmael and Bakker found, "the social connector is typically part of several different social groups and helps to bring diverse people into contact with each other."[50] Social connectors help people see beyond their horizons. "They motivate people to connect, work to find common ground and establish new relationships outside of their comfort zone, and then build these relationships into lasting communities."

The authors could have been describing the history of Canadian expats who took to the world not to claim or conquer it but to use their talents and ambitions to better it. Canada now needs to find ways to build networks around these women and men, to ensure this imaginary eleventh province is greater than the sum of our expats. In the heart of Silicon Valley, the fourth wave is doing just that, re-engineering what it means to be Canadian regardless of where you live.

3

The Optimization Game

THE NORTHERN TECHIES WHO BUILT A NEW SILICON VALLEY

Along the cedar-lined streets that lead to Rob Burgess's house, Silicon Valley unfolds like any comfortable enclave in Middle America. The winding roads, sprawling athletic fields and hillside homes, each with a pool, would blend in comfortably in Virginia or Arizona. The only palpable difference might be the Valley's most enduring characteristic, its microclimate, with a steady balm of sunshine and seventy-degree temperatures that make it an oasis between San Francisco's fog and the scorched deserts of central California. Basking in blissful isolation, the bedroom communities around Palo Alto could serve as backlot sets for the origin stories of tech entrepreneurship—of Hewlett and Packard, or Jobs and Wozniak, and their pioneering American ingenuity—each connected to the outside world only by fibre optics and a freeway system, the Valley's original social network, cut between its rolling hills. Not far from those freeways, a trained eye might spot the Stanford Research Institute, the other propeller of Silicon Valley's origin story, where the computer mouse and robotic surgery were born, and a new era of innovation began. The all-American imagery, which seems to colour the Valley at every turn, masks another side of its culture that thrives on outsiders and their intent, from the moment they arrive, to shake things up. I sensed this disruptive spirit the moment I turned on to a small road leading up to Burgess's house, where a kaleidoscope of Canadian kitsch took over the landscape. The Great White Decor was more than a nostalgic nod to the country that got him here. Since moving to the Valley in the 1990s, Burgess had been in the vanguard of Canadians developing the tools—computer graphics, video, multimedia—that help the world tell stories in a digital age. He was trying to change how Canadians in the Valley tell their story, too.

As I made my way up the circular drive, which Burgess named Maple Leaf Court, he emerged from his house in shorts and a Blue Jays golf shirt. Canada, he warned me, was a theme here. Even his main home and pool house were conceived by an Ontario designer, Elmo Starr, to look like his old Muskoka cottage. As we walked toward the wrap-around veranda, I noticed a red seat from Maple Leaf Gardens. Burgess had bought three, keeping one and giving the others to two fellow Canadians, the long-time global executive Stephen Elop and Spaz Williams, the celebrated computer graphics designer, who in different ways helped build Canada's place in the Valley. Burgess's entire estate, I was about to discover, was a shrine to Canada, from the Moosehead-themed bar in his pool house to Stompin' Tom Connors's stomping board, which he bought at auction for $15,000 back home at Casino Rama.[1]

To explain the history of Canada's diaspora here, Burgess led me to a pair of Muskoka chairs—what else?—that offered a sweeping view of the forested hills around Woodside, near Palo Alto. There was enough space here to hit golf balls from the front yard and not hit the horse farm next door (although he said his sons once did, breaking a window that cost him $1,200 to fix). It felt a bit like the entire mindset of Silicon Valley, where you can drive the ball as far as the mind's eye can see, and it won't be far enough. This is the land of moon shots—a place that, like Burgess's house, has both Canadian playfulness and American boundlessness.

As we sat down, Burgess began with his own story of departure and reconnection. He graduated from McMaster University with a commerce degree in 1979, and took a sales job with Honeywell over Procter & Gamble because the hiring manager had a nicer suit, which he assumed meant he made more money. The decision changed his life. In 1984, he jumped to Silicon Graphics Inc. (SGI), a new computer company out of the Valley that specialized in 3-D graphics and needed sales help to get its machines into the Canadian market. Knowing little about the emerging sector, Burgess devoured the field's most authoritative textbook, *Principles of Interactive Computer Graphics*, written by the pioneering computer scientists William Newman and Robert Sproull, and began at SGI Canada as employee number one. All he had was the textbook, a demo machine in his basement and one prospective software developer, Alias Research, which had no money for new equipment. Fortunately for Burgess, Alias's application engineer was Steve "Spaz" Williams, who had just graduated from Sheridan College and was one of its star students. Burgess sensed he had met a prodigy and convinced Alias, in exchange for access to SGI machines, to let him take Williams on sales calls to demonstrate them.

In the late 1970s and early '80s, Canada was a hotbed for computer-generated imagery—or CGI—talent. Studios looked north for animators, especially those from Sheridan who, like Williams, had studied under Robin King, one of the early masters of computer graphics. There was enough talent coming out of Canadian schools that several companies—Softimage, SideFX and Alias among them—decided to stay put. Canada was hot. (During a 1982 labour dispute, striking animators at Warner Bros., the studio founded decades earlier by Jack Warner—a Canadian from London, Ontario—publicly blamed Canadian animators for stealing their work.)[2] As the sector ballooned, Burgess was able to sign up many of the new players for SGI equipment, including Alias, which then developed the software that enabled James Cameron, the Canadian-born director, to create T1000, the liquid metal shape-shifting villain in *Terminator 2: Judgment Day.*

Computer animation continued to grow at a furious pace in the early 1990s, giving audiences *Aladdin*, *The Lion King* and *Toy Story*, but by then the business was morphing again, a bit like T1000, and reconstituting itself as a centralized, corporate machine rather than the sort of diffused talent network the cyber-economy had promised. In 1994, Microsoft bought Softimage from the Montreal filmmaker Daniel Langlois and his partners, after their software was used a year earlier to animate the dinosaurs in *Jurassic Park.* A year later, Silicon Graphics bought Alias Research and merged it with another acquisition, Wavefront Technologies of Santa Barbara, and put Burgess in charge, with a mandate to keep the company ahead of Microsoft in the creative space race that Hollywood and Silicon Valley had launched. They feared Steve Jobs was not far behind, with his ambition to turn Pixar into a global powerhouse.

As computer animation became the It child of technology, with *The Simpsons* as both its progeny and provocateur, more and more Canadians flocked to the Valley. Williams moved there to work on *The Abyss* and *Jurassic Park*, and later teamed up with another Canadian, Jim Carrey, to make *The Mask.* Todd McFarlane, a Calgary-born comic book creator and entrepreneur, went south to help develop Marvel's Spider-Man franchise.[3] Rex Grignon, a Sheridan grad, developed the *Jim Henson Hour*, before joining Pixar to work on *Toy Story* with other Canadians like Glenn McQueen, who crafted some of the best Buzz Lightyear scenes. Bill Reeves, a Waterloo and Toronto math grad and one of Pixar's co-founders, went back and forth between countries, writing the company's master algorithms and helping it create another piece of revolutionary software, RenderMan. (Reeves earned his PhD at the University of Toronto, developing a diagnostic tool for cardiologists using angiogram imagery, which became the foundation for some of the animation software that predicted character movement.)[4]

It was a defining moment for Canadian technology, when Toronto could have become a global leader in computer graphics, perhaps even twinning with Silicon Valley and Hollywood. There were enough Canadians in both places to make it happen. Instead, pioneers like Burgess and Williams could do only so much, deploying teams in Toronto, or Montreal and Vancouver, but never quite able to see Canada take the lead. Burgess came close in his years with SGI in the Valley, when he secretly funded an engineering team in Toronto to work on a software package called Maya that promised to transform filmmaking. His gamble paid off when the 3-D graphics application was released in 1998 and first used for *The Matrix*. Future versions of Maya have been used to make countless video games, special effects and blockbuster films, including the 2019 computer-animated version of *The Lion King*. Silicon Graphics, however, could not keep pace with the bigger technology changes underway in chip design and processing speed that ushered in the new century, and its fortunes began to spiral, taking its Toronto team with it. By then, Burgess had moved on, taking over as CEO of Macromedia, the CD-ROM giant that he turned into a software powerhouse—it created Flash, Final Cut and Dreamweaver—before selling it to Adobe, in 2005, for close to $4 billion. Burgess has since retired from full-time work and joined the boards of Rogers Communications, Adobe and Nvidia, the technology pioneer whose chips and processing units power many of the best computer games. He's also counselled a couple of generations of Canadians trying to make their mark in Silicon Valley.

There's thought to be a quarter-million Canadians like Burgess in the Valley, although the number who registered for the U.S. census as Canadian-born U.S. residents or citizens is less than a hundred thousand.[5] Whatever the exact figure, it's likely the largest population of foreign professionals in the region, and that begs a number of questions. Why does Canada continue to lose strategically valuable sectors like animation and the talent that goes with them? Why is it that Valley entrepreneurs are the ones buying out Canadians, and not the other way around? And why are so many Canadians here, working for others? Burgess took a sip of iced tea and offered one word: ambition. Canadians often choose the certainty of good over the prospect of great. In the variables of Bob McClure's formula, we have plenty of purpose but not so much risk, which means we settle for small adventures, even in the Valley.

One of Burgess's oldest Canadian friends in the Valley, Jennifer Holmstrom, has built a career around the ambition gap. Since moving here from Ottawa in the 1990s and earning an MBA at Berkeley, across San Francisco Bay, she's spent the past two decades recruiting executives, engineers and designers for Valley heavyweights. She helped Facebook staff up in its early years and since then has advised some of the region's hottest startups for GGV Capital, where she's head of talent, guiding the companies it invests in to look for problem solvers and global thinkers. For the former, there's usually a good selection of Canadians. For the latter, not so much. We don't think ambitiously enough. "It's a mindset," she said.[6]

Doug Bergeron, another active tech investor, puts our preference down to "optimization"—a pragmatism he learned as a top math student in Windsor, Ontario, but didn't hone until he was in grad school, studying systems management at the University of Southern California, which he had chosen for its abundance of good weather. In his studies, and later in his investments, Bergeron has found Canadians tend to excel as the number two in companies. He figures it's because we bring a pragmatism that balances nicely with the typical brashness of a founder. We're that programming yin to America's entrepreneurial yang. Perhaps it's our scarcity of good weather, which requires us to optimize the gift of sunny days rather than experiment with them. "I don't think of myself as an Elon Musk of the world. I'm focused on optimizing. I'm a problem solver," Bergeron conceded.[7] "We don't get one hundred bullets in Canada. Maybe we get five. My life has been about coping with those five bullets, with those limited resources, and not being centre of the universe. We don't think of ourselves as the greatest country since the Roman Empire. We view ourselves as competitive spokes in the wheel."

Donna Morris was one of those spokes, growing up in Ottawa where she worked in human resources during the nineties tech boom, until Adobe (the creator of PDFs) bought her employer and transferred her to San Jose as head of talent. In the company of twenty-two thousand employees, she discovered hundreds of other Canadians, scattered around the world, in addition to the three hundred based in Canada. "They make for congenial and effective leaders," she found.[8] "They're able to bring together disparate types of people. They're more inclusive. They're naturally good at convening people of different backgrounds." When she arrived at Adobe, Morris's assignment was to shake up the status quo, drawing on her ability to connect cultures, to be the signal string that holds a web together. In 2012, she abolished performance reviews,[9] making Adobe one of the first companies to do so. Adobe managers and employees were spending upward of one hundred thousand hours a year on the formality and largely saw it as a rote exercise that staff dismissed as "rank and yank." When Morris scrapped the process and replaced it with more casual check-ins, she made international headlines as the Canadian who killed performance reviews. In her Canadian mind, it was simply a no-nonsense way to make the best use of everyone's time.[10]

To understand this culture of optimization, and why there are so many Canadians who are part of it, Burgess directed me across the Valley, to the little town of Mountain View where his old company, Silicon Graphics, had a decade earlier sold its campus to the fastest-growing startup in history. Today, the occupant, Google, is worth close to $1 trillion,[11] having built an empire out of algorithms that optimize the way we search for information. Its headquarters, known as the Googleplex, sprawls across Mountain View and has become a trophy for the new economy, a three-million-square-foot complex of buildings that has enough of everything—swimming pools, an amphitheatre, beach volleyball courts, laundry, sleep pods and eighteen cafeterias serving free food—to ensure employees, if they don't want to leave, never have to.

It's hard to be at the Googleplex and not feel you're entering a cult. Pretty much everyone there sees the Google Way as a model for American techno-capitalism, and an assurance that human capital can be used for both economic and social good. Brainpower, wisdom and guile are central to the company, as are the vast, diverse networks of the digital age. It's stitched together by a simple mantra—"don't be evil"—that sounds dubious in the face of data breaches and oligopolistic profits, but remains sacrosanct around the generous campus. When I arrived, I found employees playing Frisbee on the many lawns or biking between buildings as if this were an endless summer of grad school. I wanted to learn more about optimization but also explore something I had heard in my travels: that the Google Way drew on the Canadian Way, through idealism, openness, diversity and, at times, naïveté. If true, it would help explain why so many Canadians were part of the company's hyper-growth story, and why Eric Schmidt, its former executive chairman, once told his chief financial officer, Montrealer Patrick Pichette, "Google is Canada. If you dropped Google in the middle of Canada, it would fit in."[12]

Google's origin story is compelling. Two Stanford grad students, Larry Page and Sergey Brin, wanted to organize the world's information by assigning keywords to every page, and then ranking those pages on the basis of their history, the relevance of their keywords and, critically, how many other web pages linked to them. It would all be coded in a secret algorithm that aimed to test the popularity and trustworthiness of information. Shona Brown, a Fredericton-born engineer and management consultant, was one of the first Canadians through the door at the Googleplex. After studying at Carleton University, Brown won a Rhodes Scholarship to Oxford, where she played hockey, and then moved to Stanford to pursue a PhD in industrial engineering. She explored strategy as "structured chaos." After completing her thesis, she wanted to return to Canada for an academic or think-tank position but found nothing appealing, so she joined the consulting firm McKinsey & Company, first in Toronto and then in California, where she made partner. She was recruited to Google in 2003, as it was preparing to sell shares to the public, meaning the company's prospective shareholders had to get ready for structured chaos.[13]

Working with Brin and Page and the rest of the executive team in those early heady years, Brown was tasked with ensuring that Google's business and workforce could grow exponentially without tipping the whole place over. Job one was getting business operations to a global scale before rivals in the search business did. Job two was a comprehensive talent strategy, what she called "people operations," to add thousands of engineers and marketers around the world while maintaining the Google Way. Although Brown thinks the link is overstated, her arrival paved the way for a steady stream of Canadians who are today all over Silicon Valley. One of the first was Don Harrison, a Halifax-born lawyer who helped take the company public and went on to run mergers and acquisitions. Next was Sukhinder Singh Cassidy, a Tanzanian-born entrepreneur who grew up in St. Catharines, Ontario, and ran Asia and Latin American sales. She went on to become president of StubHub. Then came David Radcliffe, another Carleton grad, who was brought on board to run real estate operations, helping the company create more Googleplex-like offices in its expanding empire. Deepak Khandelwal, a Saskatchewan engineer, ran global online sales and later became head of innovation at CIBC. Angus Birchall, a Canadian digital marketing specialist in New York, came aboard to build revenue-sharing partnerships for an increasingly hostile media sector. As Birchall saw it almost from the moment he arrived, "Google is a place that draws a certain personality type, and that attracts Canadians, people who are adventurous, hard-working, nonconformist and creative. The soft skills Google wants line up with what a Canadian expat is."[14]

Shuman Ghosemajumder, one of Google's early cybersecurity leaders, chalks it up to something less ephemeral than soft skills. When he joined the company in 2003, fresh from MBA school at the Massachusetts Institute of Technology, he discovered "a greater concentration of smart people than I had ever been around, and that included MIT." A rare computer geek who was also a championship debater, Ghosemajumder grew up in London, Ontario, coding games for his Commodore 64, and in the mid-nineties studied computer science at the University of Western Ontario. As a kid in London, he read an essay by Guy Kawasaki, Apple's marketing guru, whose advice on tech careers was simple: "Step One: Move to Cupertino." Ghosemajumder[15] was mesmerized the moment, as a teen, he first visited the town outside San Jose and saw the Valley's ambition through Apple. A decade later, after he'd spent time running his own internet software development company, Google recruited him to develop its ad business, based on algorithms. He went on to help build Gmail. And at each step his thinking kept coming back to that word, *ambition*, even for people. "Pretty early on, I realized Google was one giant talent play," he said. In addition to not being evil, their mantra was find the best, hire them and figure out their job later, which led Google recruiters to a lot of Canadian schools.

Later, when Ghosemajumder became chief technology officer of Shape Security, a Valley firm focused on computer-generated cyberattacks, he continued to see Canadians everywhere, and began to chalk it up to Canada's colleges and universities, which enjoy a much smaller standard deviation in the quality of education than you'd find in the U.S., or, for that matter, anywhere else. Canadian graduates in computer programming, and most other fields, are pretty good no matter where they study. Maybe not as good as those coming out of Stanford or MIT, but within a keystroke. Ghosemajumdar noticed something else about his own education: Canadian schools tend to allow more creative licence in programming than American ones do. "American schools tend to be much narrower," he found. "Deeper, maybe, but also narrower. You graduate knowing how to do only one thing." He figured that's another reason so many Canadians ended up at Google: the company wanted creative thinkers.

Shona Brown's biggest hire at Google was undoubtedly Pichette, a fellow Rhodes Scholar she'd known at Oxford, where he helped coach her hockey team. In 2008, Pichette had been chief financial officer of Bell Canada Enterprises and had just stepped down as president of operations for Bell Canada; Brown realized he was the right person to help Google expand. Her challenge was to convince Brin, Page and Schmidt to bring another Canadian into their inner circle. She described his steady hand and sage mind, and how his Canadian touch might keep Google on an even keel as it began to take in money at the rate of $10 million an hour. Anyone who has worked with Pichette knows him to be innately balanced, a trait he attributes to his Canadian upbringing. "Because of our geography, because of our history, because we're not born out of revolution, we're accommodating," he told me.[16] Once on board, he was saddled with plenty of revolutions and all the so-called science projects that make Google what it is. He would be the guy who had to scrutinize the out-there proposals that every employee is encouraged to spend 20 percent of their time conceiving. Glasses that can read emails. Cars that can drive themselves. Thermostats that can program themselves. As every big idea found its way to Pichette's desk, Schmidt counselled him to ignore the ones that aimed to reach fewer than a billion people. It was Risk + Purpose to the nth degree.

Chris O'Neill, another Canadian who came in under Shona Brown and still considers her a mentor, rapidly expanded the company's footprint in Canada and then ran the Google Glass project, before leaving in 2015 to become CEO of Evernote, a popular app for note-taking and list-keeping. At his new company, which he ran until 2018, O'Neill figured 5 to 10 percent of his 320 employees were Canadian—"and it was growing."[17] During his decade at Google, he had come to see a number of Canadian strengths. First, the quality of post-secondary education was consistently high, which is why he told the Evernote HR team to hire as many Waterloo co-op students and grads as they could. Second, he found Canadians could blend into America, while also bringing with them an uncommon worldview. "The ethnocentric view that pervades America isn't Canadian. To run a global company, you need a worldly view and Canada has that in spades," he said. Third, Canadians know they're outsiders, even when they blend in, which keeps them curious. Fourth, among executives he noticed a disproportionate number of Canadians he'd consider "Level 5" leaders, who mix an emotional touch with the knowledge, experience and discipline required of the C-suite. And lastly, generosity. His role model on that front was Pichette, who one year donated his entire bonus to charity.

When Pichette retired in 2015, he and his wife, Tamar, moved to London, England, to have a travel base from which they could pursue real adventures—climbing mountains, riding extreme bike trails and running marathons. In a farewell letter to his colleagues, which he posted online, the Canadian wrote of his personal desire to restore some balance to his life. Privately, he was also thinking about the need for society to find some balance. He worried about the earnings treadmill that corporate America had created for itself, and how it distracted big companies like Google from their original purpose and their employees' and customers' passions. America's growing wealth divide concerned him, too, and it was getting worse because of Google and its neighbours. Their shares had made a small number of people, him included, fabulously rich; their technology, while universally available and largely free, had made a small number of companies fabulously powerful, too. The world was more polarized, and neither the American way nor the Chinese model was working terribly well for the mass of humanity. It was one of the reasons why, after leaving Google, he took up a senior role with Inovia, the large Quebec investment fund, to advise Canadian entrepreneurs on how to think more ambitiously and globally. Short of government intervention, he felt it was one of the few ways to spread the wealth he saw so concentrated in the Valley. But as hopeful as he was in some ways, he also knew the world was pulling itself apart on YouTube, Facebook and Twitter, and more than a free market would be needed to fix it. As he and Tamar left Mountain View with their backpacks, Pichette wondered if, in that Canadian spirit, there might be a third way. He had already taken a stab at it, organizing a group of investors in 2013 to pay close to $40 million for sixty-five thousand acres of wilderness known as the Kenauk lands in western Quebec, near Montebello on the Ottawa River, to give to the Nature Conservancy of Canada to protect from development.[18] They added a research centre, the Kenauk Institute, to ensure Canadians learned from the land, too. He was motivated, in part, by a concern that highly successful expats don't return enough of their wealth to Canada, or do enough to inspire Canadians. Equally, he felt Canada could do more to draw on some of the early inspiration that so many Canadians had brought to Google. He still believes, "Google is the story of the world coming together."

If there's a quintessential Canadian at Google, it may be Rachel Potvin. When I visited the Ottawa-born engineer at the Googleplex in 2017, she was responsible for the infrastructure that hosted all of Google's code. That meant two billion lines of code were in her hands, giving her almost divine power over the largest and most fluid repository of computer language in history. Or as she preferred to call it, "a single source of truth."[19] Potvin's job was to protect the repository while also ensuring every coder at Google had access to it—a tension she had to manage with Canadian diplomacy. Potvin had greeted me at the Googleplex, and as we walked across the sun-drenched campus—it was eighty degrees Fahrenheit with clear skies—you could sense the energy of minds racing about, each seeming to focus on the equivalent of a moon landing for the information age. It's what brought Potvin here, and continued to give her purpose in her work. "It's cheesy," she said, "but we want to make the world a better place."[20]

Potvin's father was French Canadian, and her mother had immigrated from England, which meant she travelled to Britain a lot as kid, seeing the world through Canadian eyes. After studying computer science at McGill, she joined the Montreal office of Ubisoft, the French video game giant, where she was one of only three female developers in a cohort of four hundred. Although Potvin became the first female tech lead at Ubisoft Canada, she was always reluctant to contribute to shooter games. "I started to feel I wasn't contributing to society the way I wanted to," she told me. She left Ubisoft and, after an MBA and study trip to China, found the chance at Google to take on something more fulfilling. Despite some initial reluctance to move to the U.S. because of its gun culture, she relocated to San Francisco in 2008 and took on increasingly complex challenges, including the development of Google Cloud. It was during that assignment she discovered something about being Canadian. Three of her ten team members were compatriots, who like her saw the world of information the way Canadians tend to see health care, as something that should be free in price and equal in access. They were on a mission.

Potvin interrupted our campus walk, saying she needed a white board to continue. She pulled out her phone and opened a Google app to book a meeting room—the Googleplex, among other attributes, is a maze of meeting rooms—where she could use a white board to explain the algorithms that shape our lives and how vulnerable they are to what's called "code dependency." Once we found a room, Potvin drew a diamond for me to illustrate a special concern called "diamond dependency." Think of a diamond, she explained, in which the top point (A) is dependent on both side points (B and C), which in turn are dependent on the bottom point (D). When D changes, the impact may hit B and C at different times, which could completely break A even though the code writers for A have no idea what's coming. It's a bit like a car crash on one side of the highway that causes a pile-up of rubberneckers on the other. No traffic planner can adequately prepare for it. Yet, as computers do more of our coding, those sorts of knock-on effects have become perpetual risks. Our digital society has become like an L.A. freeway of pile-ups, leading to frustrations and suboptimal decisions on freeways all over the virtual map. When Google set out to optimize the world's web of information, it faced the risk of an endless web of diamond dependencies, but by keeping its ever-growing terabytes of code in one place, Potvin argued, Google and its army of human engineers were able to keep a handle on this complexity. It echoed Pichette's view of a third way, blending the free, even libertarian, flow of information on the internet with a bit of central control at the Googleplex.

Potvin walked me back across campus, explaining how she and her husband, also Canadian, were wrestling with a different kind of diamond dependency. It was the great expat question: Should they apply for American citizenship? They wanted their children to grow up Canadian. But they also knew their opportunities here were greater than they could find elsewhere, not least because of lower taxes and better weather. Potvin conceded Google was a cultural bubble, a bit like the Truman Show of technology. But at least it was closer culturally to Canada than much of America. We passed gaggles of young engineers—some sitting at picnic tables, some just out for a stroll—speaking in more languages than either of us could identify, often in the same conversation.

Potvin found there was a degree of community around the campus that reminded her of Canada, and was essential to her open approach to storing code. Her system would collapse if her thousands of engineers didn't implicitly trust each other, or her, at the end of the day. It's a bit like a mass transit system. Engineer it all you like, but if commuters don't trust each other to allow people to get off before others get on, chaos will ensue. At least here, in the words of Shona Brown's thesis, it's structured chaos.

In a matter of two decades, Google has grown from a university thesis idea into one of the world's largest companies, largely because of structured chaos and the underpinnings of trust among its engineers. Of course, not everything at Google turns out to be good, despite its "don't be evil" mantra. Turns out, its algorithms see evil, hear evil and speak evil, because they're constantly shaped and informed by human behaviour. And therefore Google can't help but mimic us humans, a bit like those unavoidable traffic jams. It's a function of design, as well as habit. Through Google, some evil was inevitable. Its algorithms skewed the world's understanding of knowledge, and access to it. Perhaps unwittingly, it threw the world's publishing order into something much worse than structured chaos when it drove eyeballs, and advertising, in all sorts of new directions. Perhaps unwittingly, its YouTube platform became a boulevard for bullying and bigotry, just as its artificial intelligence (AI) platforms became as biased as the men who coded it. Could those problems, and those evils, have been prevented, or at least mitigated? Could the Canadians at Google have done more to help it, and Big Tech, find a better way? Or would that have been just another pinprick of Canadian piety, the kind Americans tend to swat away like a mosquito?

Before I left, I noticed scores of Googlers lined up for the company bus home, assured their work was in trusted hands. It reminded me of that scene in *Bowling for Columbine*, when Michael Moore discovers a neighbourhood in Toronto where people are okay leaving their doors unlocked. They trusted their neighbours not because they were Canadian but because it was a good neighbourhood. We may never have it across society, but at least among Canadians, a general level of trust has ensured agreement on a host of issues—public health care is good, education should be subsidized, gun ownership should be controlled—and underscored our own mantra of peace, order and good government. We got there through a series of social bargains, which many Americans see negatively as compromise. But perhaps, as Potvin showed me at the Googleplex, it's not compromise at all. Perhaps it's optimization, a means with which to find the most efficient, least damaging way to integrate complex and competing ideas. Perhaps that's why so many Canadians stand out in the world's most competitive tech community—because they seek value through inclusion rather than victory through elimination.

For the hundreds of thousands of Canadians here in the Valley, a natural style of accommodation has paid off well. Many are here because they enjoyed a good upbringing in Canada, including cheap, and excellent, post-secondary education. Many still have family and friends in Canada, just a short flight away. Some keep vacation homes, too, on Vancouver Island, in Muskoka or along Nova Scotia's South Shore, all while enjoying California's benevolent winters and exhilarating vibe. They know that if and when they want to head home, Canada will be waiting. In that respect, they've constructed their own optimization game. But for at least one group of expats in the Valley, the individual pursuit of optimization had become unpalatable. Even though they had surfed the great Canadian wave down to California, this group felt they had not done enough to return the favour. A bit like Pichette in retirement, perhaps a bit like Google in its early years of search optimization, they realized they had taken more than they'd given. Here they were, at the epicentre of technology, and they weren't doing enough to help their own country innovate.

In 2009, on the eve of the Vancouver Winter Olympics, a small group of expats looked forlornly at the world's podium of innovation and saw we were nowhere near owning it. And then they realized they could optimize for that.

4

Putting the Crazy Back in Canuck

THE C100'S QUIET CAMPAIGN TO CHANGE A COUNTRY

The centre of the digital universe is a discreet luxury hotel that's hard to notice from Sand Hill Road, the Menlo Park thoroughfare where technology startups flock to win the support of investors and the validation of Silicon Valley. Without the help of Waze or Siri, a visitor could easily miss the hotel, nestled into the Santa Cruz hills as naturally as the eucalyptus trees that surround it. The same can't be said of its patrons, who flock to the Rosewood because they want to stand out. In the Valley, this is where you come to make a statement. At breakfast, venture capital players can be seen sizing up entrepreneurs who think they're building the next Facebook. At lunch, corporate executives from the East Coast, dressed down in Valley chic, can be heard listening to twentysomethings explain how their latest idea will change humanity. Or at dusk, in the golden glow of a setting sun, you can see clusters of self-styled disruptors, toasting their latest success by the tiered pool patio. The Rosewood is surrounded by three of America's wealthiest zip codes, with more billionaires than anywhere west of Manhattan, and no one seems to want to keep that a secret. Economically, technologically, sociologically, this is where the digital revolution comes to bask in its hubris.

On a cool, dry evening in late November 2009, the Rosewood was also where several dozen Canadians tried to get their country to make a statement, to shed its national modesty in favour of some silicon sass that everyone here seems to think is all you need to shake things up. At the time, Canada was revelling in the hype of the upcoming Vancouver Olympics, with expectations of a record medal haul thanks to a national effort called Own the Podium that targeted amateur sports spending on those athletes who stood the best chance of medalling. Could the same approach be taken in the world of technology? Could we back the entrepreneurs and expats who stood the best chance of winning? We needed to do something. Nortel was gone. BlackBerry was going. In the wake of the financial crisis, investment in innovation was headed to zero and tech entrepreneurs were pulling out of Canada as if it were Saigon '75. For a new generation of Canadians in the Valley, it was enough already. They had come to the Rosewood to figure out how to get back our digital game. If we could come together to win the Winter Olympics, they asked, why couldn't we do the same in the competitive arena of innovation?[1]

Earlier that year, with the economy back home still reeling from recession, diplomats at the consulate in San Francisco had started to mobilize expats to kick-start something, in the hopes of better connecting Canada's tech sector with the Valley. The diplomats began by inviting a small group of tech investors for lunch to explore the idea of an organization modelled after expat groups from other countries. The government would help. Chris Albinson was among the guests and couldn't get out fast enough. A tech investor, he had been in the Valley for a decade and found himself at home with its libertarian and disruptive airs. In his mind, innovation and government went together as well as oil and water—one being good for energy, the other only to dilute it. Anthony Lee, another venture capital player at the lunch, had the same impression, but the two knew something had to be done. They agreed to develop the idea on two conditions: it would be a non-profit volunteer association of company operators, founders and investors, and government would have to stay far away. As for a name, Lee suggested C100—C for Canada and 100 for the number of expats they should recruit. Someone in the room joked that the name sounded like a West Coast AM radio station, perhaps not knowing it actually is the name of an East Coast FM station, in Halifax. No matter; it stuck.

Over the spring of 2009, Albinson and Lee charted a more entrepreneurial path for the C100, and pulled in every enterprising Canadian they knew on the San Francisco Peninsula. Even though they had not met before the consulate lunch, the two dealmakers quickly saw themselves as kindred spirits, as equally passionate about Canada and Canadian entrepreneurs as they were contrasts in appearance. Born in Sudbury and raised in Vancouver, Lee was West Coast corporate, with his natty wardrobe and trim fit. He had studied at Princeton and Stanford and run a few startups before getting into venture capital in 2000. Even though he and his Toronto-born wife had been gone from Canada for decades, they did everything they could to stay Canadian, ensuring their American-born kids were dual citizens, played competitive hockey in the Bay Area and cheered for Canadian teams. Albinson preferred the dishevelled look of a disruptor, often taking meetings in jeans and a slightly untucked shirt. Raised in Kingston, Ontario, where his father taught phys. ed. at Queen's, he had opted for Western and caught the startup bug there with his first venture investment. After graduation, he worked for the Canadian tech legend Terry Matthews and, in 1999, just before the dot-com crash, moved to the Valley. He planned to stay only two years. A decade on, he still couldn't get enough of the place.

As they developed the idea of an expat network, Lee and Albinson called a couple of expat friends, Katherine Barr and Lars Leckie, for advice. Albinson knew Leckie from Kingston, where he went to Queen's and was a competitive sailor before heading to Stanford for engineering. Leckie had travelled the world for sailing and was always surprised by how proud Canadians were and how little influence they usually brought to bear. In his early years as an investor in the Valley, he had come to believe "Canada was like Minnesota"[2]—nice when present, forgotten when not. He told the Canadian duo to be bold. Barr had also studied at Stanford, but was not your typical globalist, at least on paper. Growing up on a farm[3] outside Perth in eastern Ontario, she had gained an outward curiosity from her mother, an avid traveller, and a passion for technology from her father, who taught her the coding language BASIC. She went to McGill, studied a bit of Japanese and moved to Nagano after graduation, to help with the 1998 Winter Olympics. From there, her sister, who was working for Elon Musk, convinced her to move to Stanford for a masters in management and engineering. Her sister also introduced her to the Digital Moose Lounge, a club for Canadians in the Bay Area where she discovered "our crown jewel"—our expats. She told the duo to be brash. She had learned in the U.S. to lose the subtleness of Japanese culture and the conciliatory nature of Canada, and replace them with an American competitive streak that a lot of other Canadians seemed to be missing. She had learned to promote herself, and ask others to promote her, too. In the new economy, it wasn't a zero-sum mentality, and it wasn't quite like anything she had seen in Canada. The Valley exuded a culture of "co-opetition"—a natural inclination among rivals to help each other, to share ideas and opportunities, to revel in their opponent's success and to never stop building. Grow the pie. Pay it forward. Clichés in the Valley flow like Napa wine, and everyone believes them. The C100, Barr argued, could foster the same spirit for Canadians.

To make a difference for Canada, the group agreed they had to be more than a mutual support club. They'd have to drive deals, and that meant getting government out of the way. At their next meeting, that's what they did. The consulate had convened a larger group of expats over lunch at Il Fornaio, an upscale Italian restaurant in downtown Palo Alto, and Albinson, once again, couldn't get out fast enough. Like many expats the world over, he had run away from the status quo, and here he was feeling pulled back into it, watching bureaucrats show slides and talk about bilateral trade numbers. It was then and there he knew the C100 had to be a rebel force, a kind of movement that was willing, even wanting, to shake things up. At the door he was surprised to run into the new consul general, Stewart Beck, who felt the same way. He had just moved back to San Francisco, having opened Canada's trade office in Silicon Valley in the 1980s, and couldn't believe how little was happening. His last posting was as Canada's top diplomat in Shanghai, so he understood trade and investment. With an MBA from Queen's, he also understood business. What he couldn't figure out was why every time the consulate introduced visiting entrepreneurs to investors here, nothing happened. His top trade officers, Thierry Weissenburger and Tab Borden, had been running a program to pay for Canadian entrepreneurs to come to the Valley to talk up their companies, and the startup crowd all seemed to leave with the same story: great time, no contacts. Beck wondered if the entrepreneurs could blow things up. "I agree this is terrible," he told Albinson before they left. "Can you help me make it better?"

The C100 founders reflected on what other countries were doing, which was plenty. They had taken note of how China, Britain and Mexico approached the Valley to build inroads for their companies back home. They were struck by Israel and its focus on entrepreneurship, and how it worked strategically to help successful startups connect with the world capital of innovation. You'd expect that from Israel, where every day brings with it the threat of war, and where it's widely felt that idle allies are unhelpful allies. More surprising, perhaps, was India. It was racing ahead. Albinson had been there to study the startup culture and spent time with a group of South Asian expats in California called TiE, or the Indus Entrepreneurs, who had become a driving force between the subcontinent and the Valley since launching their organization in 1992.

As the Olympics approached, the C100 founders felt they were ready to test their idea with a broader Canadian community. To show they were serious, they booked the Rosewood for a reception, hoping to recruit a nice round number of one hundred members. They even promised to designate as "charter members" those guests who signed up and paid an initiation fee of $850. Initially they wanted entrepreneurs and investors. No salaried types. They especially wanted founders, a favourite word in the Valley, where being on someone else's payroll is for chumps. Creating something is what real entrepreneurs do. When the organizers sent out invitations, they got sixty-six confirmations. Of those who came, sixty-five signed up, which Lee and Albinson figured was good enough to call themselves the C100. In the startup world, aspirations are worth more than reality.

Beck, the consul general, saw it as government doing what it should, serving as convener and catalyst for a committed group of expats who could do the rest. In this case, the group left the reception with an ambitious goal: to get one hundred of the best Canadians in the Valley to help the top one hundred Canadian growth companies that had moved beyond the startup phase.

They'd offer connections to capital, people and ideas, and give entrepreneurs as much inspiration as they could muster. To inspire this new community, the group held a kickoff dinner in San Francisco the following March, a week after the Olympics ended. Rob Lloyd, a Manitoban and senior executive at Cisco who later became CEO of Virgin Hyperloop One, gave a rousing speech comparing Canada's podium wins with the success of its expats in the Valley. He noted we had done exceptionally well in team sports. Inspired by the sudden burst of patriotism, Shaan Pruden,[4] a long-time Apple executive from Ladysmith, British Columbia, who headed worldwide developer relations, stood on a chair and led the crowd in an impromptu singing of "O Canada." "That's when we knew we had something," Lee said.[5] [6]

Forming a network was one thing; activating it quite another. To avoid the trap of most expat associations that become little more than social clubs, the C100 founders had to get busy with their purpose, which was to promote Canadian entrepreneurs and the unique links—capital, talent, advice—that Canadians in the Valley could provide. As Beck liked to remind them, "We know a lot of you aren't going to move back but you want to give back."[7] At the Digital Moose's Canada Day party, one of the C100 founders, Michael Worry, met a young Canadian, Atlee Clark, who had worked in the Canadian embassy in Washington and just moved to San Francisco with her boyfriend, looking for work and a shot at Silicon Valley. Worry suggested Clark call Albinson and Lee, as they were looking for someone to run the new non-profit. Beck vouched for her, too, as she was the cousin of a former chief of staff—a reminder of how small a community Canada can be, with every person just two or three emails away from pretty much everyone else. In Israel or Singapore, that's played up as an advantage; in Canada, it can be knocked down as elitist, even an abuse of privilege. But this wasn't Canada. Lee took her for lunch and hired her on the spot. She had no experience in entrepreneurship or engineering but lots of gumption. He figured that was exactly what Canada needed.

To make a splash, Clark[8] put together a one-day event to profile young Canadian firms, led by a then-obscure e-commerce company called Shopify. (She would later join Shopify as its first employee in the Valley and eventually move back to Canada with the company.) She then launched an event series called "48 Hours in the Valley" to expose Canadian entrepreneurs to Bay Area networks, and ensured that visitors like Michael Litt (Vidyard) and Ted Livingston (Kik), who were both getting their Waterloo companies off the ground, got the contacts they needed, through the expat network. Behind the scenes, as a founding board member and eventual co-chair, Barr turned the commitment into a second job, travelling to Canada to recruit entrepreneurs and working her network in the Valley with the intent of helping Canadians build "unicorns," the billion-dollar companies that are to tech entrepreneurs what the Olympic podium is to athletes. The C100 was soon a thing, and a leading voice for Canadian entrepreneurs at home and abroad. More importantly, it began to show Canadians the power of a diaspora, something that Israelis and Indians had understood for generations. Next, the charter members reached out to policy-makers in Ottawa to explore ways to help the Valley's venture capital largesse flow north, and for more Canadian entrepreneurs to grow their businesses to a global scale. Beck arranged a coming-out reception for them in Ottawa, at the Pearson Building on Sussex Drive where the foreign affairs department is based. Albinson, a former Young Conservative, also met with Stephen Harper's finance minister, the late Jim Flaherty, foreign minister John Baird and industry minister Tony Clement to explain how

Canada's withholding tax system discouraged U.S. investors from funding early-stage Canadian companies. It was one of the main reasons, Albinson told them, that venture funding had collapsed. Flaherty liked his thinking and changed the tax structure, which Albinson figured brought an additional $1.4 billion of venture funding from the U.S. to Canada.

The Harper Conservatives and then the Trudeau Liberals both liked the C100 because it had no political bent and genuinely seemed to want to make Canada better. The Liberals, soon after they came to power in 2015, suggested to Dominic Barton, the management guru, that he use the network to help the economic advisory council he had been commissioned to lead. He recruited Barr and fellow C100 board member Angela Strange, who were among those who talked the Liberals down from an early desire to tax capital gains at a higher rate—a decision that, they warned, would have truly led to a Saigon '75 for risk capital. On immigration, they and other C100 members also advocated for fast-track visas for entrepreneurs who needed them for specialized talent they were recruiting from abroad, and would see their companies crash if they had to wait. Their arguments were so compelling that when Trudeau heard them, he made the issue his personal cause with the bureaucracy. Another C100 founding member, Scott Bonham, was instrumental in kicking into gear a national artificial intelligence initiative, shuttling between his home in Palo Alto, Toronto and Montreal to ensure the Canadian effort was ambitious enough to make a difference in the world. Too many Canadian initiatives, Bonham feared, were designed to be the best in Canada, rather than best in the world. He later joined the boards of the Vector Institute and the Canadian Institute for Advanced Research, two of the bodies tasked with putting Canada's AI ambitions to work.

Such attitudes, and ambition, may be the biggest dividend the expat network has returned to Canada. In the past, a typical Canadian company coming to the Valley would present itself as realistically as possible; Canadians like to be seen as rational people solving rational problems. No Hollywood hype. No moon shot rhetoric. No Elon Musk crazy talk. Which in the U.S., as many Canadians have discovered, means no money. Working with Canadian business incubators like Communitech in Waterloo and MaRS in Toronto, the C100 network was able to put the crazy back in Canuck, the way the country did for Olympians in Vancouver.[9] "There used to be a stigma around Canadian entrepreneurs," Lee explained.[10] "That's now in the past tense." Albinson[11] went further, saying, "Canadians used to try to integrate. Now we're speaking up more as Canadians. In a world with more connectivity, it's now an advantage to have that worldview."

The C100 has been so successful as a diaspora network that it's been approached by companies and government representatives to franchise the model, in New York and London. When Weissenburger moved to Boston as trade commissioner, he helped a group there replicate the expat network. Beck, in his next post as high commissioner to India, tried a different approach, working with Ryerson University's Digital Media Zone to launch an incubator in Mumbai for Indian and Canadian entrepreneurs to work together, laying the foundation for a new generation of Canadians to connect with the subcontinent. If there's a challenge for these pioneers, it's the organic nature of networks. Rarely can they be designed, or designated. They just happen, driven by clusters of people who want to make a difference. The best investors know how to spot that passion in the best entrepreneurs. The best countries seem to do the same with their best expats. You can't engineer it; at best, you can harness it.

Nearly a decade after the C100 launched, it continued to serve as a portal for Canadian entrepreneurs trying to build their networks in the Valley. It runs events and produces materials, but its greatest value may be the connections that charter members like Ajay Royan provide. I had met Royan a few times in Canada and went to see him at his office in the Presidio, the old military compound overlooking the Golden Gate Bridge. The building had been leased from the U.S. military by the filmmaker George Lucas, who in turn rented out space to an assortment of new-economy types. Royan's venture capital partner, Peter Thiel, among the co-founders of PayPal, hung out here before he relocated to L.A. For a time, so too did J.D. Vance, author of *Hillbilly Elegy*, and Sean Parker, Mark Zuckerberg's co-founder at Facebook.

Royan walked me through the airy office, which had the feel of a movie set and hints of Canada everywhere. I noticed a stash of Tim Hortons coffee, alongside the Philz and Starbucks, in the pantry. There was also a bookshelf brimming with Canadian histories, including sagas of the Canadian Pacific Railway and Hudson's Bay Company. Royan, who prefers jeans and cowboy boots at work, explained the books were more than cultural touchstones. He and Thiel are avid students of history, and always on the lookout for intersecting trends as well as diverging interests. I asked Royan to explain how a Tamil, raised in the Middle East and then Toronto, educated at Yale University and now immersed in Silicon Valley, remained Canadian. His life has been a crossover since birth, which is true for a lot of expats. Born in south India, he spent his early years in Abu Dhabi, where his grandfather owned an oil services company. His family left the region during the 1991 Gulf War, when Ajay was eleven. Some of his relatives went to Singapore, others to Australia and New Zealand. Ajay's parents chose Canada. As a young teen, he read Edmund Burke and could see the liberal values he espoused reflected in the Toronto suburbs where his family had settled. Royan was struck by how "Canada was less parochial than many places. To me, Canada meant room to grow. And there was bonus: you had hacked the Americans." By that, he meant we had cracked the American culture code. We were part of America and yet removed from it. It was the sort of dichotomy an Indian expat could appreciate.[12]

When Royan went to Yale, he studied under Martin Shubik, the game theorist who was born in the U.S., spent his childhood in England and was sent to Canada during the Second World War to complete high school. He stayed on to study math at U of T and was then part of the first brain drain, leaving for Princeton to work with John Nash, the Nobel economist portrayed in the book and film *A Beautiful Mind*. Shubik was equally brilliant, although controversial among academics for his growing ties to U.S. industry. Before globalization became a buzzword, he believed international trade gave so much power to the victors that the economy, like the Cold War itself, would become a winner-take-all system. In that sort of environment, markets would lose their natural redistributive powers by driving the early leaders—the innovators—to do whatever it took to develop, and keep, a dominant share of growth. Shubik found a testing ground for this theory in postwar industrial America, advising General Electric and the RAND Corporation, and then investing, through a vulture fund, in exotic new products like mortgage bonds that preyed on the downfall of others.

Royan thought the combination of mathematical theory and market discipline was perfect. As a newcomer, he was awed by North America's "surplus capital," and especially impressed by how his first employer, Deloitte, found ways to harness it. After the Cold War, the Big Four accounting firms had discovered a surplus of talent from regions steeped in mathematics and finance—Eastern

Europe, Southern Africa, South Asia—that were suddenly open to the world. Moreover, a tradition of chartered accountancy in Commonwealth countries like Rhodesia, which became Zimbabwe, helped create a different kind of diaspora—one of financial advisers—just as the world of finance was taking off in the 1980s. Seeing how immigration was more challenging in the U.S., the firms started to park those wandering expats in Toronto, where they could serve American clients without leaving their time zone and still be accessible to Europe and Asia. Surrounded by Afrikaners and Bengalis, Royan found Toronto to be the perfect finishing school for his next move, to the Valley, which he considers "an emerging market that happens to be in the First World." He had met Thiel through mutual friends who were Yale alumni, and knew the German-born, American-raised investor was looking for outsiders, people who could see what the Americans around them were missing. In the early 2000s, Royan joined Clarium Capital, Thiel's contrarian hedge fund, and then, in 2012, launched Mithril Capital, named for a fictional middle-earth metal from *The Lord of the Rings*. Over the next seven years, he raised more than $1 billion to invest in pioneering companies. Royan's philosophy was to avoid "a concatenation of buzzwords"—the Wall Street habit of stringing together business ideas rather than crafting an investment thesis from scratch. He had another secret weapon: as a director of the C100, he had a clear line of sight on thousands of Canadians in the Valley. In his tranquil retreat near the Golden Gate Bridge, he could include those Canadians in his network of networks to follow opportunities around the world.

We watched the fog lift from the Presidio, where in the early years of the Second World War the U.S. military plotted its response to Pearl Harbor. The ghosts of history were not lost on Royan. Staring out toward the bay, he compared his strategy to a submarine and argued Canada needed to take the same approach to the world. We can't blitz our opportunities, as we'll never have the scale to sustain an attack. Mithril followed the same strategy, with a low profile, no Twitter stream and no PR strategy. It didn't even publish its portfolio, the antithesis of Silicon Valley's chest-thumping bravado. He considered it to be part of the Canada ethos, to "be excellent, be global, be quiet." Better to be like Israel, he said, constantly circling those opportunities without the notice of others. "Game theory–wise, a submarine is much smarter than an aircraft carrier," he said by way of explanation. "You surface only when no one expects it."

Like the other C100 founders, Royan was trying to instill in the Canadian network a standard of excellence. Others may prefer more profile. He cheated to execution, seeing the need for more outcomes and a greater understanding of those outcomes. Royan harkened back to Shubik's winner-takes-all game theory to make his point. In Silicon Valley, and increasingly across the digital world, there's no silver medal. Moreover, as Shubik found before his death in 2018, the ever-growing size of the digital economy is likely to encourage even more irrational market behaviour, like the kind that led Big Tech astray. The prize is just too big. Sensing the dangers of a distorted market, a bit like a tumultuous sea for a submarine, Royan in 2018 shifted his base to Austin, Texas, and opened another office in Toronto, which were both among the fastest-growing tech centres in North America.

Could Canadians restore some balance to the irrationality of Big Tech? Royan hoped so. As we were wrapping up, he excused himself to greet a lineup of prospects, most of them Canadian firms, who were gathered in his waiting room, enjoying a mug of Tim Hortons. John McCall MacBain, the billionaire Toronto founder of *Auto Trader*, was visiting from his home in Geneva.

Bob Friedland, the Canadian mining promoter, was just on the line from Singapore. Andrew Fursman, founder of the Vancouver quantum computing company 1QBit, was here, too, seeking counsel. Royan pulled Fursman into his boardroom, and within a few minutes extracted enough information about 1QBit to tell the entrepreneur that what he really needed was to focus on talent, not technology. Fursman, he suggested, had no talent strategy. Royan realized he might get an investment opportunity out of the meeting, but what he was really hoping for was to push the C100 mission, to push Canada out of its comfort zone and pull Canadians like Fursman into his tempestuous ocean of opportunity, where strategic battles are fought below the surface.

We talked a bit more back in Royan's office, about Canada's inability to see the submarines already at our disposal. We'd lost our signal with them, or perhaps never established it. While Ottawa had helped launch the C100, it was just one network, and as Royan knew, there were tens of thousands of disconnected Canadians out there. People like Shona Brown, for instance. No one from Ottawa had ever called her, even though she was one of the most influential executives at Google in its first decade as a public company. No one ever recruited her to help with, say, net neutrality, even though she was a leading thinker in the U.S. on the topic. Nor did anyone try to recruit Jennifer Holmstrom to help map out a Canadian talent strategy, even though she was doing just that for Facebook. Or reach out to Ajay Royan, whose network with Peter Thiel was more powerful than all of Ottawa's favourite venture funds put together. Our next generation of entrepreneurs like Andrew Fursman, who are building a new Canadian economy, have more to gain from Royan than they'd get from umpteen government innovation programs.

Royan left me with a hint of the frustration—disappointment, really—that Canadians here often feel: that they do more to access the Valley and its vast digital networks for Canada than Canada does on its own. Unfortunately, the costs of complacency are increasing by the year, at an exponential rate most Canadians don't appreciate. It's the nature of the borderless and boundless internet. Before I left, Royan pointed me to the row of war histories on his office bookshelf and recalled his game theory days with Shubik, a self-styled honorary Canadian who was among the first to argue the odds of war increase with the permeability of borders. In the cyber age, that means countries need to think well beyond their borders, indeed beyond geography, to secure their interests. In Royan's mind, that presents a choice: "You can build an aircraft carrier or a submarine. I tell all my companies to be submarines. Canada should be, too."

As I made my way to another part of California, to meet another tribe of Canadians, I wondered if Canada's expats could be those submarines. Surely they could develop sub-surface networks like Royan's, connecting Canadians and Canadian interests in the digital world's proverbial oceans, near and far. In his 2016 book,[13] *Seventh Sense: Power, Fortune and Survival in the Age of Networks*, the corporate director and futurist Joshua Cooper Ramo made the case that such networks had already replaced governments in terms of influence. As Royan might say, they ruled the high seas. Ramo studied science and technology elites: from the physics establishment that Arthur Kerman joined at MIT in the 1950s, to the early brains of Xerox PARC who laid the Valley's foundation, to the Silicon Graphics whizzes who flooded the Valley from Toronto and Montreal in the 1990s. He called them a "new caste," representing the biggest movement of brainpower the world had seen. Unlike in earlier migrations, this caste did not see its destination cities—Boston, San Francisco, London—as journey's end. Rather, its members saw their chosen homes as hubs from which they could expand their networks, pinging back and forth to Waterloo or Bangalore, or wherever their peers may be. It was like the C100 at global scale.

In Ramo's view, such networks have allowed us to move to a distributed age from a centralized one that dates back to the Enlightenment.[14] Power no longer needs to be concentrated, he argued. Before the digital economy, complicated structures—be they companies or computers—had to be in one place, for density and scale. That's how power centres emerged. In the digital age, computers manage all those complications. While this shift has led to a diffusion of power, it has not always led to a distribution of people. The reason, according to Ramo, is another shift from complication to complexity. Computers took away complication by doing lots of manual things for us, and then created more complexity by linking us to opportunities and threats we never before had to worry about. As a result, we need more computers at our disposal and more people in our networks. It's why so many people want to be around others who can thread IQ and EQ, with perhaps some of the cultural CQ that computers can't generate. Successful countries will be the ones who help their citizens, wherever they may be, knit together those human networks.

Caroline Wagner, a science policy professor at Ohio State University, has studied science networks, and concluded individual networks like the C100 are replacing institutional ones the world over. A single science star, she found, can bring together a global network that no university, or government or corporation, can do on its own. "Science is not a command and control system," she argued.[15] "Trained researchers move to places where they can maximize their access to resources and best contribute their talent to the pool of scientific knowledge." The same can be said for digital engineering, robotics, medical research—every field that is pushing innovation and creating new opportunities. In this specialized age, many of those specialists will want to be together, a bit like artists in Medici times. But they'll also want to be around strangers and generalists, especially those with the EQ and CQ that science often lacks. It's one reason why in the U.S., two-thirds of research and development spending is concentrated in just ten states,[16] which Wagner labelled "the geography of knowledge."[17] If you can get the best animators, or scientists, living in one place, the investors and entrepreneurs will follow. It's the Silicon Valley model. Bioscientists have replicated it along Boston's Route 128, as have chip makers in Korea's Samsung Digital City and cybersecurity hackers in Israel's Silicon Wadi. It's why Canadians have to buck the inclination to always call on expats to return home. We need many of them in these brain centres, the smartest places on earth, connecting us to their ever-growing networks.

When the urban theorist Richard Florida set out to study economic clusters in the twenty-first century, he found these concentrations revolved increasingly around creative types, and not just engineers and scientists. His most famous work, *The Rise of the Creative Class*, made the case for public policy to invest in the social and cultural foundations of cities, to lure and retain this creative class, just as governments once built R&D labs to recruit Cold War scientists. Florida is an expat of a different variety, having left his native America for the University of Toronto in 2004. In subsequent research, he discovered that in 2012 the most common word used in LinkedIn profiles was "creative."[18] He estimated a third to half of workforces in advanced economies fell into this class, which included architects, engineers, scientists, teachers, artists, designers, athletes, lawyers, doctors, managers and high-end sales professionals.[19] If governments want more of these people, he told audiences, they would need to focus less on tax rates and industrial subsidies, and more on ethnic diversity, sexual tolerance and freedom of expression.[20] You might think that as cultural conservatism grows in parts of the West, the most talented professionals would seek places that fit with their values and lifestyle, which might lead them to Canada, and keep more Canadians at home. That could happen. But as Florida found, creators still seek out peers, mentors and "cultural heterogeneity."[21] They want direct exposure to new ideas and art forms, and the density of expression that only a handful of cities can provide.

The late Fraser Mustard, a pioneer in medical research, sensed this new world of concentration and distribution when he created the Canadian Institute for Advanced Research, or CIFAR, in 1982. His goal was to use our expats to advance Canadian science by forging global networks for Canadian researchers. Since then, CIFAR has come to see its scholars, especially the ones who have left Canada, as "free agents"—individuals who want to be part of a championship team and are willing to move from team to team to get to one. It's why they seek out the best labs and universities, regardless of geography. For some Canadians, these diaspora networks smack of elitism, using as they do scarce tax dollars and public attention to support entrepreneurs and researchers who have left the country. Mustard, who died in 2011 at eighty-four, saw it quite differently.[22] He saw it as an opportunity to plug Canada into far bigger, smarter and richer networks than a relatively modest population like ours could ever create on its own. In some ways, he saw the need for a C100 before many of its members were born.

If Mustard's vision was lacking anything, it was an appreciation of the power of narrative. Networks need to do more than connect people. They need to be more than anodyne nodes linked by fibre-optic lines. They need to inspire and speak to the purpose of Bob McClure, in his formula for Canadians and our collective adventure. Israel has demonstrated that for decades, just as India and Singapore are doing today. Canada can, too. We've long been a nation of storytellers—of lyricists and screenplay writers, journalists and video stars. Such storytellers were among the earliest members of our diaspora. And they may be needed more than ever to shape our narrative, as the emotions of our planet become more powerful than any of the engineering the Valley has thrown our way.

To understand the power of narrative, I travelled to southern California to visit with one of Canada's most celebrated storytellers. He'd been out of the country for more than forty years, but wasn't sure that mattered. He still saw himself as essentially Canadian, and in Ajay Royan's view was still very much a submarine. In fact, submarines were his specialty.

5

Pragmatic Dreamers

CANADIAN STORYTELLERS IN THE AGE OF IDENTITY

James Cameron stepped back from the deck of a ten-metre-deep pool he had constructed in a film studio near Los Angeles International Airport, to have a word with Sigourney Weaver. He'd been working with the actress off and on since the 1980s, when they collaborated on his breakout film, *Aliens,* and counted her as a friend as well as co-worker. In this moment, she was also a good sounding board for his latest thinking on underwater motion. Cameron had spent the day guiding a team of actors through an underwater scene for a sequel to *Avatar,* and wanted Weaver's opinion about the intended magic of discovery he was hoping to capture. The stakes were high for Cameron. After its release in 2009, *Avatar* became the best-grossing film on record and inspired him to construct this massive tank, as well as a set in New Zealand, to film four sequels that are scheduled to start appearing in late 2021. The epic, which he wrote, will shift from forests and mountains to the oceans of his fictional world, Pandora; it will also include a new character for Weaver, whose old avatar, Grace Augustine, he killed off in the first chapter. Weaver was back because Cameron wanted to work with her again—just as he wanted to give the actress, who turned seventy in 2019, more screen time, which isn't always common for Hollywood's aging stars.

After Cameron relayed instructions to his crew, who were bobbing around the pool's surface, he returned to Weaver to get her perspective on the frames he'd just shot. They were hanging in suspended animation on a bank of screens next to the pool. The director and star studied the monitors and began talking about how human bodies move under water, absorbing the joy of life around them while struggling for the oxygen of life that sustains them. It was a bit like the Earth today, at once breathing and gasping, and why he's made *Avatar* his ode to the planet and the communities that shape it. The more he and Weaver talked about the scenes he'd just shot, the more apparent they were as a team, with Cameron as loyal to Weaver as she to him. As both writer and director, Cameron views his actors and crew as partners; it's the magnet that draws many of them back to his marathon projects. That sense of partnership is also the magnet that keeps him Canadian, forty years after he moved to L.A. as a teenager with his family.

"I love Canadians," Weaver told me when Cameron headed back to the tank. "Your humbleness, your decency is rare."

Without question, Cameron is the most commercially successful Canadian ever to make it in Hollywood, a century after a trio of Canadians—Mack Sennett, Louis B. Mayer and Jack Warner—helped build Tinseltown. His films *Titanic* and *Avatar* are the two top-grossing movies in history, thanks to the revolutionary techniques he brought to computer graphics. For all the high tech, though, he believes it's his emotive storytelling that continues to make his films stand out. It's the humbleness that Weaver called out. During another break, as Cameron surveyed his set, surrounded as it was by millions of dollars of high-speed computers and underwater cameras, he again looked more animated by the conversation with Weaver about how the human body should move, and how to express wonder. That movement, that sense of wonder, he said, almost hugging Weaver, had to be the thread of their story. In 2012, Cameron steered a submersible to the floor of Challenger Deep in the Mariana Trench, eleven kilometres below the Pacific Ocean's surface. It was the equivalent of scaling Everest, reaching a place only two humans had been, in 1960. Sure, an unmanned machine could have made the same journey, he conceded. But a robot (and this from the creator of *Terminator*) would not have captured the wonder of silence, darkness or ancient sands, just as a robot, or animator, could not match the wonder of humans moving underwater. In Cameron's Canadian imagination, this human sense of wonder is still our best approach to both storytelling and the planet. And finding the balance in that story is still a Canadian trait.

Cameron's need for balance has been a perpetual force in his career and his adult life in the U.S. In 2004, after the U.S. invasion of Iraq, he gave up his application for U.S. citizenship and began to spend more time in the South Pacific, particularly New Zealand and Indonesia. He and his wife, Suzy Amis Cameron, opened an alternative school in the Malibu canyon where they live, to foster sustainable science and more inclusive leadership. But he was never far from Canadians. In 2008, they helped launch the Green School in Bali, an international centre aimed at giving youth a balanced approach to learning and living; it's now run by a Canadian, John Hardy. With another Canadian, Chris Blair, a former Morgan Stanley banker, Cameron launched an investment fund to pursue companies and technologies to radically reduce the world's use of fossil fuels. In September 2017, the Camerons even showed up in Vanscoy, Saskatchewan (population: 339), to announce plans to build the largest organic pea protein facility in North America, along with a four-year research program with the Saskatchewan

Food Industry Development Centre, a non-profit group, to develop beans that could eventually replace meat in the world's diet. Cameron likes to tell audiences that since Suzy, a long-time vegan, convinced him to move to a plant-based diet, his energy levels are higher, his fat levels are lower, even his sex life is better. It's a matter of balance.

Cameron has applied the same philosophy to his film projects, which is not typical of Hollywood. "I try to live with honor, even if it costs me millions of dollars and takes a long time," he said when *Avatar* was released. "It's very unusual in Hollywood. Few people are trustworthy—a handshake means nothing to them. They feel they're required to keep an agreement with you only if you're successful, or they need you. I've tried not to get sucked into the Hollywood hierarchy system. Personally, I don't like it when people are deferential to me because I'm an established filmmaker. It's a blue-collar sensibility."[1]

His blue-collar ethic goes back to Chippawa, a small town near Niagara Falls where he grew up. Cameron's father worked as an electrical engineer at a local mill, and his mother raised the five kids, often telling them about her experiences in the Women's Auxiliary and in the process giving him a role model for future female heroes. As the eldest, Jim had plenty of time to explore and tinker. He built model airplanes and sent toy rockets skyward, and once made headlines by launching a hot air balloon, powered by candles, that was reported in the local paper as a UFO. Stanley Kubrick's 1968 film, *2001: A Space Odyssey*, opened his eyes, just as it did the world's, to the human side of science fiction. He had found his genre. He soon discovered his medium, too, learning to scuba dive at the YMCA in Buffalo, developing a lifelong obsession with the deep. Jim carried his sense of adventure to L.A., where his father was transferred in 1971, although, at seventeen, he struggled to find his way. After two years of college, studying physics and astronomy, he dropped out to focus on writing, only to discover he needed to also work in blue-collar jobs like truck driving to pay the bills. In his spare time, he tinkered with film and special effects, developing a skill that was not in demand until *Star Wars*, the 1977 George Lucas blockbuster, made sci-fi mainstream.

Fascinated with artificial intelligence, and the coming struggle between humans and machines, Cameron wrote *Terminator*, and used the cheapest space he could find—empty warehouses and waterways—to film it with a former Mr. Universe, Arnold Schwarzenegger. The film generated enough money for Cameron to get serious about special effects and team up with Canadians from Sheridan and Seneca Colleges for his next projects, *Terminator 2, Aliens* and *Titanic*. They changed the way movies were made. The technology, though, wasn't the hardest part. In Cameron's mind, as films became more technologically crafted, their stories had to dig even deeper to be rooted in humanity. It's why he clings to a line he considers Canadian: to "dream with your eyes wide open."

When Cameron won his first Oscar for *Titanic*, Canadians had already been coming to Hollywood for nearly a century. From the beginning they had brought the critical eye of a people who celebrate their observer status the way others declare themselves to be great powers. We are the people who grow up watching and listening, and realizing how similar we are to others, Americans especially, but not among them. For generations, that proximity has made Canadians natural Hollywood storytellers. The Canadian advantage has become a challenge, too, as storytelling, and mythmaking, become more powerful in an age of identity and time of division. Cameron sees it in his struggle to open the world's eyes to climate change and to the mistruths that got us here. Of course, that's part of being a tribal species, particularly one that can be as divided as the creatures of Pandora. Cameron knows that we like to see ourselves in stories rooted in beliefs over truths, especially ones that pit us against them. It's the survival gene—paranoia—at work. Except that now, through social media, those stories can reshape our worlds in an instant. In this age of identity, they're as powerful as any fighting force and, without mediation, just as dangerous. Which may be why mediators of the human narrative will be needed more as technology accelerates the speed of storytelling and distorts it, too. Canadians can do that. In a way, it's been the calling of Canadian expats since their earliest days in L.A.

Hollywood got its start in 1908, after nine filmmakers, working with Thomas Edison, formed the Motion Picture Patents Company to prevent anyone from controlling the rights to a film made on his cameras or other equipment from his New Jersey lab. It was an early attempt to have hardware control software, with predictable results. Software won. Filmmakers flocked to the West Coast, and its friendlier courts. They quickly discovered the sunshine was friendlier, too, allowing for open-lot shooting and endless days without the need for expensive lights.[2] Canadian-born Allan Dwan was among the first directors and producers to make the move west, along with another Canadian, Gladys Smith, who under the stage name Mary Pickford became the biggest star of her time, known around the world as "America's sweetheart." It was just the beginning of Canadian expats shaping the American dream. Al Christie, from London, Ontario, built what is thought to be Hollywood's first studio, in 1910. He was followed by Sennett, a Quebec-born comedy writer, who in 1912 created Keystone Studios to produce his own style of slapstick that grew into the Keystone

Cops franchise. With a stable of new stars like W.C. Fields and Charlie Chaplin, Sennett redefined American comedy, using his iconic pie-in-face routine as a staple for more than a thousand films. Sennett was followed by two other Canadians whose names became studio brands that still tower over Hollywood: Warner from London, Ontario, and Mayer from Saint John, who joined forces with Marcus Loew to create Metro-Goldwyn-Mayer, or MGM, the birthplace of *The Wizard of Oz*, *Gone with the Wind* and the very notion of a blockbuster, a film that could become its own franchise. They would have loved Cameron.

It was not a coincidence that many of the early Canadians in Hollywood, and on Broadway, were tied to comedy. As Lorne Michaels once advised Rob Burgess when he was building a computer graphics empire in Silicon Valley, "use humour; it's all we've got." In *Stand and Deliver*, Andrew Clark traced the pipeline of Canadian comics back to Merton Plunkett and the Dumbells, a troupe that started a musical review for front-line soldiers in the First World War and gained a mass following in the trenches by turning their talent to satire, taking direct aim at the British and Canadian commanders, who had never been lampooned in the style Plunkett developed. Long before *M*A*S*H*, they found humour in war, which Clark called "Canada's first internationally successful comedy export."[3] The troupe stayed intact after the war, making a splash on Broadway until the Great Depression ended their run. (Their members went home, including Jack MacLaren, who changed careers to pursue advertising, launching an eponymous agency that decades later became a marketing icon.)

The golden age of television created a new demand for Canadian talent, especially gag writers for late-night stars like Dean Martin, Steve Allen and Johnny Carson.[4] Norman Jewison, who moved to L.A. to direct *The Andy Williams Show*, became the de facto leader of this new clique of TV writers and directors when he began to host lunches at his Malibu beach house for Canadians trying to break into Hollywood. Monty Hall joined the crowd in 1961, after being connected by Bert Pearl, one of the founding members of CBC Radio's *Happy Gang*, who had moved to L.A. Hall then connected with the actor Lorne Greene, and the two opened doors for many of the Canadians who followed, including Alan Thicke, David Foster and Alex Trebek. Just as Greene had become America's favourite father through the TV show *Bonanza*, Hall became America's most trusted game show host through *Let's Make a Deal*, by being both the welcoming host and friendly middleman with just the right knack for delivering quips without upsetting sensibilities. It was a model Trebek took to even greater heights on *Jeopardy!* as Canadians came to be seen as the Walter Cronkites of entertainment, the embodiment of empathy and trust. As the late NPR host David Rakoff observed of Hall, and by extension his Canadian approach to mediation, "Who could be more American? And yet, remember, Monty only facilitated the deals."

Many of those early writers and performers came from CBC Radio, where they honed a Canadian knack for simplicity of language and eye for detail that made their stories universally appealing. Few Canadians seized on this more effectively than Michaels, a Toronto boy who grew up in Forest Hill as Lorne Lipowitz, developed an early love of television—he married Frank Shuster's daughter Rosalind—joined the CBC and finally moved south, first to L.A. and then to New York, to write comedy.[5] After winning an Emmy as a writer for Lily Tomlin, Michaels convinced NBC to let him launch his own comedy show, which the network insisted be done from New York because it had empty studio space there. He stacked it with Canadian writers, for a simple reason. He believed British humour was class-based, while American humour was hero-based. Post-Watergate, his new show needed to be egalitarian, a stage that would feature stars and double down on political humour, while still being accessible to a mass audience.[6] The Canadian art of mediation would be tested like never before, as Michaels deployed humour to tell America, through wars, scandals and eventually Donald Trump, about itself. One of Michaels's prized Canadian catches was Mike Myers, who he learned about from another Canadian, Martin Short. Myers had won his first film role in London, in *John and Yoko: A Love Story*, earning a bit part after the director, Sandor Stern, called him out for pronouncing *been* as "bean" instead of the American pronunciation, "bin." Stern deadpanned: "It's your lucky day, kid. I'm Canadian."[7] Myers didn't forget the joke. The son of British immigrants who had worked in London, Toronto and Chicago, he grew up learning to blend his father's English cynicism with the class-free sensibility of a Canadian suburban youth, and would go on to lampoon and yet elevate middle America through satire. In some ways, the middlebrow Canadian humour saved *SNL* as it struggled through the morality wars of the Reagan and Clinton years.

During the 1990s, CBC budget cuts led to a greater outflow of creative talent, especially to the U.S. and Britain where professional visas were plentiful. As the world moved into a more diverse age of entertainment—cable TV, video games, movie streaming—the demand for English-speaking, American-savvy and globally minded talent blossomed, from writers and directors to animators and performers. If content was king, Canadians were often the ones behind the throne. But even as they excelled on the world stage, the country that got them there struggled to turn that success to its advantage. For the most part, our cultural diaspora was a bauble to be celebrated—cheered and trotted out for official receptions and galas, but little more.

This disconnect with the cultural diaspora has baffled Elliott Lefko ever since he was a music promoter in Toronto dealing with expats abroad. Now that's he one of them, running his business from L.A., he's still perplexed. Lefko made the move in 2005, as part of a long line of Canadians trying to transform the concert world. It started with Mike Cohl, who in the 1970s changed the economics of concerts forever when he agreed to promote an entire world tour for the Rolling Stones. Cohl's shoes were filled by another Canadian, Mike Rapino, a marketing executive who grew up in Thunder Bay, and in 2005 became CEO of L.A.-based Live Nation, the world's largest live entertainment company. Lefko had watched those Canadians restore some balance to the music business, through concerts, and wanted to restore the artistic spirit, too. He had been at it since he was a student at York University in the late 1970s, at first picking bands for RPM, a nightclub on Toronto's waterfront, where he discovered Slow, a band that pioneered grunge, and then promoting Nirvana, Red Hot Chili Peppers and Arcade Fire. But he realized there was only so much he could do from Toronto. He opted to join Goldenvoice,[8] the concert promoter owned by the Anschutz Entertainment Group (AEG), and moved to southern California.[9]

Lefko still remembers arriving at AEG, and someone saying, "Hey, you're Canadian. Do you know Leonard Cohen?" As if. Lefko had been a fan since childhood, even travelling to a Greek island where the singer briefly lived, hoping to capture the same muse. With the new Canadian in the fold, AEG wanted to put his compatriot Cohen on an arena tour, in the hopes of staging a comeback. Lefko agreed to the opportunity but not the choice of venue. He thought arenas would not work for Cohen. He went to meet his Montreal-born idol, and created an instant bond talking about the poet Irving Layton. Cohen was interested in returning to the concert stage and had a plan that would see his band members wearing suits and the tour starting in small theatres in the Maritimes, to restore some of his allure. So began five years of touring that capped Cohen's career and left fans around the world with a lasting impression of the man and his style. (Cohen was a favourite at the Canadian consul general's residence in Hancock Park, where there remains a framed copy on the living room wall of "Listen to the Hummingbird," the unfinished piece also known as "Sweet Little Poem" that he recited there before his death in 2016.)

The deal helped secure Lefko's reputation. When I met him in 2016, he was back briefly in Toronto to promote Alessia Cara, who was just emerging as a performer. She had headlined as a warm-up act for some bigger names but had yet to break out of Canada. (A year later, she would headline Michaels's *Saturday Night Live* and be on her way to star status.) Lefko had opted to promote her concert at Massey Hall, to see what kind of market she could draw. He was happy with the early response to ticket sales, and, as we dropped by Cara's dressing room, told her the show would be packed. It was still a few hours until the doors opened. Lefko and I found some seats in the theatre to continue talking while he listened to the backup musicians rehearse. In the decade or so since he had been in L.A., he had come to appreciate the value of Canadian social networks in the entertainment capital. It's great for pretty much every artist who flocks there from Canada. But is there a value to Canada? Have all those expat singers and promoters, and actors and screenwriters, helped their industry grow in Canada? Could they do more than build their own careers? Ultimately, could they even form a collective beachhead for their country, the way the C100 did in Silicon Valley? Lefko wasn't sure. The music business, like the movie business, is star-based and driven by individuals. Your nationality is no more important than your accent, a useful attribute if and when it's needed for a part. On the surface, in some very superficial industries, those cultural props can be taken for granted, especially when they're as benign as being Canadian. But to those artists trying to build something bigger than their own careers—to restore balance in the world, as James Cameron was trying to do, or restore art to pop culture, the way Lefko imagined—the notion of a collective will is not only convenient, it's essential. It's what can give a diaspora purpose.

Alan Cross has been the unofficial historian of Canada's popular cultural migration for more than a quarter century, since he turned his growing celebrity as a Toronto radio host into a career making documentaries, including *The Ongoing History of New Music* and *The Secret History of Rock*. As he travelled the world to trace the roots and ambitions of rock, Cross was struck by the number of Canadian musicians he found everywhere: Japan, China, Britain, Singapore. And of course the United States. In his mind, Cross can trace this migration back to Paul Anka and Neil Young, who went south in the 1950s and '60s because there were so few opportunities for them in Canada. "It was just a dead-end place here,"[10] Cross remembered. "Even groups like the Guess Who had to go to America to get some kind of recognition. We didn't really have a music industry through the fifties and sixties. We had offices and small record labels but mostly they were branch-plant operations." In 1971, the imposition of Canadian content rules—CanCon—changed that. Seeking a new style of cultural nationalism, Ottawa introduced regulations requiring radio stations, in return for their licences, to play domestically produced or performed music at least 30 percent of the time. It worked. A domestic industry, outside the CBC, was born. No one today sees Canada as a music backwater, not when Drake has moved his studio to Toronto and the country produces global stars like Alessia Cara as routinely as hockey medals.

Through the transition, Bob Ezrin has been among the most prolific Canadian musical talents anywhere, influencing a generation of rock 'n' roll as a producer, musician and writer. One of his collaborators, Alice Cooper, called him North America's George Martin. Ezrin took Kiss to superstardom, writing the band's hit "Beth" and playing piano for it, and has produced Lou Reed, Deep Purple, K'naan, U2, Taylor Swift and Peter Gabriel. He eventually split his time between L.A., Nashville and Toronto, always keeping an ear open for Canadian talent. He found Canadians stood out musically because of our sense of open spaces, which he thinks are essential to the Canadian identity. "The silence of the north," he calls it, reflecting on the summers of his youth at Lake Simcoe.[11] Even a new generation of urban artists continue to strike him as expansive in their thinking, a bit like the northern sky: "Look at what Drake talks about. He's a deep thinker. He's a philosophical cat. So is Abel [the Weeknd]. Same with Shawn Mendes. We have a depth of humanity. We're circumspect. We check our surroundings and our place in it. We have the humanity that stars in the U.S. don't always project, especially on the male side."

Canadians have influenced Hollywood and New York for a good century. In Nashville, it's been more recent. The city couldn't crack America's Top Five for music production in the 1970s, despite it being home to Johnny Cash and Glen Campbell. By the 2000s, it trailed only New York and L.A., and accounted for most of the industry's growth.[12] Music City was also loaded with Canadians who had moved to Nashville both for its proximity (a two-hour flight from Toronto) and the intensity of its studios. One of Ezrin's early collaborators, Eddie Schwartz, came to appreciate the power of Nashville's Music Row in the 1990s, when the economics of songwriting in Canada had started to go south. Schwartz spent his early career in Toronto, writing songs for Canadian and American artists. Even after he scored big in 1980, with Pat Benatar's "Hit Me with Your Best Shot," he chose to stay in Canada so he could work with other songwriters like Marc Jordan and David Tyson, and still produce for bands like the Doobie Brothers. He wanted to raise his two children in Toronto and send them to Canadian schools. But eventually, Schwartz realized Canadian music publishers would never have the international reach of Americans, which meant they couldn't afford to pay writers. "In my day, people could pay me," he explained.[13] "There was enough money in the system in the seventies, eighties, nineties that I could wake up every morning and write. Now that doesn't exist."

The industry was returning to its origins as a centralized content machine, not unlike New York's Tin Pan Alley at the turn of the last century. Music labels were so desperate for global hits, they were willing to pay for hundreds of songs, knowing only a few would be recorded and distributed. It was economies of scale, and posed an optimization challenge similar to that of Silicon Valley. One search. Millions of results. One recommendation. When Schwartz got to Nashville in the late nineties, he figured there were about two hundred other Canadian songwriters there, even though only a few did well. In Toronto, he always worked with the singer; in Nashville, it was a division of labour. He'd show up at Music Row in the morning and be put in a writing room with a potential collaborator and the hopes of producing two songs by the end of the day. In Toronto, he had aimed to produce one song a week. The Nashville model was a volume play. If Music Row could consider a few hundred songs every week, it might find a few to take to Blake Shelton or the Dixie Chicks. American scale was not the only adjustment for Schwartz. His kids had to adjust to the U.S. south, with its subtle cultural lines and prejudices, and peculiar take on the English language. He had to stop saying "excuse me" and start saying "whaaaa" to his co-writers, and stop trying to rhyme "pain" and "again," which southern singers prefer as "agin."

Schwartz eventually made his mark. He was able to write for a living, which he wasn't sure he could still do in Toronto, and he found the U.S. to be a better platform for his mission to save music as we know it. The early days of the internet, and the challenge it posed to Canadian music labels, had driven him to Nashville, but even Music City wasn't immune to the digital revolution and the wicked economics it inflicted on the industry. Global platforms—YouTube, Apple, Spotify—were suddenly spinning the money dials that once belonged to the big labels, while new tools like blockchain were threatening to further disrupt, and perhaps salvage, the livelihoods of the creative class. (Blockchain is an emerging technology that allows members of a network to make instantaneous, and secure, transactions without intermediaries like banks or record labels.) Twenty years after Schwartz got to Nashville, the music industry was out of balance, with creators attacking distributors and with consumers at war with platforms, and headed for its most pitched battle yet between Music City and Silicon Valley. Schwartz, the Canadian, stepped forward. With the very notion of music rights in question, he put up his hand to become president of the International Council of Music Creators, the global collective of songwriters who had watched their business model dwindle as consumers everywhere downloaded and shared without consent and artists increasingly produced without direct compensation. Schwartz knew the era of the independent songwriter—the solo artist and member of a creative class who could work anywhere for anyone—was under threat. He also felt he could do something about it, in a Canadian way.

In 2018, the music world set out to redraft copyright rules, first through sweeping new European regulations, and then with a series of new trade agreements in North America, Asia and Europe. Working as a Canadian artist in the U.S., Schwartz had come to appreciate Canada's grounding in the world's two major intellectual property systems. While we respect commercial rights, Canada is also one of the few countries with author rights, which some musicians compare to human rights, meaning the artist and their work cannot be separated even after commercial rights are sold. The artist, in other words, should always enjoy some benefit from their work and maintain control over any effort to alter it. As Schwartz described it to me, artists must have "an eternal attachment" to their creations, a spirit he wanted to instill in new intellectual property agreements. The main front was Europe, which both prides itself on cultural protectionism and fears its capacity to keep pace with technology. Shuttling between his home in the U.S., his council's headquarters in France and the European Parliament in Brussels, Schwartz found himself playing the Canadian in the middle, keeping his American counterparts engaged while also reassuring those Europeans who viewed the U.S. as having a "pro-America cultural agenda." In the end, in late 2018, he helped convince the European Parliament to force the internet giants to better police copyright infringement and ensure fair remuneration for creators. (The Europeans separately introduced a tax on digital links to published content.) In his mind, it was a Canadian balance between collective spirit and individual will, melding the creative rights of artists, the commercial rights of distributors and the content rights of consumers.

If the new model sticks, and if Ottawa and other governments move to be more flexible with their copyright laws, Schwartz can see a day when Canada's creative class can work freely, as Canadians, anywhere. But in that world, can our expats be more than artists adrift in the creative sea? In a global economy, where national rules like CanCon are no more than fingers in a dike, can they continue to tell our stories? And as they take on the digital world, can they use their Canadian nature to shape the narrative arc of others? We will need them to be more than cultural ambassadors, to do more than attend Canada Day receptions or be all hometown Drake at awards ceremonies. We will need these Canadian voices to assert our collective voice in a noisy world of culture that will be on more platforms and more devices than anything we've known.[14]

For centuries, we've let the geography of open spaces inform our voice. In the coming decade, we will require a different narrative, along with different cultural rules—from intellectual property to free speech—to allow more diverse voices to be part of it. In the face of identity politics, Canada can restore some of the balance that Cameron brought to Hollywood and the introspection Ezrin took to Nashville. But surrounded by social media, our cultural narrative can no longer be left only to those with high-wattage names. In the 2020s, that narrative will need to be shaped by a new generation of storytellers using a new generation of media.

To find that cultural diaspora and see where they're headed, I realized I had to look beyond the recording studios of Nashville and sound sets of southern California to explore the disruptive platforms that all those Canadians in the Valley had helped build. The journey would lead me across the Pacific to the unlikeliest of Canadian creators embracing a most improbable audience, and to CanCon as it had never before been imagined.

6

Humour, Humility and Chutzpah

HOW TO BE A CANADIAN STAR ON ASIAN YOUTUBE

Go to any corner of the world and try to find the Canadian district. Good luck. There won't be one. Even though there are plenty of Canadian chefs, writers and DJs in those places, you won't find Canadian restaurants, theatres or clubs. There's the odd outpost, like the Maple Leaf Pub in Houston, where Canadians can find a familiar pint at the bar and a hockey game on the screen. But even those redoubts, with their barbecue and bowling nights, are more a commercial venture than cultural countenance. Perhaps this lack of collective expression is proof that our expat population is not really a diaspora, at least not yet. Perhaps it's just a population of individuals doing their own thing. Most Canadians abroad, after all, have left a good station in life, hoping to reach an even better one. They're in the profession of their choosing, surrounded by others in the same field, hoping to achieve even more than they did back home. Unlike other diasporas, whose members are pushed away by scarcity, most of these Canadians have been pulled away by abundance. They don't need each other for support, or protection, or the reinforcement of their home truths. They've got a new tribe, a global one in most cases, to build and guard their new identity. In many minds, a Canadian restaurant, theatre or club would seem so unnecessary, so parochial.

On those few occasions when Canadians do get together, it's more about the past than the future, to wax nostalgic about their shared roots. Rarely do they gather to build a shared identity, the way other global populations do with their food, song and stories. That identity, such as it is, tends to be left on the shoulders of a celebrity, major or minor, who can be trotted out to help welcome the governor general, or maybe to hand out an award at a charity run. But in the main, our storytellers have gone abroad to lend their voice to the stories of others. They're typically a film or TV star, or perhaps a journalist or author, who has made it in a new place, not as a Canadian so much as a highly competent and neutral figure who carries both a view that's unthreatening to the world and a voice that speaks gently to it. They're the channel for other cultures, and able to be so precisely because our story is so unimposing.

For decades, our diaspora quietly and dutifully served as the world's adaptable storytellers, whether it was television personality Mark Rowswell as China's loveable Dashan, or Ruby Bhatia as India's favourite after-school veejay. Even today, a quarter century after the internet rewired humanity, you can turn on a TV in London or Lahore and hear the Maritime lilt of Lyse Doucet, the neutral and ubiquitous voice of BBC News. Or you can pass a screen in New York or Nairobi and hear Toronto's Ali Velshi and his baritone voice on NBC, passing judgment for Americans on America. Because they're not associated with somewhere, those voices play well everywhere. And if they do manage to incite an emotional response, it can be pacified with a universal note of calm, and the whisper, "it's okay, they're Canadian." Heard and seen everywhere, we're the middling people, ideally suited to tell the stories of somewhere, as long as that somewhere isn't Canada. It's as if collectively Planet Canada is too shy for that, a nation of introverts who'd rather be the storyteller than the story.

Simon and Martina Stawski beg to differ.[1] They stumbled upon our introverted, indeterminate and at times inscrutable place in the world when they moved to South Korea from Toronto, shortly after university. The couple had graduated from the University of Toronto, where they studied education only to discover there were no jobs for teachers. It was 2008. The world had calmed down from 9/11, and Asia was booming, so they headed for Korea, where planeloads of millennials had landed jobs teaching English as a second language. The Canadians hoped they might land something at an international school for a year and then head to Japan. It didn't seem to matter that the only Korean they knew was from a teacher training stint Simon had done in a Korean neighbourhood in Toronto. They figured they'd get their foot in the door and work their way up to a more secure position.

Simon had grown up in Pickering, east of Toronto, aware of his family's Polish roots but immersed in a new suburbia that had so many cultures that none stood out, let alone was dominant. Martina was raised in Etobicoke, in the city's west end, where the most "exotic" person was a Japanese neighbour with a rice cooker, shiso garden and taste for dry fish. What they lacked in cultural fluency they made up for with good-natured ambition. In fact, the moment they landed in Korea, they knew they could bring a lot more to Asia than ESL. Right after clearing customs and immigration, the couple decided to make a video to assure their parents back home that they were safe from North Korean leader Kim Jong-il's latest threat to drown the South in "a sea of fire." To show just how normal the place was, they videoed themselves eating kimchi soup that Simon remembers as "spicy as hell." Maybe it was the hot food, or the long flight, but they couldn't suppress a Canadian urge to parody this new environment by turning the "Hello Mom" video into a send-up of the dangers they *weren't* facing upon arrival. It went viral on YouTube, which was then only a few years old. They're still not sure why, although there was an obvious curiosity in the cross between Martina's pink hair, Simon's cartoonish expressions and their quick Canadian wit about swimming in a sea of fire. The "Threat of North Korea" clip has since been watched hundreds of thousands of times.

I tracked down the couple because I wanted to understand what it was about their roots that helped them become video stars. Canadians are among the most popular producers of YouTube content anywhere, often using the international language of humour to spice up such common interests as cooking and fitness. We're masters of blending the foreign with the familiar. Of course, that comes more easily for Canadians trying to reach the folks next door, where they speak the same language, sing the same songs and watch the same shows. It's a lot harder on the other side of the Pacific when you don't speak Korean or sing K-Pop. For Martina and Simon, that's when a particular branch of Canadian culture—humour without judgment—came into play.

The pair discovered something about their Canadian identity as soon as they settled into their new lives in Bucheon, a city just outside Seoul that prides itself as a cultural hub. Whenever they emailed or texted their Canadian friends or relatives, they realized no one had heard of the city, even though it's home to nearly a million people and is on a United Nations list of the world's most creative cities. The Stawskis realized everyone back home was too consumed with their negative stereotypes of Korea, and perceptions of imminent Armageddon, to bother with such specifics. So much for global Canada, they thought.

"They had this image of Korea as a third world country," Simon remembered.

"Or it was going to bomb the world," Martina interjected.

The couple shot more videos and soon decided to turn their side project into a dedicated YouTube channel, which they named after their first meal on Korean soil. Eat Your Kimchi was their way of telling friends and strangers about their new lives. They discovered their Korean students loved it, too. At the time, as they settled into the local public school that had hired them, Simon was surprised by the narratives running through every ESL textbook he assigned his class. "They talked about Sally and Fred, and no one in our class was named Sally or Fred!" So he began to inject names like Jiyeong in the curriculum, and wove in Korean stories. He figured the same trick would work for their videos, and soon the couple was producing seven or eight pieces a week, taking cues from their students as they raced around Bucheon with their camera, asking every question that popped to mind. How do you use a rice cooker? How do you operate a Korean washing machine?

As Canadians, the couple felt they had an ability to observe and spot differences within a homogenous foreign culture. And they didn't mind playing dumb. It was like they had been to Rick Mercer School, only for this project they could have called it "Talking to Koreans." Here were a couple of young foreigners, blending into the culture yet still asking bizarre questions as if they had just landed from Pluto. It began to strike a chord with Koreans, perhaps because South Korea is such a cultural anomaly: equally cosmopolitan and insular, protected by Americans, suspicious of China, Japan and Russia, and hostile to the idea of immigration from anywhere. The Canadians, moreover, were less brash than Australians, less imperious than many British and less patronizing than most

Americans. More than anything, they seemed to be always poking fun at themselves rather than their hosts.

In the first few years, this "quirky little hobby," as the Stawskis called it, paid no money. Google, which owned YouTube, had yet to introduce AdSense, the program that single-handedly disrupted media by funnelling advertising cash straight to the producers of content. The platform was really just a storeroom for the world's video, not a navigation tool for viewers. There was no app, library or notifications. Even still, audience growth was exponential, and the Canadians—nice, funny, clever—became a minor local sensation. Then came Psy. His 2012 release of "Gangnam Style" became the top-viewed music video ever to hit the internet, and transformed YouTube as a global destination for mobile entertainment. The Stawskis' channel was already growing, but it didn't hurt that a couple of English speakers with an established audience, and Korea as their keyword, were on the right platform at the right time.

Across YouTube, Martina and Simon were celebrated on comments pages for a human style and self-mocking positivity that endeared them to many Asians, whose youthful optimism can be the fuel of pop culture. Even their dog Spudgy and cat Meemer became household names as the happy expats emerged as a kind of Ross and Rachel of Asian YouTube. Their audience grew into the millions, and their share of Google's new ad revenue model soared, allowing the Stawskis to quit their day jobs, open a studio, hire staff and expand into merchandising and corporate sponsorships. It was the sweet spot of expat life: they hadn't traded in their identities but they were no longer strangers in a strange land.

"As Canadians, we don't see things as weird. It's just the way the world is," Simon explained, trying to gauge the Canadian sensibility in their work.

"We were lucky—there aren't a lot of happy couples online," Martina joked.

"We happen to really love each other, so that worked out," Simon added. "People started to watch us as a reality TV show."

I spoke with Martina and Simon in 2018, a decade after they had moved to Incheon, and a couple of years after they had shifted their base to Tokyo, to build their video channel for the 2020 Summer Olympics. From their initial video, they had grown to become international YouTube stars, launched their own food and travel show and turned Eat Your Kimchi into a commercial and cultural phenomenon that had reached five hundred million views from Australia to the United States. After eight years in Korea, they had finally fulfilled their initial travel plan and settled in Tokyo, where they reoriented their work, including the food and travel show, to Japanese culture and tastes. That meant a new brand name: Eat Your Sushi. The new market gave the couple new sponsorship opportunities; it also presented a genre of food and drink they quickly discovered could be highly interactive. For one live video, made at a Tokyo sushi bar, they allowed viewers to vote on whether they should eat another sushi roll or take another drink of sake. The voting tended to go one way, and by the end of the fifty-minute video, their sentences were a string of slurs. Another favourite shtick for them was to go to a new Tokyo subway station and film themselves trying to find directions. The Mercer Effect, again. Their online numbers, with nearly half their viewers in the U.S., also earned them access to restaurants and sushi chefs they might not otherwise have been able to secure if they'd focused only on a Canadian audience.

As the Olympics neared, they found themselves looking further ahead, and wondering if they could transplant their model back to Canada. Their most active connection to home was a Canadian wine shop in Tokyo run by Jamie Paquin, a former sociology student from York University who moved to Japan in 2005 to work on his PhD and stayed to run his own import and retail business, Heavenly Vines. If they returned home, the Stawskis wondered if they could do something similar for Canadian food, perhaps if they created a video channel to showcase Toronto's international food scene, from the West Indian fare of Simon's hometown Pickering to the Chinese outlets in Martina's old neighbourhood.

Could they apply a Canadian eye to Canada, too?

Simon: "There are so many things we appreciate about Canada now. Lawns, for instance."

Martina: "I never appreciated the smell of Canadian air until I moved overseas."

Simon: "Or small talk."

Small talk may not be a defining characteristic of a diaspora but it's part of the non-threatening Canadian image that works especially well in distant cultures and disparate languages. It's essential to our place as the world's cultural interpreter, Canadians being that rare people who can listen and observe and do more than translate. Without judgment or pretence, we can find common threads that connect other cultures, and even weave those together in a bigger story. Where Canadians have succeeded as cultural interpreters, they've done so by gently playing back a culture for its people, often through satire—from the Dumbells as British officers in the trenches, to Rich Little as Richard Nixon, to Mike Myers as Wayne Campbell. Perhaps no Canadian has done that sort of comic routine for a larger audience than Rowswell, the first global Canadian voice of the *SNL* age, who went to China in the 1980s to study the language. A master of small talk and pointed banter, he became a Chinese superstar by landing a leading role hosting New Year's TV specials. Long before YouTube, he was an Asian video star, blending a Canadian aptitude for small talk with a Chinese love of banter.

At the University of Toronto in the 1980s, Rowswell studied Mandarin and won a scholarship to continue his education at Beijing University. China was just opening up as an economic force, and the country was hungry for foreigners, and foreign affirmation. As a student, Rowswell's Mandarin was good enough that, in 1988, after state TV producers saw him perform for a campus crowd, they recruited him for a New Year's special. His role would be to perform *xiang sheng*, or crosstalk, a centuries-old Chinese parlour game that has the feel of an Abbott and Costello routine. Once on air, Rowswell's sketches became the stuff of water cooler conversations across China, as he did send-ups of migrant factory workers looking for directions in the big city and bumbling foreigners arriving in China. The twenty-three-year-old Canadian was an overnight sensation, known as "Dashan," or Big Mountain, to reflect his considerable height. For a people whose collective imagination was struggling to keep pace with their breakneck social change, and who weren't given the freedom to express and explore critical ideas on their own, Dashan and his take on their tradition was like a bridge from past to future.

Although he hadn't set out to do this, Rowswell captured the imagination of millions with the same style that had worked for Canadians elsewhere. His timing was good, too. As the country struggled for international acceptance after the Tiananmen Square massacre in 1989, many Chinese felt honoured a foreigner had learned their language and style of humour. After centuries of foreign interference, they felt a further degree of validation that a foreigner—now a famous one—had adopted their ways, too. It helped they already had a favourable view of Canada, from the Norman Bethune story and images of Pierre Trudeau's historic visit in the early 1970s. In *Stand and Deliver*, Andrew Clark summed up the Dashan phenomenon this way: "Like Bethune, Rowswell embraced China. He was a friendly example to the Chinese that the West and the East could find middle ground."[2] Since then, Rowswell has gained more than five million followers on Sina Weibo, his preferred social media channel, and expanded his following on WeChat. Millions more track his "Dashan Live" tours online as he performs for Chinese audiences around the world. (In 2017, he was the only Mandarin performer at the Melbourne International Comedy Festival, the third largest of its kind in the world.)

When I met Rowswell in 2017, he was trying to come to grips with his role as a cultural emissary for both countries. Referring to his character in the third person, as he often does, he explained, "Dashan represents a Westerner who appreciates and respects China, who has learned the language and understands the culture and has even become 'more Chinese than the Chinese.' It's a very powerful and reassuring image that appeals to very deep-rooted emotions." He had come to see his talents as more than those of an interpreter, or of a friendly ally for his host country. In an earlier blog post on Quora, he had noted[3]: "Comedy, like the arts in general, is something that touches people somewhere very deeply. It doesn't matter how fluent you are unless you say something people remember, and there is no easier way to be remembered (at least in a good way) than to stand up and tell a good joke. I've done a lot of different work over the years, and at the end of a long year of hard work you often realize that the only thing people will remember is one line you said in one particular skit, because it was funny. That's the power of comedy." He had come to see himself as an artist, projecting to the world the humour and style he had developed in Canada and polished in China. It was the style of a cross-national performer—a bit Canadian, a bit Chinese—on the post-national stage of social media.

As probably the best-known Canadian in China, Rowswell continued to be deployed by both the Chinese and Canadian governments as a kind of goodwill ambassador. During the 2008 Beijing Olympics, he was named Canada's team attaché. He later served as Canada's commissioner general at the 2010 Shanghai World Expo, travelled across Canada to promote Chinese tourism, and stayed on call for whenever a prime minister or governor general visited. As Stephen Harper noted in 2012 when he was prime minister, Rowswell was more than a comedian; he possessed "extraordinary talents to build bridges of understanding."[4]

The photo ops and honorary positions, however, may hardly be the best use of his talents or his network. Like many expat performers, Rowswell feels we treat him like a prized trophy, to be pulled out at key moments to impress our hosts and guests alike. That may have worked in the 1980s, when he first went to Beijing, or even in the 2000s, when the world gathered for the Beijing Olympics and Shanghai Expo. But as the world enters a more disrupted state in the 2020s, as power structures shift away from the foundation stones of traditional diplomacy, the deployment of our diaspora will be more delicate, and powerful, than ever. Martina and Simon Stawski proved this on YouTube when they moved to Korea and then Japan, just as Rowswell is proving it again with his mass following on Weibo, with digital networks that are shaping culture and driving change. More than ever, Canadians will be in those networks, as quiet cultural leaders, interpreters and playback artists. And more than ever, we'll find those networks in Asia.

Fortunately for Canada, it's where some of our best architects of change have thrived for more than a century.

7

Architects of Change

INSIDE THE GREENING OF CHINA'S BUILDING BOOM

When Raefer Wallis set out for China, just after New Year's 2002, the world was his oyster, a place still riding high from the 1990s, when every liberal idea seemed to be a triumph for humanity. The spread of democracy. The rise of the internet. The free movement of people. And for a world charging into this new century, perhaps nothing was more significant than the opening of China: the acceptance of the world's most populous country into the WTO and its formal entry into the global club of capitalism. Fresh out of university, Wallis wanted to be part of it. He had grown up in Quebec's Eastern Townships, the child of chiropractors who raised him in a small community near Sherbrooke. His father, a New Zealander, had followed his mother back to Quebec after they met at college in the United States and was determined to keep his son's eyes focused on the world beyond Canada. By the time Raefer graduated from McGill's architecture school, he had already done an academic exchange in Europe and taken a year off for a "journeyman's walk" across the U.S., to work with tradesmen on construction projects and gain an appreciation, first-hand, of how buildings are made. Wallis was a top student, winning scholarship offers from American grad schools. But he also had wanderlust. He asked himself, "Where's the busiest place on earth?" Shanghai, he figured. "I bought a one-way ticket and was out of here."[1]

When Wallis landed in China with his London, Ontario, girlfriend and fellow architect Sherry Poon[2] (they're now married), he took an interview with a Hong Kong–Canadian architect referred to him by a McGill graduate. The architect hired him on the spot. Shanghai was in the early stages of one of history's great building booms, and there were far more projects than architects. Wallis was handed the mandate to build a suburb—and to hurry up, because there were five more projects waiting for him. He asked who the lead architect was. His new boss looked surprised. "It's you!" he exclaimed. Sensing Wallis's doubts, the other architect sat him down and put it simply: you grew up in Canada, you know what good buildings look like. He assigned Wallis three draftsmen—none spoke English—and told him to get to work on the new suburb. "I was better than most because the bar was so low," Wallis later conceded.[3] He lasted three months in the firm, before jumping to a larger outfit run by a Taiwanese American with more design ambitions and higher standards. Wallis was sent to Taipei for several months of training, and upon returning to Shanghai set up a local office for the firm to take on bigger and bigger projects. As he got deeper into Shanghai's boom, he couldn't help but notice what the frenzy was doing to the city, and planet. Everyone focused on bigger, bolder, faster, cheaper—without a whisper about quality or sustainability. He asked two close friends, Karen Wan and Sacha Silva, a roommate from architecture school, if they'd like to join him and do something about it. The Canadians could launch an entirely different form of architecture, for a society that was literally rebuilding itself.[4]

The Canadians set out in search of clients and were amazed to find a growing appetite for environmentally friendly practices.

"We noticed no one was looking at the small stuff," Wallis discovered. "There was a section of clientele who were starting to look for good-quality design, and for someone to take a project from beginning to end." The Canadians opted to focus on high-end residential and commercial buildings, realizing that Shanghai, like most Chinese cities, was starting to feel the ailments of excessive development, and it wasn't just the congested roads. Many of the new buildings that made for stunning photographs were sick, full of toxic materials that leached through every crack into the land beneath, the water that residents drank and air they breathed. In Wallis's mind, the frenzy offered a chance for new beginnings, for his life and for China. He chose to name his new company A00, after the symbol designated for the first page of any design plan, and then set out to write the first chapter of a new way of doing business in China. "The most important page in a book is the first page," Wallis told the others. "We've always seen architecture as a story. So for us, page one of the architecture story is the most important."

After a series of private residential projects, the young Canadians made an architectural statement with Asia's first carbon-neutral hotel, which they built in downtown Shanghai's old French Concession. URBN would be only twenty-six rooms, but "we wanted the hotel to scream that it was high-end, it was luxury and it was green," Wallis explained. "Without a sign on the wall having to say all that." He sourced raw wood for the walls and scoured Shanghai's flea markets for visual cues of the old city that he could place around the hotel. In one market, he spotted an old suitcase made in the 1930s and asked the peddler if he had more. "I've got a warehouse full of them!" the man responded. "They're old. No one wants old anymore." Wallis bought the entire supply, hired a local shoe-shiner to polish them and constructed a 3-D cluster of antique suitcases for the lobby wall, to showcase an earlier age of travel. "I wanted the building to look and feel Shanghai, not like Disney, which was what the city was becoming," he said.

When URBN opened in 2008, *Architectural Digest* and the *New York Times*[5] profiled the property, and a year later *Condé Nast Traveler*[6] named it one of world's hottest new hotels. Wallis's reputation was sealed. He was no longer a generic foreigner; he was the green architect from Canada. Green turned out to be the perfect calling card because, as many Chinese clients told Wallis, "You're Canadian. Of course you're going to prioritize nature and the environment." He was surprised how many Chinese at first thought he was American—they assumed Western architects were either American or French—and began to turn that to A00's advantage, too, seizing on a view in the market that he had American skills and Canadian values. "When I said I was from Canada, people would say, 'Oh, this is great. This conversation is going to be much easier. It will be much more open.'" (Americans in China also frequently mistook him for one of theirs, which helped earn him U.S. media coverage and attention from the Clinton Global Initiative—something he actually found "somewhat disheartening" when his work continued to go unnoticed in Canada.)

If Canada is going to play a bigger role in the 2020s, we'll need a lot more Canadians like Wallis out in the world's fastest-growing regions. And yet, if you wander around Shanghai with him, or scour Singapore or Santiago, you'll find precious few taking the roads less travelled. A century ago, the Canadians who went to these frontier markets were largely church workers. A generation ago, they were drillers and miners. Canadians, it was often said, were either missionaries or mercenaries. But as those countries developed their own capacities in the professions and skilled trades, the flow of Canadians waned, except for a small tribe who were a little missionary and a little mercenary as they went abroad. Some were rethinking cities and health care systems, others the way we interact with the environment. Regardless, this diaspora of frontier expats was Canada's best hope to bend the arc of human progress without breaking it.

Wallis admits to being a bit of both mercenary and missionary, building his international company from Shanghai while trying to help the world's fastest-growing cities defuse their environmental time bombs. He suspects he'd have a harder time getting the Chinese to accept him as both if it weren't for his birthplace. His nationality has gained him trust, in a place where trust in foreigners is scarce. "I attribute that to me being Canadian," he said. "There's inherently more trust in China for a Canadian than for an American." Even after the Huawei affair erupted in 2018, he found his Chinese customers and partners continued to place trust in him, feeling they could leave the bigger, bilateral tensions to their governments to resolve. Authorities in Beijing seemed to appreciate his ability to bridge Chinese developers, international suppliers and a growing list of global partners that included the U.S. State Department. "When everyone asks me, 'How's your relationship with the government? Are there tensions?'—honestly, in the last nine months, it has never been better," he told me in the spring of 2019. "Things are happening at record speed."

Wallis was not the first Canadian architect or developer to make his mark on China, nor the first to build a business there during times of bilateral tensions. The missionaries in Chengdu established a hospital with enough local touches that it gained notice among the nationalist movement, and allowed Canadians to stay when other foreigners were being kicked out. In the 1920s, another Canadian, Harry Hussey, broke ranks with his American peers by adopting what was then called an "Oriental" approach to the Peking medical school, which he had been hired by the

Rockefeller Foundation to design.[7] Hussey had left Port Dover, Ontario, as a teenager to work in a mine in New Mexico; on the side, he studied architecture through correspondence courses from the University of Chicago. Uprooting again, he moved to China, where the Rockefeller Foundation, which was trying to help open up China, saw his talents and commissioned him, thinking his Canadian background would impress their hosts.[8] The Americans then told Hussey to "forget Chinese designs and show them some good American architecture." Instead, the Canadian set out to study the ancient palaces of Peking, and copied their use of lakes and gardens to create open space rather than block out the world as Western designs of the day tended to do.[9] (He also defied British requests to introduce himself as a subject of the Crown, choosing instead to present himself to the Chinese as a Canadian.)[10]

When the Chinese saw the new Peking Union Medical College, with its echoes of the Forbidden City, they were surprised and delighted. At last, here was a foreigner who wasn't trying to impose modern concepts on their country, which was already on the brink of civil war over its identity.[11] Hussey had even included glazed tiles made in the same village, eighty kilometres outside Peking, where the original imperial tiles had once been produced. To do that, he had found the grandson of the last tile maker and convinced him to reopen a local mine and kiln that had been closed for half a century.[12] Hussey was more than an architect. He became an advocate for local aesthetics. While the world around him was reeling from the collisions of early globalization and fading colonialism, he spoke out against a modern building boom that was underway in China, calling the destruction of old buildings "vandalism."[13] The Chinese trusted him more and more, as he blended local traditions with imported technologies. One winter, when there was a terrible flood in Tientsin near Peking (as Tianjin and Beijing were then known), he was dispatched to the disaster zone to design a makeshift shelter that could be replicated for tens of thousands of displaced people. Made of reeds, mud and poles, the design became known as the Hussey Hut, the world's first mass-produced disaster relief structure.[14] The Canadian was celebrated as a cultural bridge-builder back in Peking, where over the next two decades his home became something of a neutral meeting place for the Kuomintang nationalists and northern warlords, and a safe haven for the growing number of American army officers arriving in China in the 1930s to explore ways to fend off the imminent Japanese invasion.[15]

From Chengdu to Peking, those early architects established a Canadian presence, which was soon found across the developing world where the postwar economic boom and a surge of new national aspirations demanded a new age of design. There were suddenly hired guns like Hussey everywhere, and eventually a new class of Canadian starchitects like Arthur Erickson and Frank Gehry. Our architecture schools, led by McGill, gained renown as they helped foster an innovative design culture for this fast-growing world, and showcased it at Expo 67 in Montreal. Quebec's Jean-Baptiste Louis Bourgeois had already paved the way with Chicago's Baha'i temple, dubbed the Taj Mahal of the American West, followed by the Monument Gardens in Haifa. Another Canadian Baha'i, Hossein Amanat from Vancouver, designed Tehran's Azadi Tower, while decades later the Iranian Canadian Fariborz Sahba took on Delhi's most iconic modern building, the Lotus Temple, and Siamak Hariri designed the Baha'i house of worship in Santiago.[16]

If there was an emerging Canadian theme for architects going out into the world, it was accommodation, a bit like the constitutional thinking that took flight after Expo 67. Witold Rybczynski, a Canadian architecture writer based in Philadelphia, believes Canadians had developed a special appreciation for density—ironic in such a sparsely populated country—and the need to combine old and new without damaging either.[17] He traced a lot of that to his hometown, Montreal, a city that's found a way to blend old-world walk-ups and modern glass towers, and through McGill has produced many of our best architectural minds for export. One of them, Israeli-born Moshe Safdie, moved to Montreal as a teenager, and after completing his training at McGill, made a splash with the Habitat building at Expo 67. A citizen of the world, Safdie moved between Jerusalem, Boston and Singapore, applying his signature to the world's landscape through the Khalsa Heritage Centre in Punjab, the Salt Lake City Public Library and Ottawa's National Art Gallery. In each case, Safdie's work was celebrated for its accommodation of new and old, and its views that were both inward and outward. Each of these generations of architects that were sandwiched between Harry Hussey and Raefer Wallis added to a growing global sense of design, by crossing East and West, North and South. But rarely did they stay out in the world in sufficient numbers to make a lasting effect. Instead, most of them came and left with their projects, leaving the signature of one rather than the statement of many.

Allan Zeman, one of Hong Kong's most successful developers, wonders if most expats are perseverant enough, especially in Asia, where resilience is a daily requirement. He came from Montreal to Hong Kong in the 1970s, when "no one had heard of Hong Kong"[18] (even his mother confused it with Japan). As a teenager, Zeman had imported clothes from the outpost, then a British colony, to make ends meet after his father died. It was his first exposure to a broader world, which stoked his entrepreneurial appetite—one that, back then at least, Canada could not feed. Once in Hong Kong, he opened a bar and then another, and within a decade had turned a few blocks of warehouses into a bustling club district called Lan Kwai Fong, or LKF. "I look at things not for what they are," he once told *Forbes*.[19] "I look at things for what they could be." He subsequently built a five-star resort in Phuket, revitalized an amusement park in Hong Kong, and took his entertainment district concepts to mainland China, including to the provincial city of Chengdu where Canadian missionaries first worked in the 1890s. Like that earlier wave of Canadians, Zeman believed his respect for local culture was his competitive advantage. "China is one word," he said, "but it's really more like thirty different countries, where every province and every city has its own culture." It was something Canadians could appreciate.[20]

After Zeman first got to Hong Kong, the mainland was opening up and Canada had a chance to change course, through a new generation of expats who could have been led by our architects.[21] Following the Cold War, which brought with it an unease over American triumphalism, Canadians like Hariri and Safdie were in demand for their rare combination of technical skills and cultural sensibilities. Younger architects like Bing Thom and Joseph Loh soon discovered they were actually preferred in many emerging markets—China, most of all—because they brought international standards without national judgment. It was the Hussey premium, applied to Canadians for not judging other cultures. Canadians also tended to be the ones best able to negotiate the many conflicts between developers, designers and engineers that were an inherent part of any project on deadline. "We're highly aware," said Lisa Bate, a Toronto architect who moved to China in the early 2000s. "We go to see the world, not to tell the world how to do things. We don't take. We add."[22] What other country could produce a Moshe Safdie, a French-speaking Jew who had the vision for a Sikh cultural centre in India?

As the world became more comfortable blending cultures, Canada, the most multicultural of nations, seemed to find its place. Arthur Lau saw this as he moved from Hong Kong to Montreal and then reached back into China with his work, seeing a brief moment for Canada in the second half of the twentieth century when entire generations were peacefully on the move. Born in 1936, the youngest of seven children, Lau enrolled in McGill after graduating from Hong Kong Technical College, choosing it because of the university's reputation and relatively cheap tuition. He stayed to work on Expo 67, where he was made section head for Cité du Havre and the "Man the Provider" exhibit on agriculture, and after Expo won a national planning competition to design Jackson Square, a new downtown development in Hamilton, Ontario, where he crafted a signature use of atriums and open spaces. Then, as China opened up, he saw a far bigger opportunity. In 1972, two years after Pierre Trudeau became one of the first Western leaders to recognize the People's Republic, Lau's office was engaged to design an exhibition in one of the old Expo pavilions to showcase the life of Norman Bethune. It began a decades-long relationship with China that included projects in Nanjing, Dalian and Shenzhen, and an appointment as senior advisor to Shanghai's World Expo in 2010. Just six years earlier, the president of Shanghai Expo had visited Montreal to tour the grounds Lau had helped design. He told the Montreal architect he wanted his exhibition, along with the 2008 Beijing Olympics, to be an architectural coming out for China and its designers, just as Expo 67 had been for Canada and Lau's generation.

Lau would be among the few Canadians or Chinese who were involved in both Expos—bookends, really, to an era—and he realizes what was lost in between. He believes that during the interim the two nations focused more on engineering than architecture, and not just in the literal sense. In our insatiable quest for science and casual abandonment of art, Canadians may have forgotten a bit of the human narrative going back to Hussey and what he had tried to build. Lau is now focusing his time and money building on that foundation, through a more sustainable, and human, approach to development. In his mind, we are spending a third of our lives in structures designed by people who are thinking too little about how we live and too much about how our buildings work. In 2015, when he was awarded an honorary degree at McGill, he gave the same message to the graduating class, urging his audience to think less about the structure of their work and more about its social and environmental impact. He need only point to their fellow McGill grad, Raefer Wallis.

Lau also ramped up the time he spent developing a diaspora network, wrangling McGill alumni, especially in Asia, to connect with and support the university. He persuaded the Hong Kong developer and McGill architecture graduate Jimmy Wong, before he died in 1994, to leave $8 million for a new engineering building in his name that sparked McGill's campus renaissance. He later convinced Peter Fu, a Shanghai architect who studied and worked in Canada, to support a new architecture program. Today the McGill school is named after Fu, who was typical of the new frontier expat—a global citizen who had his feet in several places, Canada among them. After coming to McGill from China, he spent nine years working in Toronto and then returned to Shanghai, where he designed an estimated five million square metres of the city's new landscape, including a multi-stage outdoor theatre built from discarded shipping containers.

Joseph Loh, a University of Toronto–trained architect, took the same view of sustainability to China in the early 2000s, after he grew tired of drawing plans for shopping malls for suburban Canada. He joined Tsinghua University in Beijing, as vice-president and chief architect, and undertook a series of environmentally focused projects, capped by a $500 million performance arts centre, art gallery and residential towers for Datong, a city of about two million people in Shanxi Province, next to Inner Mongolia. Bate had developed similar ambitions in the early 2000s when, having grown tired of retrofit projects like urban infills and restorations, she shifted her sights to China and the chance of a lifetime to do greenfield, crafting developments that would not be constrained by existing buildings or infrastructure. Once overseas, she learned the Chinese had a positive bias toward Canada, thanks to Bethune and Dashan, of course, and also the Canadian work in her field that was viewed as smart and sustainable. But there was more going on, she learned, and it was stymying Canada and our expats. Her French competitors seemed to be subsidized by their government, while American architects could rely on their alma maters—Harvard, for instance—to fund as well as promote their work through alumni networks. Canadians, by and large, were on their own, solo artists on the Chinese high wire. And when things went wobbly, as they do in China, they had no safety net.

Bate had her China moment—the tough kind—in 2004, when she took on a project called China Fengjing Maple Town. The project was part of a series of new suburbs for Shanghai modelled after different foreign locales, this one to capture the Great White North. She was told to include in her designs a replica of the Rockies and room for an RCMP Musical Ride. It wasn't just a Canadian thing. A short drive way, there would be a Venice Town, complete with canals; a Thames Town, to be identified by a pub and statue of Winston Churchill; and a New German Town, sitting next to a Volkswagen factory and Formula One track. As much as the Chinese like their own culture respected, no one does cultural clichés quite like they do. The project soon became mired in a planning swamp, though, as the local developer started cutting corners, opting to replace Canadian pines with palm trees and then a Group of Seven display. The Rockies and Musical Ride were not mentioned again. Local design institutes, controlled by the government, turned Bate's master plan into working drawings she could barely recognize. Her team's environmental vision for the natural canal town by the Yangtze River included slim steel bridges that used as little material as structurally possible, bicycle lanes (which were common in China but losing favour among planners), and pedestrian paths lined with Canadian maples. The canal edges, in turn, were to be protected by indigenous plants rather than the hard surfaces that developers increasingly preferred, to ensure the water's edge of bulrushes and lily pads acted as natural biofilters in tandem with the storm water inceptors Bate had specified be imported from Canada. The patented technology was proven to capture nearly all suspended sediment, free oil and other pollutants. Indeed, the entire project was to be a model of new technology and new planning that could bridge East and West. In its place, Bate found concrete. Everywhere. The Canadian storm water interceptors were gone, too, replaced by Chinese catch basins.

The Maple Town fiasco was emblematic of the challenges facing Canadian expats across China, as they tried to hold up global standards while dealing with local politicians and their crony business partners who often had their own agendas.[23] Bate eventually folded her company and joined the Canadian architecture firm B+H to expand its presence in China, focusing less on government contracts and more on the growing roster of homegrown multinationals—Alibaba, Tencent, Huawei—that harboured a more professional approach to development, and a more sustainable eye for buildings. They had to. China was at risk of becoming unliveable, environmentally and financially. "The attitudes towards energy performance in China are completely changing," Bate found, as she was able to put

Maple Town behind her and look for a more systemic approach to sustainable development. Ostentation would be out; building health and affordability would be in.[24]

Later, as Canada's voice on the World Green Building Council, Bate saw the maturing view of Chinese business when it came to sustainability, and how it might fit with a Canadian strength in China. Could they work together, Canadian expats and this emerging economic power? One of her allies would be Wallis, who was still in Shanghai but looking more internationally, as he began to see a global opportunity in China's struggle with pollution. Wallis and his partners had made their mark with buildings that were both energy-efficient and good at keeping dirty air out and clean water in. He had also started to do something about the landscape of toxic building products that each of his projects used, decimating the ground underneath his so-called green projects. In the middle of China's breakneck construction boom, he wondered if perhaps a different approach to labelling materials might help.

Wallis started to ask questions about materials and began demanding new products from his Chinese suppliers. The more he mentioned this to his Chinese clients, the more information they wanted. The demand for green building products seemed strong enough that he mandated that each project include at least one new sustainable material. That was easier said than done, as there was no Chinese lexicon for a growing array of manufactured, and chemically laced, building materials. This was not the age of Harry Hussey, when the choice was between ceramic tile and wood. In the early 2000s, builders were remaking entire cities without a common Chinese word for "formaldehyde."

Like the developer Allan Zeman in Hong Kong, Wallis continued to look at things as they could be, not as they were. He developed his own Chinese lexicon for construction materials, and put them online through a new database. His phone lit up with text messages from builders wanting more information about the materials he was using. He then began to hear from big international firms wanting to form a partnership with him in China. "It was out of control," he told me in 2017. He couldn't keep up with the requests. "We figured it would be easiest if we just published an online inventory. It was a defensive move. That database got a huge amount of attention."

Wallis realized he could turn his database, which he called GIGA, into a new business, and take it global. He likes to explain his strategy in terms of chicken brains and Albert Einstein. Even if you combined a thousand chicken brains, he said, they wouldn't be a match for Einstein's genius. Nor would a million chicken brains. It's one of the core principles of manufacturing, and, for that matter, buildings: the quality of output can never exceed the quality of input. If he wanted to truly change China's buildings, and from there the world's buildings, he had to help the world focus on inputs, the way the food industry did by listing ingredients and their sources. He started by developing GIGA as the Google of sustainable materials. In Wallis's mind, if you want to know the environmental footprint of a shingle, or a bucket of paint, you should be able to GIGA it. But he also knew he'd need more than a database; he'd need to build a global data hub that others could augment, refine and edit, a bit like Wikipedia. Again, it was about the quality of inputs, not just the efficiency of a search.

As Wallis began to raise capital to finance his expansion, a friend in Sherbrooke introduced him to Jean-Marc Desbiens, a software developer who had been part of the team that built Taleo, a Quebec City company that made recruiting software and was sold to Oracle in 2012 for $1.9 billion. Desbiens was looking for new ventures to invest in, and sufficiently inspired by Wallis to both put up some seed capital and assemble a team of developers in Quebec to work with the Shanghai group on Origin, the name Wallis had given his new data hub. ("Created in Shanghai, built in Quebec City, by Canadians," Wallis liked to say.)[25] Origin launched in 2018 as a hub of databases, with 150,000 products listed and another 300,000 in the pipeline. Although Wallis figured he would need to get to fifteen million for global impact, he had already won Leadership in Energy and Environmental Design—or LEED—recognition, moving Origin to the centre of the green building movement in North America. His compatriot Lisa Bate, through the World Green Building Council, was able to connect him and his clients to an even bigger worldwide network of builders and suppliers.

Information was one thing, action quite another. Which was why Wallis's next chapter for GIGA was a standard for the sensors used to monitor the chemical emissions of buildings. He first became concerned about off-gassing in 2005, when he started to use American sensors to measure the emissions of his building materials. He wasn't sure how good they were and was even more skeptical of the Chinese-made ones used by some of his developers, so he started to put data online to compare office air quality. He also wanted to show building occupants how they might be affected by both little things like photocopiers and big things like a smog day. The big things kept hitting China's cities, and while the governments had smog readers for the air outside buildings, there was no reading for the air quality inside. In 2012, when Beijing was hit by an "airpocalypse," as its smog crisis that year became known, Wallis's phone started to buzz again, this time with office developers wanting to know how they could get more information on the quality of sensors. Tenants' lives depended on it. Wallis decided to develop a new system called Reset, connecting sensors and online databases, that proved so successful he began to apply it in the U.S., where it was recognized by the International WELL Building Institute, the Passive House Institute, the Fitwel building rating system and Living Building Challenge, each leading industry initiatives that support regenerative design.

Back in China, the demand for his Origin database was doubling every year, as corporate tenants began to seek an independent bill of health for any building they occupied. (He was once asked by a Chinese builder if by "healthy building" he meant "a Bethune for buildings.") The simmering concern became a national scandal in 2018 when an Alibaba employee died of leukemia and his family sued his landlord, Ziroom, which is one of China's largest apartment providers, for failing to address a formaldehyde concern in the man's housing block in Hangzhou, where the e-commerce giant is headquartered. Thanks to Wallis's pioneering work from years earlier, the court was able to draw on an existing Chinese word for formaldehyde and force the landlord to take action.[26] Even state media played up the story as a sign of urban development running amok. Separately, Wallis started to work with the China Quality Certification Center, the world's largest such body, and its building standards association, signing agreements with both in 2019 despite the ongoing Huawei tensions. Chinese authorities were deeply concerned about their urban environmental crisis—too much, Wallis figured, to add his company or his work to the bilateral disputes with his home country. Instead, Chinese authorities started to see him, a Canadian, as a star exporter for China after Reset began expanding internationally and took Chinese-developed technology along with it. Wallis also worked with the World Green Building Council on a global air quality monitoring campaign, and from China launched a partnership with the U.S. State Department, Earth Day Network and the Woodrow Wilson International Center in Washington to expand Earth Challenge 2020, a citizen-scientist movement funded in part by Amazon that's aiming to recruit people globally to collect and log data on air and soil quality.

While little known in Canada, Wallis was emerging in Asia as a symbol of transnationalism for the 2020s. Two decades after leaving Montreal on an adventure, he had gone from being a journeyman architect kicking around the Pacific Rim to a digital entrepreneur with global reach. He told me he can't imagine leaving China, air quality notwithstanding. His three school-aged children were born there, although he and his wife, Sherry, consider them to be "unequivocally Canadian." They may send them to Canada for high school, to give them the international exposure he and Poon sought when they left Canada (and to ensure they grow up as snow lovers). They also want to ensure their children develop the sort of Canadian values Wallis has used as his calling card in China since 2002. He knows his Chinese partners tend to think he's doing something "because it's the right thing to do." It's why he keeps Origin free, to ensure equal access to his data hub. Even if it gives builders and suppliers commercially valuable information, the social good is worth more than any potential revenue from charging users for access. It's not just the Canadian in him, Wallis explained, but the architect, too, a profession that really does see itself as art more than engineering. As he put it, "we're public servants."

That sort of Canadian artistry has helped shape our presence in frontier markets for generations. Harry Hussey made it his mark in Peking, in the 1920s. Allan Zeman did the same in Hong Kong, in the 1970s. They're the sort of markets where restless individuals can find opportunities; and for those Canadians who dare to leave home, they're welcoming gateways. In the 2020s, those centres will be even more essential as gateways for globalization—hubs that feed established networks rather than just propel ambitious individuals. The networks that Canadians like Wallis are building in the world's new knowledge centres—Shanghai, Singapore, Dubai—will shape Canada's place in the world in the decades ahead, just as our collective connections in London, Paris and New York shaped it through the twentieth century. Unfortunately, when Canadians go abroad, when we go at all, we still gravitate to London, Paris and New York.

Dominic Barton, the celebrated management consultant, has been wrestling with that cultural challenge since he left home in the 1980s, gambling his early career in Canada at McKinsey & Company for an assignment in South Korea for which he was completely unqualified. He never looked back. In September 2019, he was named as Canada's ambassador to China, in part because of his ability to navigate foreign cultures. Barton was born an expat, the son of a Canadian Anglican missionary in Uganda, and had his first brush with adventure when, playing hide-and-seek, he hid in an army Jeep belonging to a young officer named Idi Amin. The future dictator found the Canadian and returned him home. Barton finished his education in Canada and joined McKinsey, with hopes of becoming an adviser to CEOs and other leaders. Instead, he was frustrated by the Canadian pace and thought of quitting, just when the Seoul assignment came up. He spoke no Korean, knew no Koreans and understood very little about Korea. He figured his ignorance made the move essential and would test his resilience. As he reflected decades later, "You can't study resilience. You learn resilience through failure, when you take risks, when you do things that make you feel uncomfortable."[27]

Over the decades, Barton became a soothsayer to the world's leading CEOs, with instant access to boardrooms on every continent. Remarkably, Canada used him sparingly. Jim Flaherty, when he was Harper's finance minister, recruited Barton for an economic advisory group. Harper also named Barton to an advisory committee on renewing and developing the public service led by the Clerk of the Privy Council, Wayne Wouters. For a person of Barton's experience and reach, it was fairly stay-at-home stuff. Justin Trudeau disbanded the advisory groups, and took a new tack when he headed to Davos in 2016, less than three months after becoming prime minister. A decade earlier, Trudeau's chief policy adviser, Gerald Butts, had worked for Ontario premier Dalton McGuinty and enlisted Barton to speak to their team about the changing world and Canada's shrinking place in it. Figuring Barton could help Canada better connect with that world, Butts and the Trudeau team asked him to set up a series of breakfasts and one-on-one meetings for the new prime minister at the World Economic Forum, the gathering of government, business and, increasingly, civil society leaders who meet every January in the Swiss Alps.

While at McKinsey, Barton was a doyen of Davos, with a commanding presence at the forum, where he threw a must-attend party at the resort town's main hotel, the Belvédère, complete with a twelve-piece dance band. He was happy to oblige the new prime minister, rounding up the likes of BlackRock CEO Larry Fink, Bank of America's Brian Moynihan and Lubna Olayan, the Saudi-born executive who from her base in London had become one the world's most influential business figures. Barton suggested Trudeau might also want to meet some Canadian expats. Mark Carney was an obvious one who the prime minister already knew, not least because Carney was known to harbour political ambitions. Having served as Canada's central bank governor through the 2008 financial crisis, he had been governor of the Bank of England since 2013 and came to Davos as one of the key players in global finance. Carney brought with him Gary Cohn, who was then the number-two executive at Goldman Sachs, where the Canadian central banker had started his career. It would prove to be a lasting connection. Even though the Davos crowd was fully expecting Hillary Clinton to be with them in a year's time as the new president, Cohn urged Trudeau to keep a close eye on Donald Trump as he geared up for the Iowa caucuses, less than two weeks away. (Cohn went on to serve as Trump's chief economic adviser and a leading "globalist" in the White House, quitting in 2018 over the president's escalating use of tariffs. During that time, he was among Canada's most valuable allies in the administration, especially during negotiations to revise the North American Free Trade Agreement.)

Barton added to the list Michael Evans, who surprisingly the Trudeau team didn't know. Evans had won Olympic gold for Canada as a rower in 1984 and gone on to a prominent business career in Asia, first with Goldman Sachs and then as president of Alibaba, the giant e-commerce platform that is to China what Amazon is to America. Few Canadians know Asia as well, or could offer deeper connections between China and Canada. There were personal ties, too, even though they'd been lost in the mists of time. Evans's father, John, who was president of the University of Toronto in the 1970s, had run unsuccessfully for Trudeau's father in a Toronto by-election, and was later a mentor to Butts. All things considered, there weren't many expats who could do more for Canada. Here was one of our most valuable expats, with commercial and political connections any nation would love to have, and yet scant detail about him in the prime minister's briefing book and certainly nothing to ignite a conversation on what Evans could do for the country. For Trudeau, it was an early signal of how little the bureaucracy really knew about Canadians abroad. Butts himself made the connection only when the Alibaba executive, who has his father's deep-set eyes, walked in the room.

Outside, Trudeau had become an instant celebrity on the world stage. But inside the Davos meeting room, he said he needed the business leaders' help. The 2015 oil collapse had sideswiped the Canadian dollar and foreign investment, while productivity across most of our economy was stalled. Voters had made clear they wanted a new deal, as well. If Canada was to advance economically in the 2020s, the new government knew it would need a new kind of global capital. At the Davos breakfasts, it also began to see the potential of a new kind of Canadian capital, rooted in the brainpower and networks of Canadian expats. Here in one place Trudeau had found a trio of Canadians—Barton, Carney and Evans—who represented one of the best lines Canada had seen since Crosby, Iginla and Nash took to the Vancouver Olympics. Properly deployed, they and thousands like them could help Canada get back on the economic podium. Trudeau pulled together his foreign guests and, pointing to Barton, advised them to get ready for more of Canada and more of Canadians. In his words, the expat force may be "low-key"—but it was everywhere.

Shortly after Davos, Trudeau's finance minister, Bill Morneau, reached out to Barton to see if he'd lead a new economic growth council, to come up with more ideas to help Canada adjust to a changing global economy. Barton agreed, and when his appointment was announced his inbox lit up with messages from Canadians on every continent. "How can we be involved?" they asked. "How can we help?" Living overseas since the eighties, Barton had always suspected there was an extensive population of expats, most of them doing remarkable things. He hadn't appreciated how keen they were to help their country. And yet, since those Davos meetings and their many photo ops, Canada still hasn't figured out how to fully engage those expats. (In 2017, Evans helped arrange for Alibaba founder Jack Ma and Trudeau to launch a major event in Toronto, connecting Canadian exporters to the Chinese market.) We also haven't figured out how to get more Canadians like Raefer

Wallis to take on the world, especially when it requires them to go to new and perhaps risky frontiers. It's a hard problem for any government to solve, as Barton would discover.

After stepping down as McKinsey's global chair in 2018, and before accepting the ambassadorship to China, Barton based himself in New York and Hong Kong, keeping a foot in two worlds. He continued to see Canadians in both. But as he surveyed the rise of the rest, he wondered how we might position ourselves. Perhaps, he suggested, with a new motto: "Small country, big impact." Over the next fifteen years, according to Barton's forecasts, 2.5 billion people will join the world's middle class, and almost all of them will be in Asia and Africa. Even more—three billion, he figures—will connect to the internet. "We've never seen anything like it before. It's about a thousand times larger than what was seen in the Industrial Revolution," he said, enthusiastically. In these places, Canada is both small country and small impact. Our relevance will be further challenged as we slide over a demographic ledge, joining the top ranks of aging countries. We'll need more of the world coming to Canada, and more Canadians going abroad, even if they weren't born there. The second part won't be easy. For a quarter century, Canadians agreed that immigration was an effective way to stanch our demographic bleeding. But as the rest of the world adjusted, we didn't come to grips with emigration, to get more Canadians into the fastest-growing markets and to meet all those new consumers and connect them, even just digitally, with our country.

Looking into the 2020s, we can continue to stay at home and hope the world finds us, in our little northern outpost. Or we can take Barton's advice and follow Canadians like Lindsay Miller to the world's new frontiers. She'd be the first to tell you, they're not waiting for us.

8

Lindsay of Arabia

THE IMPORTANCE OF BEING CANADIAN IN A MORE COMBATIVE WORLD

At a crossroads in the Middle East, where diasporas through the ages have come seeking an oasis of opportunity, Canada's best-known expat may be a horse. Northern Dancer is revered in Dubai, and across the United Arab Emirates, and not just for his extraordinary run in the 1960s when despite his small size he shattered the Kentucky Derby record. Even today, his legacy as a sire casts a long shadow across the Arabian Peninsula. His progenies are pursued by the most discerning Arab horse lovers, nowhere more than in Dubai, where his lineage was part of the remote emirate's transformation into a cosmopolitan hub. In 1981, nearly a decade after the world's first great oil crisis, Dubai's now controversial ruler, Sheikh Mohammed bin Rashid Al Maktoum, startled the horse world by engaging in a bidding war with British businessman Robert Sangster for one of Northern Dancer's offspring. Sangster won the colt for $3.5 million, double the previous record for a yearling, but Sheikh Mohammed was undeterred. He was among a new generation of emirs who saw themselves as global leaders, and in the Persian Gulf, there were few more valuable emblems of leadership than a horse. He quickly went after another

Northern Dancer foal, successfully offering $3.3 million for the horse, which he renamed Shareef Dancer. The prized horse went on to win the Irish Derby, the greatest victory at the time for the emirate and a sign of things to come. Two years later, in 1983, Sheikh Mohammed confronted Sangster in another bidding war for a Northern Dancer offspring, shattering the record again with a price of $10.2 million. The Maktoum family's place in the horse world was firmly established, as was Canada's reputation in their emirate.[1]

The rise of horse racing in Dubai, and Canada's small place in it, was not a mere indulgence by a wealthy oil sheikh. The outpost is one of seven hereditary fiefdoms that make up the United Arab Emirates, which was formed in 1971 after Britain pulled out of the region. It gained international notice through the 1970s for both its clout in oil markets and its strategically valuable location across the Persian Gulf from Iran. During those early heady days of influence, a young Sheikh Mohammed, who was third in line to the throne and the most Western-savvy of his family, had seen the need for Dubai to look beyond oil. The world of his father had been turned upside down by the 1970s oil boom—socially, economically, culturally—and the emirate at last had the chance to lead the changes sweeping the Middle East. Horses would be key to his strategy: they were an ancient symbol of Arabia that spoke to his people, and a signal to the globetrotters he wanted to bring to Dubai.

As the 1980s exploded with services—banking, air travel, entertainment, health care—Dubai got into the race for all the expat talent that went with this new knowledge economy.[2] Even as his neighbours binged on oil, Sheikh Mohammed pushed Dubai to binge on smarts, and to find ways to get the world's most talented and ambitious expats to move there. As he said to his advisers, "How can we race a horse without a jockey?"[3] To get those jockeys, Dubai established a new kind of class system in the 1970s, luring expats with a simple promise: enjoy the comforts of the West and tax-free status of the East, as long as you don't stir the political pot or question the ruling family. Overnight, it changed the culture and economics of an emerging international elite of professionals known as transnationals. With its accommodating climate (if you can stand desert heat) and easy air access to Europe, North Africa and the Indian subcontinent, Dubai became an expat destination. Even movie stars wanted to be seen in the newly sporty city, with its seemingly cosmopolitan rulers and their horses, unaware of what was perhaps happening inside the royal court. Enthusiasm rose with the new century, which the Maktoums believed could belong to Dubai. In 2000, they sought to secure their country's place as a global hub by staging the Dubai World Cup, with enough prize money to attract top race horses from around the world. They won it with their own entry, Dubai Millennium. His forebear: Northern Dancer.[4]

By then, the flow of people between Dubai and Canada had surged. After the first Gulf War, the South Asian expats who had found opportunity in Dubai during the 1970s oil boom realized they couldn't count on the region as a home forever. They had seen what happened to their fellow expats in Kuwait and realized it was time to seek new sanctuaries. Canada came calling, with an ambitious immigration program and a desire for a new breed of economic migrant who could help spirit our resource-dependent economy into a new global age. For the Dubai crowd, living uneasily in the volatile Persian Gulf, Canada seemed perfect. Syrians, Tamils, Lebanese and Pakistanis—all those who had flocked to the Gulf during the oil boom could now flock to Canada as dual citizens, a custom Ottawa established in the late 1970s. They could have the best of both worlds, planting one foot in the security of Canada and the other in the ambition of Dubai. Those "astronauts," as they were called for all the time they spent in the air, had come to symbolize the post-national world of the 1990s and the globalization it promised.

After the 9/11 attacks, though, Dubai had to change again. It was not only on the front lines of another war zone, its rulers realized the internet explosion of the 1990s could be an even more disruptive force. While other Arab countries tried to shut down the internet, to contain political unrest, the Maktoums saw it as a gift, a kind of drilling rig for the knowledge economy that its oil-heavy neighbours never really understood. In 2002, the rulers announced their intentions to make Dubai a new kind of global centre for entertainment, design and finance. It was about as bold as a little outpost could get. Arabs had just launched the biggest attack on America since the Second World War. A war was underway in nearby Iraq. Across the Gulf, Iran had been labelled an international pariah by Washington. And here they wanted to build something that would be a cross between Manhattan, Las Vegas and Hong Kong? Sheikh Mohammed, who was emerging as the heir apparent (and in 2006 would formally take charge of Dubai), was unflustered. He said there was almost nothing his emirate could not do.

Dubai started its ambitious new chapter with international finance, to ensure more of the $1 trillion of Arab money that was invested in the West actually flowed through an Arab centre rather than through the City of London or Wall Street. Next up, the emirate outlined a vision to pour billions into health, media and technology, to make Dubai a kind of Silicon Valley for the Middle East and North Africa. To do both, it would need a new generation of global thinkers—not the traders and financiers who came out of the 1970s petrocraze but cosmopolitan connecters who could put Dubai on a new map of smart cities. A kind of Singapore on steroids. The city-state's extravagance knew no bounds. The palm-shaped Jumeirah resort, built into the sea at the turn of the new century, was like nothing the world had seen, until it saw Dubai's 160-storey Burj Khalifa, the world's tallest structure. Or the Dubai Mall, the world's second largest after West Edmonton, spanning twelve hundred shops and built around an ice-skating rink. Dubai thrived on a conviction that it could bend nature to its will, from the indoor ski hill it built to the archipelago of man-made islands that were designed to look like the continents of the world. Even as the rest of the region struggled through the aftermath of 9/11, this little city on the edge of a desert was setting a new standard for international communities.

Lindsay Miller arrived in Dubai in 2007, just as the U.S. was building its troop surge in Iraq and threatening war with Iran. The Toronto entrepreneur and design specialist was used to Middle East volatility. She had spent her early childhood in Libya where her father, the celebrated firefighter Mike Miller, was based, and later watched him gain global renown when he and his Calgary company extinguished hundreds of Kuwaiti oil field[5] fires set by Iraqis retreating from the 1991 Gulf War. (He was awarded[6] the Kuwait Liberation Medal and Order of Canada for his work.) Lindsay spent most of her youth in Calgary, and in the mid-1990s enrolled in film studies at the University of Toronto, hoping it would take her abroad again. She had adventure in her blood and something else she had taken from her father: a desire for impact. After graduation, she trained to be a pilot and worked for a time as a flight instructor with the Sierra Academy of Aeronautics in California's desert, training Air China crews. The 9/11 terror attacks put an end to that ambition, and Miller returned to arts and entertainment, first with her own music video business, and then working for the National Film Board of Canada and Toronto

International Film Festival. The Middle East was never far from her mind, though, and after completing an MBA at York University she decided on more adventure. She had grown up listening to stories about her great-grandfather in the North-West Mounted Police and watched her grandfather and father build up their company, Safety Boss, which not only fought fires effectively but did so in environmentally minded ways that their competitors seemed to miss. Her father called it "Canadian work ethic," which Lindsay felt she could take into a very different Middle East than the one he had known. One of Dubai's sovereign-owned companies, the Tecom Group, wanted to build a media and internet city, as part of the emirate's grander plans to create a new-age Manhattan in the sand. It aimed for a dash of Hollywood ambition, too, with a studio city and film and television commission. A Canadian with frontier grit and Toronto polish would be ideal to help. Miller had spent summers in Dubai as a university student and still had family there. She knew the potential for film as a business opportunity for the region, as well as a way to nudge social change. "I felt if it could be done right," she said, "it could really shape society."[7]

As Miller discovered, almost from the moment she landed, there's no place quite like Dubai for expats. The city is home to at least forty thousand at any given time—global citizens who run its celebrated airline, its resorts, banks, hospitals, and new technology centres. In Sheikh Mohammed's mind, these were his jockeys. In her new job, Miller was tasked with building out the film industry, and told not to trim her ambitions. Dubai, she discovered, is open to any idea, "as long as it makes money." She helped land the filming of *Mission: Impossible—Ghost Protocol*, and travelled the world to sign up partners for the emirate's fledgling studio scene. From Berlin to Amman to Hollywood, everywhere she went she met receptive audiences; everywhere, that is, except Canada. "People in other countries are hungry," she said, recalling her early business trips on Dubai's behalf. "I found the Canadians were stereotypically complacent. Their attitude was, 'If it doesn't work out, it wasn't meant to be.'" Had the Canadian work ethic of her father's time been lost? "I still believe it's there," she said, "but I think it's fair to say its impact is compromised by a low appetite to compete."

Oddly, while her compatriots at home weren't convinced of the Dubai vision, she found people elsewhere eager to take a meeting with her because she represented Dubai and she was Canadian. "Being Canadian, already people were cutting me some slack," she said. "They knew I didn't assume I'm the smartest person in the room. There's a deep humility in our culture. I always felt I had to back up my point of view with strong logic. I just couldn't say, 'That's how it's done where I come from.'" Miller's ability to move between cultures helped her land her next job, developing a design district for Dubai that was meant to rival Shoreditch in London. And her local partners once again offered a reminder: don't think small. Even though the global economy was still reeling from the 2009 recession, she was asked to help build the world's most ambitious project for design perhaps in her lifetime. Costing more than $1 billion, Dubai Design District—or d3—would be unparalleled. The district would span eleven buildings and house ten thousand designers and two hundred firms, from Hugo Boss to La Perla. While physical size was important to the district's backers, they also wanted d3 to transform the place of Arab design. Miller had watched what was happening globally with designs like the *abaya*, and felt d3 could do more. She even wondered if it could impact twenty-first-century style the way Germany's Bauhaus movement and Harlem's renaissance influenced previous ages. If d3 got it right, she thought, Dubai could be part of a cultural transformation in the region and perhaps globally. She saw the chance for impact.

"We started to see design was really cross-pollinating with fashion and there was a great opportunity to bring it all together," she said.

To help make Dubai the new frontier of global design, Miller knew she'd need more than jockeys. She'd have to build the kind of innovation culture she saw in the Toronto film community, where friends and rivals find ways to work together on common needs like training programs and industry standards, and are open to the free flow of creative talent and entrepreneurship. That would mean attracting a very different kind of expat to Dubai, and getting a bit more permission from government for those expats to do their thing. Every foreigner in Dubai knew the unspoken rule: they were there to do their thing, and do it well, but not to shake up the place, say with culturally offensive designs or politically threatening messages. Could the jockeys still make a difference? Miller was about to find out. She launched negotiations with Parsons to become the district's education partner, and convinced Chanel to set up its regional headquarters in d3. The district's tenants soon included Dame Zaha Hadid, the celebrated Iraqi-born British architect who died in 2016, furniture providers Artemide and Preciosa, and an array of fashion houses such as Burberry and Dior. Once it was launched, d3 also became the foundation stone for Dubai Design Week, prompting *Wallpaper**—the creation of Canadian Tyler Brûlé and one of the world's leading design publications—to refer to the emirate as the "cultural capital" of an Arab design renaissance.[8] The bigger mission, the one Miller had signed on for, was on its way.

With three small boys under the age of seven, Miller and her husband prepared to move back to Canada in 2018, to raise their family in what they thought was a more stable region. Dubai had the artifice of Canada—Tim Hortons, Joe Fresh, BeaverTails, Second Cup—but not the sort of social integration they knew they'd get back home. They knew there was always the risk of war in the region, and growing concerns about human rights. In 2018, Sheikha Latifa, one of Sheikh Mohammed's adult children, released a video in which she said she had tried to flee Dubai only to be captured and forcibly returned by armed men and held against her will in a palace.[9] The 33-year-old's plight became a global *cause célèbre*, prompting Mary Robinson, the human rights champion and former president of Ireland, to visit Dubai to confirm her safety. Then, in July 2019, the ruler's sixth wife, Haya Bint Al-Hussein, a Jordanian princess and former Olympic equestrian, moved to London and announced she was leaving her husband, also fearing for her safety. She applied to Britain's High Court for legal protection for herself and her two children.[10] While unproven in court, the allegations did as much to damage Dubai's worldly image in the West as its glass towers had built up.

For Miller and her Jordanian husband, there were plenty of reasons to move back to Canada, but as they packed up, they realized there were other parts of a frontier economy they'd not find easily back home—global ambition most of all. The couple cancelled their Calgary plans, unpacked and bought a house in Dubai, registering their sons in local schools while Miller took on a new role with her former boss, Amina Al Rustamani, the former CEO of Tecom Group and a director of AW Rostamani Group, one of the largest family conglomerates in Dubai. An American-educated engineer with a PhD from George Washington University, Al Rustamani had set out to develop Dubai's entrepreneurial culture and was already ranked among the Middle East's most powerful women. With Miller, she wanted to launch a boutique investment fund called MENA Moonshots, using the acronym for Middle East and North Africa, to see what disruptive technologies could bring to one of the world's fastest-growing regional economies. Their early focus would be education, as they looked for technology firms to help transform learning. They felt the Middle East, with its young population, was the perfect petri dish to test and grow good ideas. A year later, Miller felt she had made the right choice. "There's just a different attitude toward risk here," she told me. "Even my own appetite for risk has changed. In Canada, it's kind of a bad thing to be ambitious, to be competitive. Here, it really is a horse race. You better win or you'll be out."

For as much as she can build in Dubai, Miller finds it to be a greater struggle to build bridges back to Canada. On occasions when she's approached Canadians for investment opportunities, she'd gotten a cold shoulder, as if the country wanted to say, "We're all right, thanks." She was told by government officials that Canada didn't really need small investments like the ones she was developing. If so, it would be Canada's loss, and not just because of the Gulf money she represents. We'd be missing out on the extraordinary network Miller now can access in Dubai. She doesn't understand her country's reluctance. When she looks around, she sees expats from places as diverse as India and Egypt working together to help each other, with their countries lending a hand. She even sees it in her husband's Jordanian community, where there's a belief that "if there's another Jordanian, you have to help them out. You have to go the extra mile." She paused to reflect on a difficult home truth: "I don't see that with Canadians."

One reason is that across the Gulf States, our expats tend to focus largely on building their own careers or businesses, when they could be lending their time to something bigger for Canada, as Beth Hirshfeld has done. For a decade, Hirshfeld was a lawyer, political staffer and entrepreneur in Toronto, until she decided to take her consulting business international, moving in 2015 to Dubai. She was drawn by its informal motto: "If you can dream it, you can be it." Dubai's business sensibilities and savviness added to its allure, so much so that when Hirshfeld arrived, she couldn't believe there weren't more Canadians. In addition to her consulting business, she became executive director of the Canadian Business Council of Dubai and Northern Emirates, which she thought should have at least 50 percent more members given the number of Arabs she met with connections to Canada—a relative or business contact, or time spent studying here—and the universally positive view of our country. Yet in markets like Dubai, as Hirshfeld realized, we don't appreciate how aggressive our competitors are, including with their own diasporas.[11] She discovered "Canadian nice" gets you a cup of tea and not much more.[12]

In the 2020s, Canada's greatest economic challenge will be innovation, to create entirely new businesses to offset the flatlining and eventual decline of our older industries. We'll need to use our brainpower and creative enterprises to transform the way we live, work and play, and while we will do it in a very different way than Dubai, we can learn from its ability to connect with the world. Like the little emirate, we can't do it on our own, not with our population, which is roughly the same as greater Shanghai. We can start, however, by connecting with more Canadians who know these places best, which means the ones who are living, working and playing there. That sort of networking used to be done best by multinational corporations like Microsoft and General Electric, which for decades moved their most enterprising employees from market to market to build businesses and develop careers. Today, that kind of international networking is done more effectively through stealth, by entrepreneurs and researchers who have their own networks rooted in individual knowledge and relationships rather than institutional might. In the digital age, the most effective intellectual property—the oil of the innovation economy—will belong to those people who can make those distant connections.

Joel Finlayson has spent much of his career watching Canada struggle with that, as we tried to plug into the world's talent sockets. He went abroad as a management consultant in the early 2000s, and went on to try to help Saudi Arabia build its health care system. Finlayson knew the Middle East well, having spent part of his childhood in Riyadh, where his parents worked for fifteen years as physicians. After completing his education in Canada and Britain, he was eventually dispatched back to the Gulf by Monitor Group, the consulting firm founded by Harvard management guru Michael Porter. Monitor was keen to bring along Canadians like Finlayson to help him advise the Saudis on economic diversification and social services like health care. A few years after the 2008 financial crisis, Monitor was sold to Deloitte. Finlayson jumped to PricewaterhouseCoopers and then joined a Saudi client, before setting up his own health care development company to import Western health care services and technology, largely from Canada, to the Gulf region. His wife, Deborah Beatty, was equally keen to stay in the region; as an executive, and previously head of digital with the media company Astral in Toronto and Montreal, she had joined Apple to lead its efforts across the Middle East and North Africa. Like Lindsay Miller, Finlayson and Beatty knew the further the region got from 9/11, the more they'd be seen as model jockeys for the new Dubai, and its ambitions to be a technology and innovation leader for the region.[13]

From his base in Dubai, Finlayson turned his focus back to health care, which may be the Middle East's greatest social challenge and Canada's greatest opportunity. As every Arab government knows, their populations are chronically ill. A third of Saudis are diabetic. The country has no screening for breast, or other common, cancers. And even though there are plenty of hospitals, many of which were designed by Canadians, primary, home and long-term care are almost non-existent. Finlayson hoped technology, and Canadian know-how, could help bridge the divide. He was hired to create a health care incubator for entrepreneurs and engineers developing wearable technologies, sensors for remote monitoring, diagnostic algorithms—anything to keep the region of four hundred million people from sinking deeper in a health care crisis that it was ill-equipped to treat. The management thinker in Finlayson saw health care as business gold. He got the social and geopolitical imperatives, too. After the collapse of oil prices in 2015, Arab governments realized they couldn't keep spending their way to social harmony. Saudi Arabia, especially, knew it would run out of oil money within the lifetimes of many of its people, and had to think about switching horses, the way the Maktoums had done in Dubai. They needed smarter management systems, the kind that Canadians are good at designing and especially good at integrating in foreign organizations. But as clearly as Finlayson saw the opportunity for Canada, he couldn't convince Canadians to take much interest. He struggled even to get attention. "Canadians are unmotivated to venture abroad," he said. "A lot of people don't even want to take their passport to a foreign embassy. It's part of our mentality." When I spoke with Finlayson, he had been at a dinner the previous evening with a group of Indians, who had come to Dubai and were on their way to Saudi Arabia. A generation ago, they might have been migrant construction workers. Today, Indian expats are just as likely to be health care professionals and management consultants angling for the deals Canadians used to think would fall into our laps. Finlayson saw the same drive among his European, Asian and Australian colleagues, who actively pursued opportunities in the region with the support of their shareholders and governments. "We're too cozy," he noted of Canadians back home. "We'd rather sell our businesses than expand globally. But our economy depends on international growth."

The general distaste for adventure among Canadians is challenging more than economic competitiveness; it's starting to erode Canada's relevance in fast-growing markets like Dubai. For too many Canadians, going abroad is still seen as going against the grain. But as Hirshfeld learned when she landed in Dubai, foreign opportunities are an ingrained part of the business and professional culture in Germany and Britain, and now India and China, whose expats are all over the Emirates. We need to appreciate a hard truth: in the quarter century since the first Gulf War and the upheaval it brought to the Middle East, Canada has gone from a preferred destination for people, and a fabled breeder of horses, to a distant land that can be ignored, or worse, impugned, as Finlayson discovered in 2018 when Canadian relations with Saudi Arabia collapsed over human rights. Even though Canadian universities had trained more Saudi doctors than any other country, Riyadh pulled its support for overseas students in Canada after the Trudeau government protested the Saudi detention of two women including Samar Badawi, the sister of jailed blogger Raif Badawi.[14] The diplomatic tensions worsened after the killing of Saudi journalist Jamal Khashoggi, and opened the eyes of many expats to the shifting sands of diaspora politics. If the Saudis could recall their students from Canada, what would stop them from expelling non-essential Canadians? Similarly, if Canada could arrest a prominent Chinese executive like Huawei's Meng Wanzhou, as happened on December 1, 2018, what was to stop Beijing from rounding up Canadian expats, as it did in the weeks that followed?

Expats have always known their status and privileges depend, ultimately, on the relationship between homeland and host country.

Expulsions, even forced detentions, are known risks. But in an increasingly nationalist world, when governments are less inclined to play by international rules, today's expat is at more political risk than ever. Even if they're Canadian. We're a smaller power than before, and although we used to be able to rely on our allies to show solidarity when standing up for our citizens abroad, those days may be waning, too. Such risks will make it more challenging to convince Canadians to head to the twenty-first-century's frontiers, and to invest some of their lives in places like China and Saudi Arabia, or, for that matter, Dubai, where the power and privilege of expats is undergoing its own transformation. But if we stay home, and let others—be they Indian or Russian or Chinese—help those countries grow and transform, the world will be less for it, as will Canada.

For decades, our expats have helped drive reform in some of the world's most important emerging markets. In the 1970s, hundreds of Canadian engineers working for Northern Telecom, as Nortel was once called, built Saudi Arabia's modern telecommunications system, leaving a legacy that for decades was celebrated by every Saudi with a phone. The commercial contract was important to Nortel, but the personal networks that evolved alongside it were valuable to Canada, and important to our image in the Kingdom. Canadians also built the backbone of the Saudi health care IT system—modelling it on the Canada Health Infoway—as well as its national disease surveillance program.[15] For very different reasons, Canada in recent years became one of the top sources of engineers for Saudi Aramco, the giant, state-owned oil company—a cadre that could have been engaged to Canada's benefit during the diplomatic fights of 2018, had Ottawa cultivated those relationships in more stable times.

We witnessed the value of our diaspora during the North American Free Trade Agreement (NAFTA) negotiations, when influential expats in the U.S. were approached by the Prime

Minister's Office and embassy in Washington to quietly lobby anyone—business leaders, celebrities, senators—who might have some bearing on the White House. It worked. In the years ahead, we may need to do even more of that, from China to the Persian Gulf. But it can't start with a random phone call in the middle of a crisis. Such networks take years to build, and strengthen.

Andrew Padmos, who runs the Royal College of Physicians and Surgeons of Canada, has spent forty years watching Canada build those sorts of networks in regions like the Middle East, and then squander them. Padmos studied internal medicine at McMaster in the 1970s and began practising in Calgary, when he went to a medical conference in Philadelphia and was struck by a pitch from the international arm of Hospital Corporation of America. The company, now called HCA Healthcare, was offering jobs for his specialization, hematology, in Saudi Arabia. The romance of a desert, perhaps stemming from *Lawrence of Arabia*, captured his imagination, and by the end of 1978 he was working at King Faisal Specialist Hospital and Research Centre in Riyadh. He would later discover the expat community was known as 3D—depressed, destitute or divorced. Even though he was none of those, he stayed fifteen years. When Padmos finally returned home, in the early 1990s after the first Gulf War, there were about 250 Canadians working in the hospital. The Saudis knew it was time for change. Their physicians had been coming to Canada on their own since the late 1970s for specialist training, and were numerous enough to warrant their government's support. The Saudis asked Canada to build out the program, eventually training a quarter of the country's nearly twenty thousand doctors in a program that became an international model, and remained so until it fell victim in 2018 to the diplomatic fight over human rights. Feeling the Trudeau government had attacked their government and society, Saudi authorities called for repatriation of all eight thousand Saudi university undergraduate students and the more than one thousand medical trainees in Canadian schools. (About nine hundred medical trainees remained in Canada at the end of 2019, under an agreement that allowed them to complete their training.)[16]

As Padmos has witnessed since the late 1970s, bringing Saudis to Canada and sending Canadians there is fundamental to a more sophisticated relationship. Other countries don't leave it solely to their embassies to build those bridges. "The Brits and Americans treat their expats as business; Canada treats ours as a bad smell," he believes. "There's a Canadian market advantage in places like the Gulf, but our government seems to be studiously disinterested." It's one reason Americans may be far ahead in the race to develop Saudi Arabia's new health care system, and gain a share of the $2 billion the Kingdom wants to spend on medical training for one hundred thousand new professionals over the next decade.[17]

The race is not just about business contracts or diplomatic influence, or the success of a handful of Canadians. It's about Canada's influence in the twenty-first century. Through expats like Lindsay Miller, we have the chance to help societies such as Dubai grow as more than commercial crossroads, by embodying the diversity and openness their citizens so admire from Canada in contrast to what they see from their own rulers. Through Raefer Wallis, or those like him, we can ensure countries such as China have the technology and skills to grow sustainably, and ensure Canada benefits from that technology, too. The ideas and enterprise of Canadians may yet be our most valuable export; that is, if we encourage more of them to take to the front lines of change, wherever those may be.

Our aid workers and human rights advocates have been pushing a Canadian view of progress for generations, in their quest for justice. At home, they're often viewed as a nuisance by business, even by government. But through their experience, in every corner of the world, they may have shown the lengths to which Canada needs to go to keep up with progress.

9

Justice Hunters

TAKING PEACE, ORDER AND GOOD GOVERNMENT TO A BROKEN WORLD

Whether it's in business or diplomacy, the arts or aid work, Canadians who go abroad often find they have a unique voice in the world. Some were raised to recognize it. Others need time in a foreign land to feel the tug of a greater purpose, and the desire to give voice to it. They've gone abroad not just to pursue their own interests or ambitions; they're out there because they're Canadian and need to speak up for principles that feel Canadian. For the better part of a century, these voices were some of the most respected anywhere, because their country was among the few that could speak up for others and be heard. Collectively we mattered. We were muscular enough—economically, militarily, diplomatically—to defend our interests yet moderate enough not to impose those interests on others. But as Canada's relative standing receded and the world got messier, through an age of terror, economic disruptions and an explosion of disinformation and distrust, the power of that voice began to weaken. Respected yes, but no longer essential. For Canadians going abroad to make a difference, it was time for a different conversation.

Joanne Liu felt that voice early in life. The fourth child to immigrant parents from Guangdong, she was raised in Quebec City, where her family owned a Chinese restaurant, and came of age during the province's language wars of the 1970s and '80s, when her mind turned to the world beyond Canada. A voracious reader, she was captivated by *The Plague,* Albert Camus's existential story of a disease sweeping the Algerian city of Oran when it was ruled by France. She drew further inspiration from *Et la paix dans le monde, Docteur?* (*The Good Doctor*), a book about a physician with Médecins Sans Frontières serving in Afghanistan during the Soviet conflict. As she told me years later, "This doctor was all by himself in the lonely mountains and this experience had made him feel useful. I thought this was the kind of meaning I'd like to have in my life."

Liu was inspired enough to sign up for Crossroads International, a Canadian volunteer organization that sends people, typically young adults, to developing countries to experience life and communities on the frontlines of poverty. Her first assignment was Mali. She went on to study medicine at McGill, focusing on pediatrics and eventually pediatric emergency care, which she pursued at Université de Montréal and New York's Bellevue Hospital. In the late 1990s, she went back to West Africa with Médecins Sans Frontières, working in Mauritania as the only doctor in a refugee camp that housed forty thousand Malians, mainly Tuaregs. From this point, she was committed. MSF next sent her to Sri Lanka, at the height of the civil war in the 1990s, followed by missions to more than a dozen other countries over the next decade, before she signed on, in 2005, to become president of MSF Canada. Splitting her time between Montreal and the field, she led missions to Afghanistan, joined the early responders to the 2010 Haiti earthquake and went to Syria just as the Islamic State of Iraq and the Levant, or IS, was emerging as an international threat. She was getting a good sense of what "the good doctor" was all about.

Médicins Sans Frontières has been around since 1971, created by French volunteer medics and journalists in the wake of the Biafra and Bengal famines, and has grown to be a force of sixty-eight thousand people in seventy-four countries. When it was founded, the postwar model of multilateralism was beginning to fray, and a new generation, connected by television, wanted direct action. George Harrison's Concert for Bangladesh, at Madison Square Garden that August, had changed the course of international aid by turning it into a mass activity fuelled by celebrity. Over the next two decades, as cable news created an endless loop of war and suffering, fundraising went mainstream and non-governmental organizations (NGOs) like Médecins Sans Frontières became household names. Their front-line heroics were part of the appeal, but their effectiveness was equally rooted in an ability to build human networks, which, by the end of the twentieth century, would begin to change the global pursuit of justice from an institutional affair to one that was also powered by individuals.

In recognition of this, the Nobel committee awarded its Peace Prize in 1999 to MSF, and invited its international president at the time, Canada's James Orbinski, to address the ceremony in Oslo. It was in the same city, in 1957, where another Canadian, the diplomat and future prime minister Lester Pearson, also received the Nobel Peace Prize, for his role in ending the Suez crisis. Pearson used the Oslo stage to appeal to the great powers for calm and to step back from the brink of war. A half century later, Orbinski, an emergency room doctor, used the same platform to praise the courage of individuals in standing up to crimes against humanity, and implored those same great powers to bring the perpetrators to justice.[1] The Canadian speeches in Oslo were bookends to an era that in the twenty-first century would have to make room for peace and justice in a post-national age.

In 2013, Liu was named president of MSF International, the role Orbinski had held. His Nobel speech stuck with her, especially his argument that "Humanitarianism is not a tool to end war or to create peace. It is a citizen's response to political failure. It is an immediate, short term act that cannot erase the long term necessity of political responsibility." The work of MSF was merely a bridge, and as she took up her new role in Geneva, those bridges were coming under attack. The failure of the Arab Spring, the ongoing success of the Taliban in Afghanistan and the struggles of governments in places like the Central African Republic and South Sudan just to hold those countries together—there were plenty of forces to suggest the international order that Pearson envisioned and Orbinski defended was being challenged anew. And across the West there was a diminishing appetite to defend it. This wasn't the world of George Harrison and celebrity fundraising anymore. In the wake of the financial crisis and amidst growing pressures of migration, walls were starting to go up, and altruistic worldviews were at risk of looking out of touch, as Liu would quickly discover in West Africa, where an Ebola crisis had ravaged the region and shocked the world.

In August 2014, a year into her term, Liu travelled through the Ebola zone and stopped at a treatment centre in Monrovia, the capital of Liberia, where she encountered an intolerable scene. As the virus swept through West Africa, no hospital, health department or international aid organization, not even MSF, had been able to stop it. The Monrovian treatment centre became a place for dying more than for healing. To the McGill-trained doctor, it wasn't just Ebola at play, or the pernicious speed with which it was consuming communities; among the West Africans, there was a sense of despair, even profound hopelessness, and soon a sense of panic in the world around them. Reports raced through Western media that a new killer virus was on the loose. When infected aid workers were repatriated to the U.S. and Europe, TV screens lit up with images of a hemorrhagic fever jumping borders. And yet, the most courageous move that summer that many governments could muster was to threaten to seal their borders, including to medical workers like Liu who were desperately needed. The Canadian sat down with Liberian president Ellen Johnson Sirleaf and her cabinet to come to grips with the crisis. "The president was so overwhelmed I felt sorry for her," Liu recalled later. The doctor had more bad news to share. While MSF had hoped to open an Ebola treatment centre with four hundred beds in Monrovia, her agency couldn't keep up with the crisis. Of its twenty-eight staff in West Africa, fourteen died during the outbreak. She promised the Liberians she would do everything she could to tell the world of the catastrophe.

Liu thought of herself as someone who could navigate her way around danger zones. Yet here she was, needing something that wasn't in the aid worker's handbook. Her hands as a doctor were of less use than her voice to the world, which she realized she had to use to shake governments into action. She went to work banging on doors and tables, talking to media and working her message up the chain of command. From her MSF base in Geneva, she spoke to every country mission at the United Nations that would listen. She badgered Canadian diplomats and politicians she had taken on aid missions. Then she got her break. On September 2, after meeting with Deputy Secretary General Jan Eliasson, she was invited to address the UN General Assembly. The U.S. delegation pushed for MSF to brief the UN Security Council, too, which a field nurse in Liberia did by video link, marking only the second time—HIV/AIDS was the first—the council had debated a health issue. As Ebola threatened to rattle a tenuous international order, Liu arrived at the UN with a speech, "Admission to Failure," that impressed and rattled the diplomats. She recounted horrors she had witnessed in Monrovia and called for the major powers to step up with both civilian and military resources. After the speech, she went to the Russian, Chinese, Cuban and Israeli missions, and gained their support. "It helped that I was Canadian," she realized, seeing how others knew she didn't come from a superpower or speak for a country trying to pressure them. Her nationality didn't hurt either when she focused on three permanent members of the Security Council—Britain, France and the United States—that had colonial roots in the Ebola zone and still maintained a significant presence. They agreed to not abandon or isolate West Africa. Barack Obama went further, committing three thousand troops, emergency hospitals and hundreds of thousands of home medical kits to the region.

For Liu, the 2014 campaign reaffirmed her commitment to the MSF credo of *témoignage*, or witnessing—the responsibility to bear witness to crises and speak out about the human suffering inflicted on so many by war, poverty and disease. She knew her work as a doctor was not just about providing medical service or saving lives. It was about providing voice, which is often the most powerful weapon Canadians have. The ability to do both is why Canadians were part of the creation of multilateral aid in the 1930s, and why Canadians are found in disproportionate numbers in global organizations as diverse as MSF and the International Criminal Court (ICC). Our passport gets us into places like Syria and Yemen. Our approach to public health and experience in remote medicine are well suited to crisis zones, too. And Canadians generally are appreciated for our signature to most UN efforts, as well as our appreciation for community, understanding of minority and indigenous rights, and fluency in the two leading languages of international assistance. "Send us a Canadian," Liu was once told. "You don't have a colonizer's attitude."

For all those benefits, Liu has also come to see the limits of Canada's global engagement, including with expats like her. While she and MSF staff tend to see themselves as citizens of the world, even though that makes them targets in many conflict zones, they know that on the international stage, governments still matter, and Canada's is not what it used to be. When Liu took up her post in Geneva, the Harper government was on the outs with many non-government organizations. Justin Trudeau enjoyed a honeymoon abroad, but that, too, lost its glow when his government curtailed international aid. As much of the world turned inward, Liu was astonished Canada didn't do more, or ask Canadians to do more. The U.S. under Donald Trump had pulled back from humanitarian work, and the British were too consumed by Brexit to focus on humanitarian crises. "There's absolutely no doubt we're missing an opportunity," Liu told me in 2019. "There's a vacuum of leadership in international governance."

The limits of Canadian influence struck her at the UN General Assembly in 2017, when she went to New York to give voice to another concern that had been overshadowed by the Ebola crisis: the disturbing increase in attacks on hospitals, including by Western forces. Two years previously, U.S. planes had bombed an MSF-supported hospital in Kunduz, Afghanistan, killing forty-two people and destroying the facility. MSF refused to stay silent. Despite the organization's reliance on the co-operation of governments, the agency had a greater concern, which was international humanitarian law and the loss of a common understanding of its role. Medical facilities had long enjoyed special legal protection. Without that, the work of MSF, and every other aid group, might be imperilled. Liu denounced the U.S. bombing and spoke out against a growing pattern of impunity for such attacks. In just two years, she noted, MSF had recorded more than 150 attacks on its facilities. She even suggested the attacks be considered war crimes. In 2016, another MSF-supported facility was bombed in Aleppo, Syria. Liu didn't care who the perpetrators might be. She went to the UN with a simple and clear message: "Medicine must not be a deadly occupation. Patients must not be attacked or slaughtered in their beds." MSF's voice, along with the International Committee of the Red Cross, emboldened the UN Security Council to accept a resolution condemning any attack on medical facilities and personnel. The resolution was backed by eighty countries and passed unanimously. Liu's voice had been heard.[2]

When I first met Liu, in 2017, to talk about her influence as an expat, she said she feared the world had given up on its postwar commitment to human rights, the one that Canadians had helped shepherd through the early days of the UN. She was especially concerned about the unwillingness of the UN, and World Health Organization, to criticize member states for putting the health of so many at risk. The emergence of private initiatives like the Bill & Melinda Gates Foundation did little to ease her mind because "Gates is not accountable to the citizens of the world." It was time, she felt, to hold the feet of governments to the fire. In September 2017, she wrote an open letter to the governments of Europe, challenging their attempts to toughen immigration policy and asking bluntly, "Is allowing people to be pushed into rape, torture and slavery via criminal pay-offs a price European governments are willing to pay?"[3]

Among the challenges of the twenty-first century is just that: to see humanitarian assistance as a political endeavour, and for Canadians to see a role in both. If Canada is to matter to the world, then the Canadians who can be found on every front line need to be engaged in a very different manner, not just as distributors of aid or facilitators of training but as a bridge between countries and as a witness for people. In other words, *témoignage.* "We need to be sure every nation has a voice and a vote," Liu told me, thumping the table as she spoke. "If we don't, we will regress to a point where only the rich will have a say. We're too interconnected for that. We need to save the world from itself. My goal is to put the health of people in front of politics. We need the courage to do that."

Canadians have been carrying that courage to the forefronts of global struggles for more than a century, and were out there well before the death of colonialism or birth of multilateral aid. Starting with George Mackay in Taiwan in the 1880s, and then the Presbyterians in West China, Canadians introduced the idea of capacity building, teaching skills so locals in time could meet their own needs. That led a group of Canadian expats to help launch UNICEF at the end of the Second World War. Then, as dozens of countries gained independence from colonial powers and struggled to get their own public services up and running, a new generation of expats scattered to the four corners, doing more to shape Canada's image in the world than any government initiative had accomplished on its own. Much of that was driven by idealistic baby boomers heading out into the world in the 1960s and early '70s. Ed Clark, who eventually became chief executive of TD Bank, went to Tanzania for two years with a team of economists from the University of Toronto to help to its president, Julius Nyerere, reorient the old colonial economy. Sheldon Levy, who went on to become president of Ryerson University and a deputy minister in the Ontario government, went to Kenya where as a computer programmer he was tasked with coding its international trade management system. At the forefront was an agency then called Canadian University Students Overseas, or CUSO, which was formed in 1961 and by the end of the decade became the dominant channel of Canadian aid, and expats, to the world. CUSO volunteers designed Ethiopia's school system, and populated Bhutan's with so many teachers that Bhutanese were often asked where they learned "Ontario English." In 1968, more than seventy CUSO volunteers went to northern Nigeria, where Canadian missionaries[4] [5] had worked a century earlier, and within a decade were so many in number—at one point, a third of its overseas workers were in the West African country—that Nigerians began turning to Canada more than its former colonizer, Britain, for post-secondary education.

The whole concept of an expat was somewhat fresh to Canada, and Canadians couldn't have been more naive about it. Bob Jones, a CUSO alumnus, remembered going to Montreal, in 1969, for a three-week orientation program that included "Introduction to Swahili," along with a heavy dose of Marxism. He remembered, "During the period of language training, we also had a number of very interesting speakers who talked to us about the country and history and colonialism."[6] Their speakers included a member of the Black Panther Party. "For young, naive, not very well-travelled Canadians, it was a real eye-opener," Jones said later. As education progressed in developing countries, and new technologies emerged, Canadian aid workers realized they were less and less valuable to their adoptive countries. The world had become more connected, and more complex, and integrated thinkers—the ones who could see the dependence of public health, for instance, on economic policy—were needed.

By the 1970s, a need for this kind of approach to global health was apparent to John Evans, the medical innovator, cardiologist and free-thinking academic who joined forces with Fraser Mustard to create a pioneering medical school at McMaster. The school would become a pipeline for Canadians wanting to take on the world, just as Queen's and Toronto had been a century earlier, but with a very different mindset. As health care became increasingly complex,[7]

Evans and Mustard felt Canadians needed to embrace simplicity. They felt that with more medicine and medical technology than previous generations ever could have imagined, a new generation of doctors needed to learn, once again, to listen. The two rooted their new school of thinking in "evidence-based medicine," with a focus on the social conditions of health and epidemiology. There would be no courses or textbooks, they said. Their students would learn from patients.[8] Evans later became president of the University of Toronto and, after his failed run for the Trudeau Liberals in 1978, moved to the World Bank, where he was one of the first to argue for health as an economic investment, not a social cost. His systems thinking transformed how health was seen in the developing world, and led to what his youngest son, Tim, called "an awakening." Global health was no longer "an eccentric part of missionary work," said the younger Evans, who followed in his father's footsteps to become one of Canada's leading health voices in Washington.

Although Tim Evans had been out of the country for decades, he still saw himself as a "nomadic Canadian." I met up with him at a Starbucks in Toronto when he was on a short visit to the hometown of his 1970s youth. He could scarcely recognize the city, or its traffic, but felt the underlying values hadn't changed. He called Canada "my foundation, my heritage, my motor." His three children, all born abroad and now young adults, called themselves Canadian, too. As a young adult in Canada, Evans had set his eyes on the world when he joined Canada World Youth, first travelling to Quebec, then to Senegal, where CUSO's presence was beginning to fade in the setting sun of benevolent volunteerism. "Once I saw a different side of the world, I saw everything differently," he said. After finishing his undergrad at the University of Ottawa, he went to Oxford in the mid-1980s to study agriculture economics, focusing on the effects of river blindness on farm production in West Africa. He was convinced health was a key determinant of labour productivity and development, the primary reason that led the World Bank to lend money to West African countries to fund river blindness programs—as an economic investment.

After leading health programs at the Rockefeller Foundation, Evans was hired by the World Health Organization, where he discovered "the golden glow of Canada" and its subtle influence in other countries. He often felt he was given more credibility than he figured he merited, largely because of his nationality and a subsequent assumption that "I was someone who could navigate conflict fairly." It was also assumed that he, as a Canadian, had an innate sense of what a just health care system looks like and how it should perform. He developed that sense of health equity during his medical residency at Harvard, when in Boston he saw disparities he had never encountered in Canada. Later returning to his studies, at Harvard, he teamed up with two titans of global health, Paul Farmer and Jim Kim, who in 2012 became president of the World Bank, and began to promote the idea that social conditions, namely poverty, were a greater ailment than many diseases. If governments could focus on those conditions, rather than pouring billions into symptoms, they argued, the payoff would be enormous.

In the early 2000s, Evans tried to bring this thinking back to Canada. He and his wife, Alayne Adams, a social scientist who had worked for three decades in global health, from West Africa to the slums of Dhaka, joined forces with several other Canadians working in the field, including James Orbinski, the former MSF president, to create a school of global health at the University of Toronto that would partner with the Rotman School of Management. They ran into a bureaucratic wall. The university wasn't interested in global health at the time. Later, when Evans was at the World Health Organization, he was approached by Paul Martin, who was prime minister at the time, to lead a G20 initiative on pandemics. The idea collapsed along with the short-lived Martin government. In 2011, the Canadian Academy of Health Sciences appointed fifteen people, including Evans, to an Expert Panel on Canada's Strategic Role in Global Health. They concluded Canada had an opportunity to twin health and foreign policy, and to seek out individuals—our diaspora—who could show Canadian leadership in the world.[9] Again, no result.

Evans expressed a frustration with his country. We were good at health care at home, he felt, and good at sending humanitarian workers abroad. We were even good at raising our voices when needed, and at bearing witness to the world's horrors. But when it came to integrated thinking—to helping the world navigate the complexities of public policy and human choice—we tended to get shy. It wasn't for lack of talent, or experience. Like his father, Tim Evans was known, and in demand, in health circles around the world. Just not in his home country. "I see lots of talented people out there who just aren't tapped because they're not part of the formal Canadian bureaucracy or a cabinet appointment," he said. "It's a travesty, because they have outstanding expertise and experience and a willingness to contribute."[10]

Over the course of a century, many of those expats had shifted their work from action to design, and perhaps a little from heart to head. In the communications age, their voice would be needed, too, and perhaps more valuable—and certainly more powerful—than anything Canadians had previously brought with them. To better understand this long humanitarian arc, from medical missionary to systems designer to communicator, I met up with Lyse Doucet, a veteran correspondent I'd known since the early 1990s, when I was based in New Delhi for the *Globe and Mail* and she was stationed in Islamabad for the BBC. Doucet is now chief international correspondent, and her maritime lilt had been the BBC's voice to the world for the better part of three decades, and since 9/11 the one most often used to explain the traumas and tribulations of a post-terrorism world. Even if she's not a household name in Canada, she may be the most influential Canadian at work today in terms of the households she reaches abroad.

Doucet asked me to meet her at London's Frontline Club, a converted three-storey factory building in Paddington that's now a watering hole for journalists returning from the world's hot spots. The walls are crowded with the war zone photography of Robert Capa and James Natchwey, and the memorabilia of a media age gone by. There's a cell phone that took a bullet and saved a life, typewriters that survived bombings, and articles of clothing stained in blood, each there to remind future generations of the reporters and photographers who went before them. Press freedom, Doucet explained as we made our way up a narrow staircase, is a baton.

For someone who had been in most major war zones of the past quarter century, Doucet exhibits remarkably few battle scars. She stopped at every table, greeting people like an upbeat schoolteacher welcoming back her charges from summer break. She matched a story from Iraq with a tale of her own recent foray into the region, to the United Arab Emirates for the WorldSkills Competition. Her fellow correspondents might have seen the trip as a journalistic pink slip, a ticket to the land of soft features, but Doucet couldn't contain her passion. Skills and automation, she told a camera crew who were suddenly enthralled by her storytelling, would be more powerful than any army in tamping the age of terror. "The Middle East will topple without better education," she declared, without losing her trademark smile.

After we found our table, she continued to explain why she had focused on human development as the trigger story for the 2020s. Wherever she found herself, whether it was Baghdad or Badakhshan, she sought out young people, especially young women, to understand and record their views of the future. It was a bit of a Canadian thing, she said, to forgo the muscular voices of power for the views of the underdog. "Maybe," she offered, "it's empathy."

Doucet can't remember when she first got hooked on world issues. Growing up in Bathurst, New Brunswick, she was fascinated by a missionary aunt in Japan who came home every seven years. She later picked up a book on international development, written by a Bathurst resident, and realized it was what she wanted to do. After an undergraduate degree at Queen's, and a master's in international studies at the University of Toronto, she joined Crossroads International—the same NGO that sent Joanne Liu abroad—to teach in Côte d'Ivoire for four months. She was hooked, although not on aid. She saw herself as a storyteller for the millions who could not get theirs on the nightly news. Perhaps because of her Acadian and Irish roots, the underdog story felt natural.

She stayed in West Africa as a freelance journalist, feeding the BBC until it posted for a reporter in Islamabad to cover Pakistan and Afghanistan in the final days of the Cold War. Doucet got to Islamabad in time to cover the swearing in of Benazir Bhutto as Pakistan's prime minister (and the Muslim world's first female leader). Three weeks later, on Christmas Eve, the Canadian was in Kabul watching Soviet troops prepare to pull out. She stayed for a year. In 1994, she moved to Amman to open a BBC bureau and then a year later to Jerusalem to take over as Middle East correspondent, a job that would test her Canadian mettle for neutrality. Nowhere else is the underdog narrative more hotly disputed, perhaps because everyone thinks they are one. Doucet discovered this one evening at a reception in London, hosted by the American University of Beirut, which had invited her to join a group of eminent alumni in the city to meet Prince Charles. Once in the receiving line, she overheard Arab guests telling the prince their stories of loss. When it came her turn, she felt compelled to share hers, telling the prince, "I'm of Acadian ancestry, a people expelled from eastern Canada by the British in 1755, and some Acadians would like an apology from your mother the Queen." Her Arab friends looked at her with newfound respect. The prince looked at her and said, "History can be so unkind."[11]

Capturing history, and explaining it, has long been a Canadian tradition. Indeed, for as long as there's been international reporting, there have been Canadians in conflict zones, in front of and behind the camera. If there were an American war correspondents Hall of Fame, it would have a special wing for Canadians, from Kathy Gannon and John Burns to Morley Safer and Arthur Kent. When Jeffrey Kofman joined ABC News in the 1990s, the late Canadian anchor Peter Jennings pulled him aside and reminded him to always guard and protect his "engaged but detached view," as he knew it was something Canadians developed uniquely while growing up with U.S. television. In 2003, when Kofman broke one of the biggest stories of his career, about serious discontent among U.S. troops stationed in Fallujah, he was vilified by the right-wing press. Drudge Report referred to him as "Canadian and gay," which he found amusing since he had already outed himself in the *Advocate*. But for Kofman, it was a reminder: "We have a more global outlook. We do not see it as our destiny to rule the world. Middle powers have a certain humility about their place in the world."[12]

Like humanitarian workers, Canadian journalists enjoy privileged access to places and people that others don't get. Our passports, our comfort in other languages and cultures, our easygoing nature tend to open doors. But like Liu, Doucet knew the world of her youth was not the world she covered today. It was one thing to be a spectator in an objective age, when institutions like the media established the world's fact set and moderated its conversations; it was quite another to be a journalist in a sea of subjectivity, when everyone felt they had a voice that had to be heard. The very nature of *témoignage* needed a rethink. The witnessing that Mackay initiated, and Liu championed, was suddenly in the hands of everyone with a phone. Would independent reporting be needed anymore? Doucet believes it is, more than ever. She has seen enough bloodshed and hardship to haunt a person for a lifetime. Yet, in her stubbornly upbeat manner, she continues to search for better ways to tell stories and ensure their impact on the world's conscience is indelible. Even as her subjects gain their own channels to speak directly to the world, she believes mediation will remain the keel of humanity.

Doucet is an active member of the Oslo Forum, a group that convenes and supports conflict negotiators, and a trustee of Inter Mediate, the British charity devoted to the advancement of mediation in war zones. This style of advocacy journalism was not in vogue when she first went overseas. Even as late as the 1990s, before the internet turned communications on its head, news reporters were expected to capture and share facts, and nothing more. A decade or so of social media has gutted that belief, not least because the public now sees and accepts how media select what to report on. Who's to say the Arab skills crisis isn't as important, or interesting, as the latest Arab political crisis? More than through story selection, though, Doucet stands out because she listens to people who are unknown to the nightly news viewer or online news browser. It's why the BBC shows her in countless promo shots, her head covered by a shawl, quietly taking notes as others—women, usually—speak. To listen, the promos could say, is to witness.

This sense of empathy is one of the reasons so many Canadians are at the forefront of both media and social justice. But if there's a twenty-first-century test of that empathy—and a challenge to our sense of voice—it can be found across the English Channel, at the International Criminal Court in The Hague. Canada played a central role in the court's creation, and Canadian lawyers remain central to its functioning. You might expect that from a country designed by lawyers, as Canada was, but for the Canadian legal minds who are trying to establish a new era of international law, the ICC's awkward adolescence is rife with frustrations, between those who witness atrocities and those wanting to act on them.

James Stewart faced these tensions almost the moment the ICC's member-states elected him in 2012 as deputy prosecutor, tasking him to bring to justice those accused of some of the world's most heinous war crimes. For anyone in global affairs, the ethnically rooted conflicts and war crimes of the 1990s were no longer top of mind. New forms of atrocities were on the rise, particularly in the Middle East, Central Asia and West Africa, while many governments were beginning to retreat behind the curtains of nationalism. In fact, international justice—something Canadians helped develop—was being questioned anew by both conservatives and liberals for falling short of its promise. Stewart knew he had to prove the critics wrong.

Born in Montreal and educated at Queen's, Stewart had been a prominent Crown attorney in Ontario in the 1980s before taking an unpaid leave in the nineties to move to the forefront of international justice and a new model being tested in the wake of the Cold War. He worked as a prosecutor for the International Criminal

Tribunal for Rwanda, in Arusha, Tanzania, and then for the International Criminal Tribunal for the former Yugoslavia, in The Hague, serving in both places under another Canadian, the prominent justice Louise Arbour. Stewart moved easily between French and English and found it just as easy to move between cultures, including in Tanzania, where he met his Kenyan wife. He also brought with him a pragmatism that the international system would need as it struggled to build support for the court, especially among those Americans who wanted to close it. "We seem to get along well with people," he told the *Globe and Mail* in 2013, shortly after his appointment to the ICC. "We seem, because of the nature of our own country, to adapt well to people of different backgrounds."[13] When I spoke with Stewart in 2017, two of the three ICC trials underway were led by Canadians; much of the court's grunt work of justice was done by their compatriots, too, because, as he said, "We tend to put people in the field who can do the job. We're not obnoxious. People trust us."

The idea for an international court to try crimes against humanity emerged after the First World War. While it faded with the demise of the League of Nations, it found new purpose after the Second World War, gained currency in the 1980s as a means for Caribbean nations to pursue drug traffickers, which appealed to U.S. Republicans, and deepened its traction after the Cold War, when many countries sought a new balance of power through international law and the ultimate hope for right over might. In the absence of duelling superpowers, scores of countries saw the idea of a court as a means to hold unchecked warlords to account. The UN moved ahead cautiously with special tribunals on war crimes, focusing on the 1994 Rwandan genocide and the brutal wars in the former Yugoslavia. Then, in 1998, at a special meeting of the UN in Rome, a statute to create the court was endorsed by

120 countries (and rejected by seven, led by the U.S., China and Israel). The ICC was born, a permanent body governed by statute to pursue crimes against humanity. No sooner had the court opened its doors, however, then controversy entered. After issuing its first arrest warrants in 2005, the court took another seven years to render its first judgment, in 2012, convicting a Congolese rebel leader, Thomas Lubanga Dyilo, of exploiting child soldiers. To many at the time, the decision exposed the ICC as a victor's court, where political opponents could be marched off to oblivion. The heavy weighting of African cases added to worries it would focus on marginalized countries and duck some of the world's more geopolitically contentious battles. In 2016, nine of the court's ten actions were against Africans (Georgia being the exception.) A year later, South Africa threatened to withdraw from the Rome Statute after the ICC's judges rebuked[14] its government for failing to arrest Omar al-Bashir, who was then president of Sudan and wanted on charges of genocide and war crimes against his people, while he was in the country for an African Union meeting. South Africa didn't follow through on the threat, although that same year, in 2017, Burundi became the first member-state to leave the court[15] after Stewart's group opened a file on crimes against humanity in the small country that continues to be ravaged by ethnic and political violence. As for the major powers that control the UN and thus any enduring system of international justice, interest in the court continues to be temperamental. The Trump administration would like it gone, while Russia, China and Israel—each a player, diplomatically or militarily, in various conflict zones—want no part of an international system of justice.[16] Still others, notably Western Europe and Canada, continue to push ahead and staff the body with their expats, believing international justice is not just a moral imperative; it's in their national interests to secure a world that

hews more closely to peace, order and good government. In 2017, the Trudeau government nominated Manitoba's Kimberly Prost, a former judge from the Yugoslavia war crimes tribunal, to the court, as the first Canadian judge on the ICC since Philippe Kirsch stepped down in 2009. The rhetoric from Trump's Washington notwithstanding, Stewart remained undaunted. He had watched a quarter century of geopolitical tensions occasionally slow the progress of international justice but never stop it.

This quiet resolve can be found in the diaries of George Mackay, and the speeches of Joanne Liu, and no doubt among the generations of justice hunters who came between them. Few of them went into the world for Canada's benefit, although a fairer approach to international justice, in all its forms, was in Canada's interest. And yet, as the twenty-first century unfolds, attacks against this calling continue unabated. Truth tellers are smeared as "fake news." Rights advocates are portrayed as agenda seekers. It's a fight most justice hunters are used to. Many even enjoy it. The same cannot be said of Canadians who take to the global business stage.

Whether an executive, adviser or entrepreneur, every business operator abroad knows they rely on international law and justice, and the circuit breakers the international liberal order provides for capitalism. But as the Canadian business diaspora criss-crosses the world, its members have felt the tailwinds of that order fading. The very countries expressing doubts about the justice hunters had become the ones questioning the market hunters, too. On the eve of the 2020s, global capitalism was at risk of an existential crisis. Decades earlier, Canadians had helped design the principles of a global economic system that served as a buffer between mercantilism and Marxism. With populism again on the rise, and its advocates challenging the idea of a market economy, could Canadians again transform globalization?

10

The Opposable Minds of Globalization

HOW TO REWIRE CAPITALISM AND SAVE IT, TOO

If you had to name a place and time for peak globalization, London 2012 wouldn't be a bad choice. The Summer Olympics had embraced the tenor of our times, with its hip opening ceremony and group hug for global diversity. London was among the undisputed business capitals of the world, the financial crisis notwithstanding. The city remained an essential crossroads of diplomacy, too, a place where the world could gather to try to resolve its troubles, be they the Arab Spring or Benghazi debacle or Russia's meddling in democracy. In almost any field, London was the place to be, a global capital that was comfortable in its cosmopolitan skin. So comfortable that at the height of the 2012 celebrations, the city took little notice of what the rest of the country was thinking. It wanted a different deal. Four years later, when the Brexit vote startled the world, no place would be more rattled than London, which voted massively to stay with the European Union while so many others rushed for the exit. The discontent among Britons wasn't just about the EU. It emanated from a sense that the global elite, and all those expats who considered London home, were the new carpetbaggers, a new caste of transnational citizens who had gamed globalization to their favour. The view was gaining currency elsewhere, too. To listen to the political debate in Birmingham—England or Alabama— you might think that two centuries of expat progress, going back to the Scots who left London for Halifax, had come to a crashing halt. Moya Greene saw it differently.

As the Olympics got underway, the Canadian had already been CEO of Britain's Royal Mail for two years and was preparing the five-hundred-year-old organization for the most controversial privatization since Margaret Thatcher's time. Greene was the first non-Briton and first female to run the Royal Mail. When she arrived in 2010, the state-owned enterprise was, in the words of its own chairman, "balance sheet insolvent,"[1] which quickly threw Greene into the crosshairs of a public debate, raging since the financial crisis, about the purpose of business. Decades of labour unrest had weakened the Mail and rendered it seemingly helpless to fight the rise of Amazon and society's general shift to digital communications. And now the government wanted to sell it off, threatening the old-style service that many Britons depended on and the lifestyle its employees had come to assume. Greene didn't mind the challenge. As a civil servant in Ottawa in the 1980s and '90s, she had been put in charge of the privatization of CN Rail and the deregulation of airlines. Then, after several years on Bay Street, she joined Bombardier to help it expand in Europe, and in 2005 took over as CEO of Canada Post to help it cope with disruption. If nothing else, challenges were her forte. But as the Canadian executive took on her biggest one yet, to get the £10-billion-a-year Mail ready for new owners, she knew the financial crisis had changed everything by throwing capitalism into a dimmer light. The world over, and especially in Britain, employees, regulators, customers and the voting public were no longer giving business the benefit of the doubt. Even for a transformation project like the Mail, she'd need a different approach.

I met Greene at the Royal Mail's headquarters, which is a curved art deco slab of a building on the north bank of the Thames. The entrance to the monolith is marked by large plinths, each topped with a stone carving of horse and rider, known as *Controlled Energy*. It's an apt metaphor for Greene's Canadian management style. While Brexit was causing chaos outside, she seemed at peace as she welcomed me to her modest office, where she worked between neat stacks of files and briefing books on a large table. I asked if it was daunting to lead an organization that was established by Henry VIII and had invented home delivery, the post box, stamps and air mail. She didn't think so. In fact, while the British sense of history may have brought the Royal Mail here, she felt it was her willingness to come at things from the present that helped the organization absorb reforms that would make Henry VIII's head spin. "People here maybe have too much history," she said as we sat down at her table. "I believe I saw it differently because I'm Canadian."

Governments going back to Thatcher had tried to privatize the Mail, but it had been through so many labour disputes and had lost so much money, no investor wanted to touch it. Why would you, when you could just buy Amazon shares? To build confidence, Greene knew from the moment she arrived she'd need to win over three groups: her regulators, to allow her to innovate with pricing and delivery models; her managers, to seek more diverse thinking; and her unions, to allow for a more collaborative approach to labour relations. She insisted it was a team effort on each count, as she says was the case at CN. But she also appreciated how her Canadian way, even in distributing praise, didn't hurt. "We have to do something really wrong to lose people's confidence," she said. "I'm not sure if that's true if you're German or French. It's definitely not true if you're American."

Among the first big challenges, she explained, were the regulators who told her not to do anything radical. It was astonishing. The whole parcel delivery business was in the throes of a revolution, and they didn't want anything radical? She calmly explained what Amazon was up to, and that it could effectively do to the Mail what Facebook had done to the greeting card business. They got it, and gave her permission to be more radical. Next up, she had to change the Mail's culture. She went to her executives and said she needed more women, more visible minorities, more gays and lesbians, more disabled—more of everything Britain was becoming. It was the only way she knew to make the place open to new ideas and see new opportunities. She had learned that from the 14 Bus. As a newcomer to London, she had started to ride the double decker to work, and quickly noticed how it looked nothing like her workforce of 150,000 employees. She told her board the Mail needed to look a lot more like the 14 Bus. Oh, and she wanted to make the changes while cutting twenty thousand jobs. To speed things up, she told her diversity leadership council to give her a mandate, with specific goals, so she could tell staff she was following staff instructions. Finally she turned to her management team, to talk about the challenges ahead. Many of them continued to blame the unions. "I had managers who just stood there, arms folded, saying 'They're unmanageable,'" she recounted. That's when the Newfoundlander in her came out. "I'd say, 'I think you're unmanageable. Your attitude is going to kill the company.'"

Confrontation was a way of life in British labour, where the MO was strike first, negotiate later. When Greene arrived, the Royal Mail had just endured three disastrous strikes. In the previous year alone, it had suffered fifty-eight labour disruptions—not the record potential investors wanted to see. "Disputes are inevitable," Greene told the union bosses. "How disputes are handled is not inevitable." She explained the Canadian approach to labour relations, asking her union leader to sign a non-aggression pact. He agreed to make strikes the last resort, not the first. She then introduced the union to a Canadian style of mediation, suggesting they turn to a third party for ideas they might otherwise miss. In Greene's rookie season, just one year after the fifty-eight labour disruptions, it recorded none. The organization went on to eight consecutive years without a strike.

On October 15, 2013, the Royal Mail was listed on the London Stock Exchange, which valued the enterprise at £3.3 billion and placed shares in the hands of 99 percent of its employees. Putting equity in the hands of staff was critical in Greene's mind, and a small victory for those wanting to make globalization more diverse and better distributed. She chalked up the approach to a pioneering spirit she found common among Canadians, who tend to prefer a co-operative management style. "We see what's possible," she said. "There's a saying here: 'put it in the long grass.' We don't say that. Maybe it's because we're honest-to-goodness pioneers." For her efforts, Greene was knighted a Dame, a greater recognition than she had received at the time from Canada, which did not reach out to her during her years as one of the leading executives in Europe or as one of the most accomplished female CEOs anywhere. Even when she sat on a council of European CEOs, where she found her colleagues had "a soft spot" for Canadians, her own country didn't ask her to help advance Canadian interests. Pity, as the British might say. She was willing.

After retiring in 2018, Greene was named to the Order of Canada, and says she still cherishes her home country, for the education and career in government and business that prepared her for the Royal Mail. She talks as if a team of Canadians had even stayed with her as she moved abroad. But despite such attachments, some frustrations with Canada linger. You can hear them as she gently slaps the table and allows her Newfoundland voice to thicken. Despite Canada's potential, she's concerned a new generation of Canadians aren't willing to take on the world, or even move abroad to learn about it. "We have to stop being so parochial," she stressed. "I tell every young person I meet, it's the first thing any international organization will look for, is international experience. They want to know, 'Can this person find their way outside their own cocoon? Can they form new networks and get on with it?'"

The kind of globalization she envisions for this new generation is very different from the ones that preceded her, going back to the first Canadian businesses that came to London before Confederation. Those early years of globalization were powered by steamships and entrepreneurs like the Cunard family of Halifax, and led to a transformation of economies around the world. Soon, Canadian multinationals like Brascan and Inco were sending Canadians to far more places than London, as they built hydro dams in Brazil and mines in Indonesia. That was the industrial version of globalization. A postmodern version was crafted more recently and shaped by three seminal events: the launch of NAFTA in 1994, the creation of the eurozone in 1999 and China's entry into the WTO in 2001. In this new economic order, Canada was still on the global stage but rubbing up against a new cast of economic players who were bigger and, in many ways, more ambitious. The ensuing race for global scale in the early 2000s led to a hollowing out of corporate Canada, with foreign companies devouring mining, metals and forestry companies, just as they had swallowed the computer graphics industry in the 1990s. Suddenly, there weren't as many Canadian multinationals to send new generations of expats abroad. If a young Canadian wanted to pursue a business career on the world stage, they'd have to go on their own, as J.C. Curleigh did when the new globalization was starting to take shape.

Curleigh set off for London in the 1990s when Europe was

coming out of the Cold War and heading into the unchartered terrain of a true common market and shared currency. The world had never tried this before, to have nation-states surrender their power over interest rates, regulations and government budgets—in short, their economic sovereignty—to a transnational movement. Corporations were suddenly in the driver's seat, and they'd need people who could keep them from crossing the lines of different cultures. A new age of corporate diplomacy was needed.

As a Nova Scotia kid and army brat, Curleigh had grown up on military bases across Canada and the U.S., and for a time in Belgium, when his father was posted to NATO headquarters in The Hague. The itinerant upbringing proved to be good training. After studying commerce at St. Mary's University in Halifax, he moved to London where he worked in marketing for Mars, the candy company, and then joined Salomon, the French ski company. He was in the right place at the right time. In 1997, as Europe's open market took shape, the German sporting goods giant Adidas bought Salomon for $1 billion. The Germans had been worried the Americans (and that meant Nike) were about to steal their game, and if they didn't the Chinese one day surely would. Adidas was especially keen on TaylorMade, the golf equipment company Salomon had bought in the 1980s but never taken to a global scale. To create their own global force, the Germans knew they needed to make peace with the French, and to do that they figured they could use a Canadian. "I was brought in as the diplomat,"[2] Curleigh said bluntly. His first assignment was to shuttle between the German and French camps, a bit like his father once did at NATO. Curleigh found the French to be laissez-faire, except when it came to defending the French way of doing things. The Germans, by contrast, were brutally direct. Then there were the others around him, like the Dutch who were always clinical and the Brits who tended to be passive-aggressive, always polite and always scheming. Curleigh just smiled and carried on, convinced that "If you put Adidas and Salomon together, we could take on Nike, which was having its way with everyone. I saw synergies where others saw culture clashes."

After Adidas, Curleigh went on to run Keen, the Portland footwear company, and then, for six years, was president of Levi Brands in San Francisco. In 2018, he moved to Nashville as CEO of Gibson, the iconic guitar company. Through each move, he continued to summer in Nova Scotia, to ensure his three teens—Scotia, Olivia and Alexander (as in Keith)—learned to pick blueberries and play softball. He also ensured they carried Canadian passports, and not just for convenience. It was a symbol of the approach he found made him successful at every stage of his international business career. "We have a balanced global view that's objective," he liked to tell his kids. "I don't think of objective as lacking passion. Just watch us playing hockey. We have passion. It's just a matter of balance. Canadians don't make big promises, but the promises we make, we keep."

Dominic Barton saw this Canadian approach when he took over as global head of McKinsey & Company in 2008. The soft-spoken, often self-deprecating business leader knew the Canadian style had helped make him a favourite of CEOs around the world, and he saw it in other Canadians he met along the way. In almost any meeting, anywhere, he could identify a Canadian as the one asking questions, and actually listening to the answers. Barton came to see his country as a "we" culture, not an "I" culture. "You don't see a lot of Canadians going around saying 'I did something.' Canadians are usually running around behind the scene, getting things done," he said.[3] He also began to note some of the attributes that were essential in the emerging age of globalization that he and McKinsey were piloting for so many countries and companies.

Reliable. Dispassionate. Conciliatory. At ease in any culture. And willing to subordinate oneself. Those attributes, he discovered, helped explain why Canadians were so often found in deputy positions in international organizations, serving as a sort of non-threatening, nondescript adhesive for multinationals trying to glue the world together. In this new century of globalization, with so much emphasis on being number one, Canadians were becoming the classic number two, the people who could maintain an even keel while advising the captains of their organizations of the mood onboard and the conditions ahead.

That worked for many Canadians seeking business careers in the last stage of globalization, when markets everywhere were opening up. But after the financial crisis, and especially after the Brexit vote, Barton found global businesses looking for a new kind of leadership, embodying everything he had come to see in Canadians abroad. In this more complex world, there was a growing imperative for diverse worldviews that could pull together competing, and at times conflicting, perspectives and integrative minds that could stitch them together. Roger Martin, the management thinker and former Rotman dean,[4] labelled it the "opposable mind."

In his travels, Martin has found this mindset to be common among Canadians, including himself as he toggled between academia and business and between Canada and the U.S., where he's now based in Miami. His 2007 book *The Opposable Mind* made the case for a business brain that did much more than accommodate divergent views; it actually melded them into new ideas, by seeing what everyone else was missing. Through profiles of globally minded Canadian entrepreneurs like Isadore Sharp, the founder of the Four Seasons hotel chain, he explained how integrative thinkers usually found new options rather than simply picking the best option available, as often happens in the zero-sum world of American capitalism. Bruce Mau, the Canadian design guru in New York, told him such minds "revolve around the plural."[5] Martin concluded such minds were shaped by three things: our stance, our tools and our experience. Our stance is where we come from, and for many Canadian expats it was a multicultural, inclusive upbringing. Even for those who had been gone for decades, Canada wired their decision-making brains through public schooling, universal health care, income redistribution and even something as distant as federal-provincial power sharing. It's how they got to the plural. Martin's second factor, tools, includes motivation, and on this count Canadians can fall short. We are not always a motivated society, at least not like the Germans in their quest for efficiency or Americans in their embrace of creative destruction. It's why many Canadians look elsewhere, to be around others with the same drive. As for the third factor, experience, it's what most expats have in spades, having moved around like Moya Greene or J.C. Curleigh. They've experienced big parts of the world, and let it shape their thinking. They just don't have a ready platform to share it with other Canadians.

I thought of *The Opposable Mind* when I went to see Brenda Trenowden, an international banker who had been worrying about the risks of globalization since the 1980s when she left Halifax for Queen's and on to Hong Kong, where she parlayed the emerging-markets boom into an international banking career that eventually took her to London. She has been there since 1991, witnessing the most remarkable quarter-century of globalization the world has ever seen and, along the way, a growing confidence among Canadians who are part of it. "People trust us more," she told me when we met in London's financial district. "They're more open to us. Going abroad as a Canadian has always put me in good stead."[6]

That trust factor had put many Canadians in the front seat of globalization. But in the depths of the financial crisis, as international capitalism fell from grace, Trenowden felt she had to do more than be a complacent passenger. She had seen the power of finance to transform communities in places like Bangladesh, and also watched its vulnerabilities when a reckless pursuit of profit prevailed. Among the subtler crises for business, she thought, was a lack of diversity, and it wasn't just a matter of representation by ethnicity or gender. It was a lack of diverse experiences, and of a plurality of networks, that deprived decision makers of the critical thinking—the opposable minds—needed to avoid the inherent risks of a free market. In London, the boardrooms of her clients looked nothing like the city around it, and that was limiting the influence, and success, business could have in the world.

Coming out of the crisis, Trenowden felt, capitalism had some catching up to do with history. As one step, in 2010 she joined a small group of executives led by Helena Morrissey, a British finance executive, to see how they could change the way business approached gender balance. They formed the 30% Club, a business initiative to get large companies to commit to that percentage of women (at a minimum) on their boards and to get CEOs to commit to that level for their senior management teams. She discovered there was a Canadian network ready to help. "We decided the only people who could make a difference were the people in power, and that's typically men," she told me. Morrissey convinced Mark Carney, soon after he arrived at the Bank of England, to speak publicly about the issue at an event around the International Monetary Fund that Trenowden had organized. Trenowden then recruited Jim Leech, a fellow Queen's alumnus who was running the Ontario Teachers' Pension Plan, which has major investments in Britain and around the world, and Tom O'Neill, another Queen's alumnus who was global head of PricewaterhouseCoopers, to push the cause on CEOs. The movement spread quickly. But even as the 30% Club took off from London to other business centres, the initiative's international expansion almost missed Canada. Initially, Trenowden's co-founders fixed their sights on Hong Kong, in part because no one from Canada was fighting for their attention. Trenowden persisted, connecting with Beatrix Dart, a professor and diversity advocate at the Rotman School, and Victor Dodig, the CEO of Canadian Imperial Bank of Commerce, to get a Canadian chapter going. They officially launched it in Toronto in 2015, putting corporate Canada at the forefront of a global movement. Had it not been for the persistence of one expat and her global network of Canadians, the moment for Canada might have been lost.

As we enter a new and more contentious time for globalization, Canada's opposable minds are up against some fierce oppositional forces, and they're showing few signs of abating. Trump's tariff wars. Brexit. A rising sense of nationalism in emerging markets like Brazil, India and China. As these storm clouds continue to gather, the risk grows that they will discourage younger Canadians from leaving home. Even by default we may emerge with our own softer nationalism, which Canada would suffer for. Not only is our economy too small to meet the aspirations, and expectations, of our nearly forty million people on our own, we're not big enough to meet the ambitions of all those Canadians who are globally minded—especially those in the fast-growing knowledge economy who, like the Canadians in Silicon Valley, want to be in the global hubs of expertise and to bring Canada with them. For this new generation, we will need to recognize that globalization isn't going away, not in a world where we buy on Amazon, watch on Netflix, share on Instagram and talk on Skype. In a world that runs increasingly on those platforms, we will need to value the emerging intangible supply chains in which people and ideas are more powerful than plants and infrastructure, and should move about as seamlessly. To seize on this new global economy, and its raw materials of intellectual property, brands, databases and customer lists, more Canadians than ever will need to be out there, physically and virtually, ensuring we're part of it. Unlike in the last stage of globalization, when multinationals set the pace, this new stage will be led by individuals, most notably entrepreneurs, creators and professionals, and the people networks they can build. In other words, Canadians.

Adam Boyes sees this demand for a new kind of Canadian expat everywhere he goes, as he builds teams of developers and gamers to plug into the fast-growing supply chain of internet gaming. Born and raised in Abbotsford, British Columbia, Boyes is the CEO of Iron Galaxy Studios, a video game developer founded in Chicago in 2008, which he knows he could locate anywhere. More than location, his success depends on digital supply chains and the teams he can build to connect the producers and buyers of video games anywhere in the world. His business, like much of the intangibles economy, really does transcend borders. Boyes discovered this transformation in trade early in his career, helping build EA Canada, as part of the Electronic Arts gaming empire, and then when he made his mark at Sony, as the executive in charge of helping developers build games for PlayStation. As he negotiated his way between the creative brains of *Final Fantasy* and the marketing gurus of Sony, his Canadian intuition for diplomacy and accommodation was invaluable. "Growing up in Canada, you want to have everyone happy,"[7] he told me. In business, that means "we care about each other regardless of the costs." Among his Japanese partners, he's seen as trustworthy and respectful of risks. Among his U.S. partners, he's seen as globally ambitious. "Being Canadian," he concluded, "is one of the greatest business assets I've come across."

The opportunity for Canadians in his sector could be enormous. With nearly six hundred active studios across Canada, video game development is no longer a garage industry. It employs forty thousand Canadians and adds $3.7 billion a year to the economy. Canada's position on copyright and licensing—key points of tension in the globalization debate—will help determine if the sector grows or shrinks domestically. But a bigger, perhaps more hidden opportunity lies with expats like Boyes who can be found around the gaming world. They came out of schools like Sheridan College, which produced a generation of world-class talent, and continue to emerge from a deep pool of companies in Montreal, Toronto and Vancouver that got started with the help of government incentives and now produce some of the world's best games. For those like Boyes who went abroad for opportunity, they can be—and should be—the industry's best ambassadors, ones who can connect Canadian developers and designers to the supply chains of a new, more virtual form of globalization.

That won't be easy as this new globalization gets tougher and tougher for smaller players and smaller countries. Just ask Brad Katsuyama, who tried to take on the power brokers of Wall Street. Katsuyama is the Canadian hero of *Flash Boys*, the best-selling Michael Lewis book about the world of high-speed stock trading and how the young grad from Wilfrid Laurier University and a team at RBC Capital Markets in New York took them on and won. It was a story of principle in the age of globalization, and of a group of techies and traders who didn't like the oligopolistic advantage that others were seeking through the digital universe. The Canadians set out to restore fair competition in the market in a game that was costing pension funds and other big investors billions. Underdogs do that. During his research, Lewis shared with Katsuyama one of his insights about Canadians: "You didn't find the fight. The fight found you, and you fought back."

While *Flash Boys* became a bit of an American legend—a classic underdog story—Katsuyama struggled with the next phase of globalization. He left RBC in 2012 to start his own company, to take the fight to an even bigger arena, assembling a team to build a new kind of trading platform called Investors Exchange, or IEX, that would be a virtual David to the New York Stock Exchange's Goliath. He had long been frustrated by the NYSE and its ability to extract fees from everyone who walked through its doors, from the companies wanting to list shares to its own members needing market data and access to the trading system.[8] To fight back, Katsuyama envisioned a competitor exchange that would be entirely digital and filed an application with the U.S. Securities and Exchange Commission (SEC) for a licence. Irked, the NYSE sent a team of lobbyists to Capitol Hill to block the move, while another exchange, Nasdaq, threatened legal action. Katsuyama responded by doubling down on the David shtick. Michael Lewis had made him a cult hero in Middle America, among that singularly American tribe of day traders and Main Street investors who believe, deep in their hearts, they can beat Wall Street. Katsuyama decided to put them to work for his cause,[9] encouraging his followers to write to the SEC. He then turned his charm on the New York and Washington media and beat the Americans at their own game, prompting one NYSE executive to call him "unAmerican" for going after an exchange founded in 1792. He shot back: "I'm okay with that. I'm Canadian."[10]

In 2016, the SEC granted IEX a licence, and since then the exchange's daily volume has exceeded that of the Toronto Stock Exchange and London Stock Exchange. But his fight against the bigger forces of Wall Street was far from over. Most listed companies have opted to stay with the Big Board, as NYSE is called, and while Katsuyama thinks they're paying too much, the companies say they're getting value. It's a bit like how capitalism, and its offshoot globalization, have always worked—as a negotiated compromise. When I visited Katsuyama at the IEX office, on the fifty-eighth floor of the new World Trade Center, he hadn't given up the fight. Rather he seemed feistier than ever. In jeans and a neatly pressed shirt, he showed me around the expanding office, which unlike most Wall Street shops had its own games area and a new mantra: "Fairness. It just might be the biggest disruptor in the stock market." The whole place exuded "innovation"—the latest buzzword in business that really just echoes Martin's opposable mind. Innovators aren't out to break things, per se. They want to build what others can't yet see. With his opposable mind, Katsuyama felt his footing as an outsider was key; it's why he hired so many other newcomers to New York and even called them "a band of renegades." About half of his hundred employees were immigrants. The biggest nationality on his founding team was Canadian.[11]

I left Katsuyama to go uptown, to hear from another pair of Canadian business thinkers who would never be called renegades but often spoke with an opposable mind. Their focus was global capitalism and they felt it urgently needed a shake-up. Dominic Barton and Mark Wiseman, a prominent investment executive, had teamed up in 2014 to launch Focusing Capital on the Long Term, an initiative of business leaders and major investors wanting to disrupt the old approach to global capitalism. They had first connected on the issue in 2011 when Barton wrote an article entitled "Capitalism for the Long Term"[12] for the *Harvard Business Review,* imploring readers in the wake of the financial crisis to rethink the system they had designed. He wanted boards and CEOs in North America and Europe to get their heads out of the next quarter, even the next decade. Barton plans his schedule the way an elite athlete prepares a training regimen, and when he was running McKinsey he aimed to speak with two CEOs a day, wherever he was in the world. In those meetings he was struck by the short-term mindset of his Western clients, who genuinely struggled to think beyond the next five years (which not coincidentally was as long as most would last in their jobs). His clients in Asia, by contrast, seemed quite comfortable talking about planning cycles lasting twenty-five years. It wasn't just an East versus West thing; it boiled down to a view of capitalism and its purpose. In his research for the *Harvard Business Review* article, Barton had spoken with Wiseman, who at the time ran the Canada Pension Plan Investment Board (CPPIB), and was impressed by his view that when he was moving its $250 billion[13] of assets around the world, to ensure there was enough to pay pensioners down the road, he rarely thought about the next three months. "Our quarter is the next twenty-five years," Wiseman had told him.

After the article appeared, Wiseman called Barton and asked, "What's next?" Surely, he thought, the piece was good for more than publicity value. That's when they decided to use it to launch a movement. Barton agreed. He had heard enough complaints from clients about their inability to build sustainable business models or uphold commitments to employees and communities when hedge funds and activist investors were pushing them to shake every loose nickel from their operations just to boost the stock price. It was something Canadians could appreciate, having watched the hollowing out of the resource economy in the last wave of globalization. To get their idea off the ground, the pair reached out to Larry Fink, the founder of investment giant BlackRock, who pulled in Andrew Liveris, then CEO of Dow Chemical, and, with Wiseman's help, Cyrus Mistry, who was then chairman of the

Indian conglomerate Tata Group. From there, other big names rolled in, among them Randall Stephenson, the chief executive of AT&T, and Lim Chow Kiat, the head of GIC, Singapore's sovereign wealth fund—names that would find an instant hearing in most of the world's boardrooms, in a way Canadians might not get on their own. It's the power of networks.[14]

The Barton-Wiseman initiative may not put an immediate end to quarterly capitalism, but it can give governments, regulators, executives and investors a bit of a safe space, and intellectual fuel, to explore ways to make that happen. In another article[15] for *Harvard Business Review*, just before launching their initiative in 2014, the Canadian duo warned that nothing less than the future of capital markets, and their ability to match savings and investment, was at stake. But a new approach to capitalism, indeed a new approach to globalization, will require more than a clarion call. Investors will have to accept different kinds of information than quarterly profit numbers. Regulators will have to demand more transparency in how companies assess their results. And governments everywhere will have to ease up on the rigid rules and regulations that have stymied entrepreneurs and company builders in so many places, and return to a more principle-based approach to capitalism.

Fewer rules, more principles: that tends to be a very Canadian approach to the law. It could be the approach Canadians bring to the next era of globalization. In fact, it's an approach one Canadian has been preaching for decades, in the very place where globalization found many of its earliest believers and today faces some of its harshest critics.

11

How Very Canadian

EXPORTING LEGAL PRINCIPLES TO COMBAT POPULISM

Even from a distance, every stone wall and wooden door at Oxford University seems crafted to keep the world at bay. Established in the 1100s, long before Britain saw itself as a global power, Oxford's insularity is by design. Its role for centuries was to develop and protect England's aristocracy from the venal forces outside its gates. While the university accepted its first foreign student, a Finn, in 1190, it was much more effective as a bastion for the elite, and in recent centuries a prep school for the architects and agents of an empire. Oxford's cloisters only started to catch up with a changing world in 1902, when Cecil Rhodes—one of those agents, who had run both a business empire and the racially divided Cape Colony in South Africa—established a trust and scholarship that still bear his name. Rhodes wanted to bring students from around the empire to its intellectual heart, to both learn its ways and inject some global thinking into the old place. He wanted the Rhodes Scholars to change Oxford, and by extension the world.[1]

As the number of international students rose, the small university town became an international crossroads, as famous for speaking up for the oppressed, through its namesake charity Oxfam, as it was for defending the privileges of the powerful. Soon, it was turning out a very different kind of elite, graduating a new generation of world leaders, from Indira Gandhi and Benazir Bhutto to Bill Clinton and Tony Blair. Briefly, in the 1960s, as the revolutionary forces of youth and technology rampaged through the world's campuses, Oxford tried to build another wall. A landmark commission, led by Oliver Franks, advised the university to maintain its place as a society of learning and resist the American idea of integrating academia with the world outside, but it was too late. The new generation had already taken over Oxford and was turning its bucolic isolation into a hub for internationalism, with Canadians in the vanguard.[2]

Probably the first Canadian to make a mark at Oxford was George MacKinnon Wrong, who studied there in the 1880s, before returning to Canada to launch the University of Toronto's history program. He was eclipsed by William Osler, the medical pioneer who created bedside clinical training and moved to Oxford in 1905 to teach medicine. But it was the Rhodes program in the twentieth century that created a twin pipeline for Canadians to get to Oxford and for its worldview to flow back to Canada. By mid-century, Canada had become the dominant source of Rhodes Scholars, thanks to our easy access to England and affinity with British culture, and the program's philosophy that seemed very Canadian in its emphasis on inquiry over argument and understanding over conviction. Among the Canadian Rhodes, John Turner became prime minister, Bob Rae Ontario premier and Chrystia Freeland deputy prime minister, while the program became a launch pad for global Canadians like John Evans, Mark Carney, Dominic Barton, Patrick Pichette and Jennifer Welsh. They got more than an exceptional education. In bringing so many Canadians to the centre of global debate, Oxford helped Canada reposition itself as a serious player in the postwar liberal order, and in the rise of globalization.

Although America set the standard for globalization, Oxford laid many of the intellectual foundations and principles. The university has long been a training ground for liberal thinkers, from Adam Smith, the Scottish economist who urged countries to open up to global trade, to E.F. Schumacher, the German mathematician who urged companies to become more aggressive on efficiency, through global scale. It produced some of the greatest proponents of globalization, too, led by Margaret Thatcher, who opened Britain's economy in the 1980s, and Manmohan Singh, who did the same for India in the 1990s. It even produced many of the engineers of globalization, like Guy Hands, who pioneered private equity, and Tim Berners-Lee, who built the World Wide Web. Martin Wolf, another alumnus, ensured globalization had a supportive, if critical voice, through his influential columns in the *Financial Times*, while Rupert Murdoch, class of '53, ensured the new economic order had a base of support elsewhere, notably America.

One of the masters of this new global elite, Timothy Endicott, still marvels at the revolutions these walls have seen, and wonders about the ones that await. As the Canadian dean of Oxford's law school, Endicott enjoyed a degree of intellectual sway over Britain's approach to globalization, and brought with him a detached view. He may lack the celebrity of a Mark Carney or Moya Greene, but in some ways might rival them for lasting impact on this country, which still sees itself as the world's commercial and legal crossroads. In fact, Endicott's work on an idea known as vagueness in law offered Britain an approach to property rights that could yet bridge an economy that is both rooted in the Magna Carta and transitioning, awkwardly, to a new international order. It is innately Canadian.

I went to see Endicott on a sticky summer day, when the high streets of Oxford were crowded with tourists and prospective students from every corner of the world. He greeted me at the porter's lodge of Balliol College, the perch from which he guided the law school. Balliol is a gardened fortress that was built in 1263, five hundred years before the British and French agreed to a legal foundation for Canada and laid some of the seeds for the concepts of vagueness Endicott now teaches. From the porter's lodge, we walked through a series of gates and courtyards that led us to the college's grand hall and its portraits of former prime ministers, statesmen and other worthy alumni dating back to John Wycliffe, the radical theologian who first translated the Bible into English. It wasn't just the political and business classes that made this their finishing school. C.S. Lewis dined here, as did fellow authors J.R.R. Tolkien and Lewis Carroll. It was here at Balliol, in 1930, that another Canadian, Lionel Gelber, used his Rhodes Scholarship to launch a diplomatic career that helped establish the state of Israel and, for decades after the Second World War, promoted the growth of a transatlantic alliance, with Canada as its bridge. They were ideas Gelber had picked up from another Oxford graduate, Lester Pearson.[3]

For Endicott, the tour of Balliol's walled gardens was a reminder of the need for openness, and, especially in a digital age, for the world's universities to continue to open their gates to other cultures and ideas. He knew his adoptive country was increasingly sour to that notion and happy to lampoon academic elites like him. As a constitutional authority, he also believed the legal principles he taught to be essential to the survival of the liberal economic order, and indeed the best way to prevent the world from retreating further from it. Endicott moves and speaks with a mouse-like quietude, which seems befitting of a Canadian whose work is to keep the world from the many traps that politics is laying. After a brief tour of Balliol, we settled into the Fellows' dining room for lunch, sitting down at a table with four other professors and students.

By coincidence, two of them were Canadian, including the legal philosopher Leslie Green.

Endicott came to Oxford in 1991, not long after starting his academic career teaching corporate law at the University of Toronto, where he had studied. The son of an Anglican minister (and brother of Marina, the novelist), he was born in Golden, B.C., raised in Nova Scotia and got his first exposure to liberal elites at Toronto's Upper Canada College, where he was a champion debater and rugby player. He studied classics at Harvard and then Oxford as a Rhodes Scholar, practised law for a time in Toronto and returned to Oxford for a doctorate in legal philosophy. He specialized in legal language and the concept of vagueness, a Canadian idea that had inspired some governments to keep laws rooted in principle rather than precision. In the minds of lawmakers and judges, vagueness was a way to leave legal decisions open to interpretation rather than bind the law to any original intent, perceived or declared. Vagueness may not sound like a prized national export, but Endicott saw it as one of Canada's more enduring gifts. He believed a common understanding of language, however vague, was just what the world needed to keep it from fracturing again.

As we worked our way through the bland fare of a campus kitchen—lasagna, mixed greens, bread—Endicott spoke in a gentle voice that lacked any hint of a quarter century in the south of England. He explained his own journey of academic leadership, and what it might mean for Canada's role on the world's campuses. After he returned to Oxford to teach legal philosophy, he grew concerned about a divergence of global ambition and national identity. Through the 1990s, most of the world seemed to be signing up for a new deal, with more open access for goods, services, ideas and people. The Thatcher-Blair, Gandhi-Singh compact of globalization was holding up, although how this new world order would settle disputes within this framework remained unclear. Surely, Endicott thought, if one law school could tackle these emerging vagaries, it was Oxford. And then he discovered Oxford was designed more to welcome the world than to take it on. The law school, for one, was operationally "shambolic." Its excellent reputation notwithstanding, the school was run by a board that had no real control over course material, faculty recruiting or fundraising. Anything that might be considered strategic, and therefore normal in a North American university, was considered alien and intrusive at Oxford. Endicott did that typical Canadian thing and volunteered to fix it. In 2007, he became the first official dean of law in a school that went back to 1869.

Like Cambridge, Oxford is a federation of colleges, each with the money and ambitions of a medieval fiefdom, and about as much management savvy. Professional schools, like law, are run independently, intersecting with the cloistered colleges only when needed, such as meal times. Endicott was able to reorganize the law school's administration and finances, but realized it needed more than new management. Oxford Law was out of synch with the world around it, teaching the rules of law with little regard for the economics of law. It was as if the twentieth century hadn't happened. At the time, British academics considered themselves to be above crass American tort law, with its emphasis on a victim's needs rather than a defendant's duties. But in a global economy, where individuals felt increasingly powerless, the idea of a victim's needs was gaining currency. Seeing the need for principled pragmatism, Endicott set out to develop a new intellectual framework to address British principles and American economics, with a more pragmatic approach that seemed very Canadian and might even bridge what he called "a cultural gap between Britain and the U.S. that can be as big as the ocean."

Many Canadians think that ocean can be bridged by international agreements that resemble the Charter of Rights and Freedoms. Endicott does not. His early academic work, with its focus on vagueness, was rooted in 1950s Quebec, when courts turned to the concept to challenge the arbitrary political methods of the Duplessis era. Consider the example of dangerous driving, which the public generally prefers to be left loosely defined. The same with corruption, be it local or international. Although laws can't say what dangerous driving or corruption entails, Canadians are generally happy to let their judges call it when they see it. In Endicott's mind, this concept can be more powerful than precision, especially when political abuse is evident. But he also sees limits to vagueness, which was never meant to give courts the power to define laws as has happened in the Charter era. Such an approach, Endicott argued, can lead to a "completely unacceptable" role of judges in policy-making, particularly when the opponents of a government decision find a way to persuade judges to see a choice as arbitrary. In those cases, courts seeking precision will both risk public alienation and restrict the law from evolving with changing social norms, technology disruption and other forces that can't be predicted. In some ways it's what drove Britons to reject the European Union, the feeling that they were being subjected to the EU's precision rather than the original principles that had brought Europe together.

Within Oxfordshire, the vote to remain in Europe was overwhelmingly positive. But just outside the walled town, the vote to leave was equally so. Endicott was not terribly surprised. While many forces inspired the Leavers, a primary one was a desire for Britain to regain authority over laws and their interpretations, and for citizens to regain control over the way they lived. Many of the Leavers wanted to ditch what they perceived as a rules-based nanny state, and return to a principle-based society, the kind Endicott believed worked in Canada. That approach to law, he believed, could work for globalization, too, by presenting a new kind of principled pragmatism. It won't be easy. A delicate balance between courts and legislatures, parliaments and constitutions, and judges and politicians, has long been the anglosphere's legal trip wire. Canada, for the most part, has held the mean, balancing popular will with prescribed intent to determine what's legitimate. It's why Canadians tend to defer to statutory bodies: we trust administrative authority, unlike the British, who prefer parliamentary authority. It's why Canadians tend to approach legal questions with flexibility: we know answers can change with the times, unlike Americans, who prefer the permanency of their constitution and its perceived intent.

After my lunch with Endicott, I walked along Oxford's crowded Broad Street, away from the new Weston wing of the medieval Bodleian Library, and out Woodstock Road to St. Antony's College, where Margaret MacMillan, the Canadian historian, was wrapping up a decade as warden. I found her packing boxes in her small study, lined with books about national identity and its often toxic effect on history. (She had some eclectic works, too, like a tome on Canadian-Finnish relations for which she'd written the forward). MacMillan was preparing for a new chapter, in which she would divide her time between her hometown of Toronto, where her family and academic roots were, and her adoptive home of Oxford, where she kept a flat. I wanted to speak to her about national identity in this transoceanic age, and the international principles needed to guide it. But before we could sit down, MacMillan spotted an icon that she thought might aid our conversation: a Canada 150 hockey jersey. It was a gift from the government, from one of those expat initiatives that felt good in the moment and was quickly forgotten.

After MacMillan put the jersey aside, I asked her to explain why Canada's nationalist instincts had eased, while in many other places those instincts surged. Surely it was about more than court rulings or EU regulations. The world over people were struggling with the very concept of nationhood and identity, even though we knew, as her bookshelf attested, they were often the sparks of war. MacMillan put down the jersey, and responded with her own rhetorical question: "What is it about identity? Why do we feel the need to be Finnish or Norwegian?" I turned the question back to her, asking what it meant to be Canadian. She laughed and fell back on clichés such as "to be not American" and "to be modest." But there was something more pressing on the Canadian identity, especially for those like her who lived and worked outside Canada. It was about symbols, the kind that laws try to codify, even at the cost of vagueness. In a world straddling nationalism and post-nationalism, torn as we are between personal identity and digital anonymity, MacMillan feared symbols were mattering again in all sorts of new and dangerous ways. Many of those symbols were what people sought when the law didn't go their way. As a student of modern Europe, she knew the dangers. We both looked at the hockey jersey, knowing it was about as dangerous a symbol as Canadians could produce. But in many places, more inflammatory icons of nationalism—language, clothing, religious symbols—were once again being used to divide people and build psychological walls around communities, in the name of identity.

Like Endicott, MacMillan saw some hope for a return to global principles, especially as the world moved beyond the last era of globalization and its flurry of prescribed rules from new bodies like the EU. Such hope might increase if the world could adopt a kind of global federalism, guided by universal principles and national rules. That would be the sort of asymmetrical order Canadians are very comfortable with, and one they could help lead. As MacMillan noted, "We understand federalism in a way the British don't. We tend to like reason. We tend to like compromise. We tend, in style at least, not to be authoritarian or top down." If Endicott were with us, he might add, "We like principles."

For a new generation of Canadians at Oxford, this return to principles was not just a theory to be debated behind medieval walls. This emerging generation, the global millennials who will shape Canada's place in the 2020s, had set out to blend the sanctuary of their schools with the storms of the world, to drive change and not just study it. They were taking Endicott's approach to principles and adding practice to it. After my visit with MacMillan, I met up with one of them, Emerson Csorba, who was studying at Oxford between stints running a consulting business. After graduating from the University of Alberta, Csorba had moved to Cambridge and then to Oxford to pursue a PhD in theology. The Edmontonian wasn't looking for an ivory tower experience. He was using Britain's two best campuses to inform his international consultancy as it worked with clients on social networks and big data projects in Latin America and Israel (while also trying to help the fledgling Alberta Party back home). When we sat down, he began to explain his pragmatic approach to the world, including his pitch "to encourage Alberta firms to think more broadly about how they source ideas." Alberta voters, too. He was concerned that Europe's growing insularity might make its way to Canada, even though we, more than most, can't afford to disconnect from the world. That's especially true for Alberta, which during his years abroad lost both foreign capital and foreign confidence in Canada's ability to manage its considerable petroleum resources. Csorba believed that by taking a greater lead on global issues, as he was trying to do, Alberta, and Canada, could turn globalization back to our favour, using some of the principles that had guided our economy for generations.

To show how, Csorba introduced me to another Canadian he had met at Cambridge, who had gone in the opposite direction along the Milton Keynes corridor, moving to Cambridge for her PhD after completing her masters at Oxford. Ellen Quigley had barely settled into Cambridge in 2012 when she discovered its challenges on climate change. Environmentalists had seized the campus agenda, and as a western Canadian she was aware how difficult that could get, for Cambridge and for Canada. Over the next few years, political pressure mounted on campuses worldwide to cut ties with the fossil fuels industry, particularly any company connected to Csorba's and Quigley's home provinces of Alberta and Saskatchewan. Cambridge was in the activists' crosshairs. In 2016, the university's endowment fund blacklisted oil sands companies as well as coal stocks. More generally, as one of the world's oldest and most celebrated schools its position on fossil fuels would set the tone for campus debates everywhere. A study group[4] commissioned by the university had already concluded oil and gas companies played a role in "systematically misleading the public on climate change" and were "complicit in human rights abuses." It suggested oil and gas stocks were both an environmental challenge and a financial risk to the endowment's long-term interests, and recommended an action known as "considered divestment," which would keep the university from investing in coal or oil sands companies but not bar fossil fuels altogether. On some campuses, the divestment movement echoed a similar campaign among universities in the 1980s to boycott South Africa for the racist apartheid policies that Cecil Rhodes had crafted. Quigley preferred a more measured approach, to ensure the world moves rapidly away from fossil fuels, but not so rapidly as to destabilize communities or economies.

The more Canadians I met abroad, the more I realized how many of them were at the centre of such raging debates. And yet, they were rarely the ones raging. Instead, they had quietly inserted themselves into conversations, usually seeking a common ground to bring people together rather than keep them apart. Quigley was cut from that cloth. Growing up in Saskatoon, she had come to value consistency, not least because she attended the same elementary school that her grandfather and father went to. Unlike them, she was not going to stay put. She attended Harvard to study English literature and then veered into oceanic history, fascinated by how currents shaped history, from the slave trade to global warming. After four years back in Saskatoon as a community organizer, followed by her masters at Oxford, she stayed on in Britain to advance her global climate research. Her doctoral thesis focused on the impact of economists, and their education and political leanings, on the public view of social and environmental issues. On the side, she began to explore the field of sustainable finance. In both realms, in economics and sustainable finance, she discovered a narrowness of perspectives and declining interest in competing positions.

Perhaps it was a Canadian thing, or just the opposable mind at work, but Quigley felt the Cambridge debate needed more points of view, and more curiosity among those who held them. She reminded me of the Dominic Barton line about Canadians being the ones asking questions in meetings and actually listening to the answers. It was essential to our approach to vagueness, this fundamental understanding that the world evolves and evidence changes as human behaviour, social norms and technologies take effect. It's why Canadians, through generations and across diverse regions, have tended to be less polarized. We want to be around others with differing points of view. It's why many Canadians, as easygoing as we can be, get our backs up when governments try to prescribe behaviours, norms or technologies. We prefer to stick to principles over prescriptions. Nowhere is this approach more challenged, though, than in the climate debate in places like Cambridge, where many environmentalists believe global warming is so intractable we have no choice but to prescribe a new approach to our economy, investments and lifestyles.

Wondering if there might be a common ground, for Cambridge and Canada, Emerson Csorba, the Oxford student, had assembled a group of about twenty Gen Y Canadians, including Quigley, to meet with Mark Carney, who was trying to bridge some of the same gaps on the world stage. In July 2019, they sat down with Carney at Ditchley Park, near Oxford, where he had just delivered the Ditchley Annual Lecture on the grounds of an estate where previous generations of Canadians had worked with British and American leaders during the Nazi blitz to keep the North Atlantic alliance intact and then after the war to build a new global order. The focus of his speech, fittingly, was multilateralism and what we could learn from finance. As governor of the Bank of England and from 2011 to 2018 chairman of the Financial Stability Board, an independent body created after the crisis to monitor the global financial system, Carney had pushed countries to see the need to balance financial capital and natural capital, even to see them as mutually dependent. He had encouraged banks and insurance companies to develop a new approach to risk, to see climate risk as financial risk and to price it accordingly. In his view, the growing exposure of financial institutions—or, for that matter, university endowments—to assets that could be devalued or wiped out by climate change was as serious a risk as any bubble in the housing market. He thought shareholders, not to mention pensioners and university administrators, should know about it through better disclosure. His argument fit well with the Barton-Wiseman view of capitalism needing better data to inform long-term decisions. But getting the world to co-operate on a common model had become both the business and diplomatic challenge of our times, with Europe going one way, the U.S. another and a range of big carbon emitters—China, Russia, Canada—caught in between, waving our arms for action while dragging our feet to get there. As Carney prepared to wind up his term in England, he urged Quigley, Csorba and their generation of Canadian expats to continue to push for the sort of multilateralism—the common ground—that could bring those different countries and aspirations together. It's what Canadians did well.

Back at Cambridge, Quigley hoped to restore a more principles-based approach to the climate debate, although she increasingly was of the mind that time was not on the world's side. Along with a few other students who shared her concern, including a fellow Western Canadian, Farhan Samanani, she formed Positive Investment Cambridge, to conduct scores of interviews, analyze research and collect a diversity of opinions on how to think about the university's investment portfolio. She found an intellectual ally in her fellow Canadian, Stephen Toope, not long after he arrived at Cambridge as vice-chancellor. Toope was accustomed to campus politics from his days at UBC and Toronto, and not surprised when at his first open meeting on campus, in March 2018, he faced about five hundred students. They were overwhelmingly anti-oil. They wanted the university to divest. But as Toope calmly explained, that would be a decision beyond the vice-chancellor's powers. While listening, he encouraged the students to wait for the experts to report back, and perhaps focus on the university's governance model. In other words, if you don't like a decision, don't demand that it be changed; explore how it was made.[5] Maybe even look for new options.

Under Toope, Cambridge continued to pioneer how universities approach climate change and their role as thoughtful leaders in a divided society. He brought in a Canadian, Ian Leslie, to advise the administration on decarbonization, and another, Paul Casciato, to lead the university's communications on sustainability issues. Quigley joined his team, too, as an advisor on sustainable investment for the university's chief financial and investment officers. Even as much of Britain was turning inward, Toope was trying to keep Cambridge's focus on the bigger world. There were plenty of other nationals involved, of course, including a lot of Britons. But a Canadian style of debate—informed, open-minded, what the improv teams call "yes, and"—was having an effect.

I asked Quigley what Canadian values she brought to the Cambridge debate that, say, a globally-minded Briton, Australian or Indian might not. She paused and then suggested an ability to listen and interpret different views, and an antipathy for social structure. Canadians move around more, not always geographically but between social groups, especially compared to her English neighbours. Britain, she found, and it wasn't just Brexit, was more uptight, at once complacent about its place in the world and displeased with that world. Canadians like her brought a more positive view—that most things aren't as bad as they seem, and yet they can be improved more than we realize. It sounded like Moya Greene's pioneer theory.

Quigley offered to introduce me to other Canadians who were developing a more principles-based approach to globalization, in all its forms. While she was focused on climate, and Csorba on politics, their friends Logan and Tookie Graham saw technology as their tool for changing the world. Still in their early twenties, the Vancouver siblings were both at graduate school at Oxford, and each pursuing tech careers: he in artificial intelligence, she in blockchain. Oxford may appear old, but inside its stone walls you can find some of the most ambitious tech projects anywhere. I met Tookie at a startup hub called the Oxford Foundry, overlooking the canal that for centuries has brought the world to this university town. It was December and the canal was already frozen, glistening with the glow of Christmas lights festooned along the adjoining medieval laneways. She had just joined a blockchain startup, Veratrak, run by another Canadian at Oxford, Jason Lacombe, who was hoping to use the technology to improve pharmaceutical supply chains. (They had met, as Canadians seem to do at Oxford, through mutual friends on the ice hockey team, on which Lacombe played.) Using IBM's Hyperledger Fabric, their company's system would allow regulators, doctors, patients—anyone, really—to know the origins of each element of a drug. Graham's focus was on ethics, sensing that an emerging challenge for blockchain would be the human component, as it was for so many new technologies. She wondered, could you code blockchain to be ethically responsible, to differentiate between different sources of data based on their trustworthiness? Could a machine tell which sources to trust? And critically, when things go wrong, as they can with pharmaceuticals, who would be held responsible, ethically and legally? Graham didn't have an answer, but in her work with tech teams around the world—Israelis, Japanese, Chinese, Indians—she found a collaborative approach was usually what got her to one. She liked to include other Canadians for that reason, that we're open, curious and inclusive. "I see diversity as a massive opportunity," she said. "If you create anything with just one group of people, it's a huge missed opportunity for everyone, yourself included."[6]

Tookie and Logan Graham inherited this worldview from their parents—their father is an architect, their mother an entrepreneur and former nursing professor—who took them abroad whenever they could, put them in French immersion (rare in Vancouver) and shared their home with international students from places like China, Japan and Turkey. Tookie did her undergrad at UBC, then moved to Silicon Valley to work in tech and eventually start her own consulting company and on to Oxford to complete an MBA. Her side gig with Veratrak wasn't her only venture into the arena of business principles at Oxford: while at the Saïd Business School, which is among the world's best, she discovered it had no standalone ethics course, so she and a friend organized a three-day seminar in April 2017. It focused on gender issues, the cultural roots of ethics and how global businesses can balance universal values and local norms, material the school used for an elective course in its MBA program.

Logan, meanwhile, was trying to bring the same discipline to artificial intelligence, which was the focus of his PhD at Oxford. When he arrived, advanced software technology was entering an existential crisis that would shake Silicon Valley to its core. From the explosion of misogynistic material on social media to its manipulation of democracy and free speech, Big Tech had seen its early twenty-first-century honeymoon come to a crashing halt. Logan, who was on a Rhodes Scholarship, had intended to study economics, but the spread of AI globally in 2016 and 2017 convinced him to focus his research on AI, and what could be the most powerful technology ever seen, to better understand the risks it posed to humanity. Oxford's walls had seen some of philosophy's greatest minds, from Thomas Hobbes to Aldous Huxley, wrestle with the advent of technologies. In their footsteps, Logan was hoping to develop new ethical standards through a group called the Rhodes Artificial Intelligence Lab. He especially wanted to understand how the benefits of technology could be better distributed. Think of disease detection, or climate mitigation, he suggested. Do the benefits go to those who can afford them? Or to those most in need? Or to those who can make the best use of technology for others? In his research, Logan found that the Rhodes ethos—to ask questions rooted in curiosity not conviction—echoed his Canadian upbringing and its foundation in principles over rules. He figured the same approach, rather than a rush to more regulations, could help the lords of technology find their moral footing. In Europe, he saw the benefits of the General Data Protection Regulation, which was the EU's attempt to better protect individuals and their data, despite the objections of tech giants that hold so much of that data. In the U.S., he saw the benefits of a less restrictive system and what it could do for innovation by those giants and the many startups that want to disrupt them. He had reached out to the Canadian government to see if there was a different course he could help chart.[7]

In their few years abroad, the Grahams had developed a more critical view of Canada, fearing we'd lost our place in the world and even lost our relevance in places like Oxford. While they were both compelled by the U.S. and its special ability to commercialize technology, Logan had an eye on China, too, where he thought the next chapter of AI was already being written. The siblings felt technology was changing business, capitalism and the global economy in ways we weren't even close to understanding, and they weren't sure where Canada was on any of it. They also weren't sure how they could help Canada secure our place in this changing world order, although they'd like to. They were raised to believe they were part of something bigger than themselves, which seemed to echo the Barton-Wiseman concern for capitalism and the Carney view of how to better use it. Could they have the same impact? Here were two of the brightest and most ambitious young Canadians I had met, the kind who could lead the country through the 2020s and '30s. But like them, I didn't see the country making an effort to sign them up for these bigger challenges, let alone put them in charge. Instead, they were starting to slide into the grips of other, more determined countries.

They weren't alone. The global impact of Canadian millennials is at risk, and not just in terms of influence. Even as their generation connects itself digitally with the world, the number of young Canadians going abroad is in decline. Through the 1990s and 2000s, when Britain was flush with money for universities, it recruited Canadian academics in droves. At Oxford, there were more than a hundred Canadians on faculty, led by John Bell, the celebrated Alberta-born immunologist who went as a Rhodes Scholar in 1975 and never returned to Canada. In spite of that surge, Oxford in 2018 recorded only 342 Canadian students. Cambridge had even fewer. In the early 2000s, at the height of Cool Britannia, the British census counted only 204 Canadians in Cambridgeshire.[8] Endicott had expressed to me a concern about the trend, as it indicated a retreat to North America. Whenever he returned to Toronto as a guest lecturer, he found his law students wanted to pursue their studies in the United States more than anywhere else, because it was closer, in geography and in law, and richer in job prospects. He feared too many Canadian students preferred the U.S., if they looked abroad. Most didn't. While our teachers and researchers were running some of the world's best universities—Cambridge, Stanford, Berkeley—a dwindling number of students were following their path.[9]

The risk of a further retreat is greater than we might appreciate. We're heading into an age that will be more interconnected than humanity has ever known, and yet Canada won't be one of those connectors if we're not out there in greater numbers. For decades, governments have taken a laissez-faire approach to the ebb and flow of our global population. An outward-looking Canada will need a more considered path, and there's no shortage of ideas from other countries to follow. But first there needs to be an awareness that we're losing touch with our global Canadians—an awareness that needs to start in Ottawa, where most bureaucrats rarely think about our diaspora and few politicians know we have one.

12

Diaspora Diplomacy

WHAT WE CAN LEARN FROM ISRAEL, INDIA AND IRELAND

For as long as humans have organized themselves outside the family unit—first tribes, then dialects, then nations—there have been diasporas, and with them diaspora politics. But the voluntary, organized and commercial movement of people as we know it today didn't accelerate until after the U.S. Civil War, when the United States and Canada needed people to populate their frontiers. Soon, there was demand for immigrants in Australia, Argentina, Brazil and parts of Africa, and the emigrants that responded became the new weapon of diplomacy. As international travel and the spread of liberty enabled humans to move in ever-larger groups all over the planet, their governments back home discovered the power of diaspora politics, and with it a need for diaspora diplomacy. Germany was one of the first to see this power when in 1913 it changed its laws to grant citizenship to children born outside its borders, creating for the first time a legal diaspora based on descent. Poland, Czechoslovakia and Hungary followed suit, investing in overseas programs to keep their diasporas tethered to the motherland. Italy went further, supporting more than fourteen hundred Italian associations around the world to exert its cultural and political influence, and to keep tabs on this new force lest it help foment rebellion back home. By 1910, more than two hundred thousand overseas Italians had joined expat associations in the U.S., while in Buenos Aires membership reached fifty thousand. Rome strengthened the diaspora bonds with funding for cultural groups, community organizations and Italian language media that continues, albeit diminished, today. As Tara Zahra wrote in *The Great Departure*, "Many Italian officials explicitly viewed emigration as a substitute for colonial conquest."[1] The hyphenated diaspora was born.

The rise of globalization moved entire business sectors across oceans, and with them went people. By the 1960s, humans were volunteering to move like never before, as old economies struggled and new technologies, and the industries and cities they powered, replaced frontier land as a draw for immigrants. East Germany allowed 293,000 people to leave in the sixties, in return for cash from the West German government.[2] In the same decade, Yugoslavia lost 4 percent of its population to migration. But as much as the world was changing through telephones, television and jet travel, our notions of emigration were still rooted in the Book of Exodus, as a humanitarian response to crises rather than an individual right to opportunity. The United Nations had enshrined "freedom of exit" in the 1948 Declaration of Human Rights, and the 1957 Treaty of Rome placed freedom of movement at its core. But it took the intensity of the Cold War, and the Helsinki Accords of 1975, to shift these vague rights into policies that would open borders to the free and voluntary movement of people.[3]

By the 1980s, as a new phase of globalization took hold and the world began to flatten, the economic power of migration began to overwhelm countries that had stuck to a command-style economy. More than a million Poles travelled abroad in 1981, seeking jobs and livelihoods in Western Europe and North America that their struggling homeland could not compete with. Humans were the new currency. In 1985, five members of the European Union signed the Schengen Agreement, named for a town in Luxembourg where the agreement was reached, to allow the free flow of people between their countries. The group soon expanded its membership to ten, launching a daring experiment that would transform modern Europe and spur a period of progressive migration, as borders fell, economic demand grew and people everywhere sought opportunities they could see on their smart phones. At least they did until 2015, when another wave of migration, ironically, crashed a half century of progress on the shoals of nationalism.

For the better part of our first century, Canada was at the controlling end of these floodgates, and happy to be there. Whether run by Conservatives or Liberals, Ottawa focused its people strategy almost entirely on immigration, to populate the western provinces and keep pace with a rapidly expanding United States, even though by 1900 one in five Canadians—1.8 million at the time—lived in America.[4] We weren't able to do much about it, as Britain controlled Canada's citizenship and border policies until the Citizenship Act of 1947 (when on January 3, William Lyon Mackenzie King, the prime minister, became the first Canadian citizen). The door was open to a new era of migration that eventually would allow Canadians to come and go, no longer as British subjects, but as people whose identity transcended both ethnicity and geography. Thirty years later, with a new Citizenship Act in 1977, the identity of Canadians began to be defined by the rights of citizens, regardless of where they lived, and soon those rights became the foundation stone of a Canadian diaspora. Although Canadians had been going abroad since Confederation, the 1970s brought with it new economic challenges and pushed Ottawa to pursue more open borders, for goods and services and for people in search of opportunity.

Starting with NAFTA in 1994, Ottawa ensured that professionals enjoyed freedom of movement, allowing managers to head to the *maquiladoras*[5] and computer programmers to uproot more easily for Silicon Valley. Unfortunately, Canada didn't match our trade strategy with a people strategy, at least not the way Australia, India, Ireland and so many others did in the early 2000s when they began to see their diasporas as a strategic asset. In terms of collective action, the best Ottawa could do was the 1993 launch of ROCA, the Registration of Canadians Abroad, which was basically an emergency call list for consular officials. At its peak, a decade later, ROCA had registered only 170,000 expatriates, or fewer than 10 percent of Canada's global population.[6]

Jeremy Eves encountered this kind of national insularity when he moved from Ontario to the United States in 2005. As the U.S. economy recovered from the dot-com bust and 9/11, the software executive found he couldn't keep up with the job offers, starting first in Chicago, then in Houston with Matrikon, an Edmonton-based company that was later bought by Honeywell, and finally in Nashville. Although Eves knew career migration was the American way, he wanted to bring Canada along, to help his country and also find ways to help other Canadians in a place that was at once familiar and foreign. In short, he wanted to be part of a diaspora. In Houston, after he and his wife saw the Tragically Hip play at a local bar, they realized there was no formal Canadian community in the city and so decided to launch a Canadian Club of Houston, from an office in their garage. The club quickly grew to fifteen hundred members and ran regular social gatherings along with three bigger events a year, on Canada Day, Canadian Thanksgiving and a game night at the now defunct Houston Aeros of the American Hockey League. Eves recalled,[7] "A lot of people used it for networking, a lot of people developed really good friendships, lifelong friendships.

I think we probably sourced several marriages." But any larger government connection was "very ad hoc," typically a last-minute notification of a ministerial visit. Other countries had sophisticated and well-funded diaspora strategies to help expats build such networks, and occasionally stand up for their homeland's interests. Canada's strategy seemed to be the equivalent of dial-an-expat. Eves didn't get it.[8]

Perhaps more than any other Canadian abroad, Rob Hain has had to play that role of Mr. Canada, the go-to expat in London who is expected to pull together a crowd on short notice. He also knows what it's like to be overlooked on the more important stuff—in his case, international finance, which he spent decades working on—and how much the country is missing as a result. Hain grew up in Prescott, Ontario, and went to the University of Toronto, where he was so bored he opted to study abroad in third year, in Edinburgh. He was gone. After completing his studies at Oxford, majoring in anthropology, he accepted a job in financial services that took him from London to Zurich, with a stint in Winnipeg with Investors Group. He finally returned to London with Invesco, the large U.S. investment manager, and a few years later launched his own company, City Financial, with a business partner, using their expat network to create a quiet Canadian force that eventually employed 180 people and managed $4 billion in assets. It's a telling story. Hain's business partner and CEO was Canadian, as were thirty-four of their thirty-five fellow shareholders. They wound down City Financial in 2019, and Hain became executive chairman of Sound Diplomacy, a strategic consultancy also founded by a Canadian ex-pat to help cities and regional authorities extract more economic benefits from live music. But for all he has built in business, Hain feels that every time he tries to build something for Canada in London, he is largely on his own. For several years on

July 1, he and another Canadian, lawyer Derek Linfield, helped turn Trafalgar Square into a giant Canadian party, largely with funds they raised from other Canadian businesses, including Tim Hortons, which erected a pop-up outlet, and Bombardier, which once moved a subway car to the square for the day. In 2017, the government threw its weight behind a Canada 150 celebration, including a hockey game featuring Mark Carney (who as a student played goalie for both Harvard and Oxford). Hain saw each opportunity as "a big advertisement for Canada to the world."[9]

Hain has moved internationally several times with his Swiss-raised Canadian wife and become a bit of a student of diasporas and their ability to get attention. The Dutch, he thinks, are the best at it, turning much of London orange for their national day. The Americans are good, too, turning the Fourth of July into a London festival. "The challenge that any diaspora has is the absence of a reason to get together," he has found. "Some people have language or religion to bring them together. Or food. Canadians don't wear our identity on our sleeves. We don't need to huddle together to give ourselves confidence. We don't need to be part of a community. Apparently, we can survive as individuals on our own."

As a country, we have to work harder to create the glue that can bind expats with each other and with Canada, especially on days other than July 1. When he was still running City Financial, Hain showed me around his office, just off the Thames in the heart of the City. There was nothing visible to identify the place with Canada, or for a visitor to associate him with his homeland, other than his accent and polite ways. Our ability to blend in—so valuable to expat careers—is also our collective liability. I asked Hain what mattered more for expats: joining a community network, throwing and attending great parties, or working with a larger collective to achieve something greater for their country? He answered quickly:

the latter. "Canadians have a lot to contribute to the world. We're well-nourished, well-educated and very peaceful. I just don't grasp why we're not doing more with it."

At their core, nation-states exist for a handful of reasons: to enhance a culture or language; to develop and protect economic interests; to provide sanctuary to a common group, and defend against others; and, more recently, to organize public services and finance them.[10] Increasingly, many nation-states also see their diasporas as an opportunity to strengthen their raisons d'être in the broader world. Israel sees its diaspora in a unique light, for reasons of religious purpose, historic persecution, regional security and, more recently, economic growth and investment. Although there are millions of Jews globally with inherent ties to the country, the government counts only eight hundred thousand expats connected to a national population of 7.8 million.[11] Its population strategy is designed to see both numbers grow. The country's well-known Law of Return establishes rights for any Jew to become an Israeli citizen.[12] Since 1952, shortly after the state of Israel was founded, it has also conferred citizenship rights on anyone born to an Israeli anywhere in the world. Those overseas citizens can even vote in Israeli elections, provided they come to Israel to do so.

India's diaspora strategy also dates back to its formative years as a newly independent country hoping to mobilize a large and growing global population to speak up on its behalf. In 2004, the government deepened that relationship with the creation of a Ministry of Overseas Indian Affairs, headed by a cabinet minister and given responsibility for two established classes of global Indians: non-resident Indians, or NRIs, who are citizens living abroad, and overseas citizens of India, or OCIs, who are former citizens or their descendants. Both groups gained special privileges to invest, travel and work in India,[13] while the more than twenty million NRIs also enjoy the right to vote. To maintain ties, especially for generations of Indians born outside the country, the ministry has since added programs such as Know India—a three-week course for youth to learn about advancements in science and technology—and a summertime Study India Program. More recently, it made Pravasi Bharatiya Divas (Non-Resident Indian Day) a bit of a festival, held every second January to celebrate expats "who have contributed to enhancing the country's valour and global status."[14]

Ireland has taken a different tack, coming to see its global population as much more than expats. The country of 4.4 million has, by its count, another 3.1 million Irish citizens living abroad and eight hundred thousand Irish-born who are now citizens of other countries. And then there's the estimated eighty million who it counts, perhaps with a bit of Irish embellishment, as an "affinity diaspora."[15] To get beyond the flowery rhetoric of national pride, the government in Dublin created an Irish Abroad Unit as well as Enterprise Ireland, an entity that supports thirty overseas Irish business networks, plus a charity channel called Ireland Funds that raised €300 million for Irish causes and inspired diaspora foundations in India and Brazil.[16] (Not to be outdone, Scotland targeted forty million people globally who it considered "ancestral diaspora,"[17] reaching out to them for tourism and "homecoming" events—a tactic Ireland has copied.)[18]

For many of the world's fastest-growing countries and economies, these sorts of diaspora strategies are now a key part of foreign policy, perhaps *the* key part. According to the World Bank, there are two hundred million people globally who have chosen to move to another country, and are presumably open to helping their homeland.[19] Among the biggest sources relative to its population is New Zealand, which figures about 20 percent of its population lives abroad, mostly in Australia. That outflow inspired the country to launch a Kiwi Expats Abroad program to track and engage people, and a World Class NZ program to connect with star expats. Australia, with one million expats from a population of 22.5 million, has gone further, requiring all overseas residents to vote in national elections for the first six years of expatriation—a system that not only maintains a bond with the diaspora but feeds into a national database called the "smart traveller program."[20]

In 2016, a research team from the University of Toronto's Munk School of Global Affairs examined the diaspora strategies of two dozen countries, and found most to be more advanced than Canada in terms of policy.[21] Israel, India and Singapore were most widely recognized for their diaspora work, the study found. Singapore was especially ambitious with its overseas communities. When it discovered close to 5 percent of its 5.5 million people had moved abroad, it didn't panic or implore expats to come home. Instead, the government saw its overseas professionals as a secret weapon, to build trade ties with China, the U.S. and Europe, and launched an Overseas Singaporean Unit to track and support them. The government then developed a Facebook page and online news portal, and fostered overseas community groups in New York and London, to spread information for students and professionals abroad, and to explain services to those looking to move home.

No country focuses more strategically on its diaspora than China, which tracks forty million overseas Chinese and aims to stay connected with them through an array of hard and soft efforts, ranging from cultural hubs called Confucius Institutes to some thirty Chinese language newspapers published in Europe.[22] It's part of China's ambition to be a leading global force in the 2020s. Even those countries that seem to be turning inward—the United States and Britain, among them—have developed active policies for their expats. In terms of voting, Britain still has one of the most generous systems, allowing most of its five million expats to vote for the first fifteen years of their overseas residence, provided they register for each election.[23] Since the Brexit vote, the British government has also turned to its expats to promote trade and investment, and to kick-start new relationships on every continent. The United States has preferred a more indirect relationship, ensuring its six million or so registered expats maintain the right to vote, which among other things allows the government to maintain a good map of overseas Americans,[24] although in that American way it has left mobilization efforts to private partisan groups like Republicans Overseas and Democrats Abroad.

To strengthen bonds with their diasporas, most countries offer a sliding scale of privileges—from the tangible, like social security benefits offered by Australia, to the symbolic, like the diaspora pins distributed by France,[25] to special banking privileges like the ones created by Vietnam and Nigeria to help manage the billions of dollars of remittances flowing every year from their expats.[26] Seeing the need for cultural bridges, Armenia established a Ministry for Diaspora with programs to bring overseas Armenian youth to the country for short visits, in the hopes of reimagining Armenia as "a globally networked nation" rather than a landlocked country[27] in the Caucasus. Armenia's neighbour and historic rival, Turkey, saw political advantage in its diaspora and built an array of networks for the four million Turks in Western Europe and half million more across North America, the Middle East and Australia. In the 1990s, Finland got in the game when it discovered approximately six hundred thousand first- and second-generation Finns lived abroad, representing more than 10 percent of the country's population of 5.2 million.[28] The government saw overseas Finns as a critical resource, and in 1997 established the Finnish Expatriate Parliament, made up of Finns from eight global regions who meet every two to three years in Helsinki to consider issues of importance, vote on key policies and provide feedback to the government. A small council of global leaders meets twice annually. Estonia jumped that step altogether, establishing itself as Nation State 2.0 with a new form of global citizenship that allows anyone, anywhere, to sign up electronically to be Estonian. Its ambition is a digital diaspora that could, in theory, include the entire planet. Entering the 2020s, pretty much every country with a significant overseas population had a diaspora strategy. Except Canada.

In 2017, I sat down with civil servants in Ottawa to better understand the hands-off approach to our diaspora. More so under Justin Trudeau than in any government since his father's time, the federal government had been bashing about in every aspect of Canadian life, from marijuana and assisted suicide to skills training and infrastructure finance. Like it or not, Ottawa was back—but not, it seemed, for our expats. Global Affairs Canada had taken some small steps, the bureaucrats told me. They had reached out to expat networks for a few key policy reviews, notably on foreign aid and defence, speaking to Canadians in roughly sixty-five countries. They had also launched a career development program to identify up-and-comers and place them in key international organizations. They credited the effort with helping place scores of Canadians in international institutions such as the prestigious Conseil Européen pour la Recherche Nucléaire, or CERN, nuclear research lab in Switzerland. But for the most part, they felt Canadian expats didn't want Ottawa mucking about in their lives, micromanaging their careers, intervening in their business interests, or recruiting them on contentious issues. And then there was privacy. Would Ottawa even have the right to know who was where and doing what, at least without their consent? I hadn't heard those concerns from many Canadians abroad. To the contrary, I found most expats I interviewed yearned for contact and for a country that thought more ambitiously about them and what they could do for Canada. They understood that for every opportunity we missed, other countries were swooping in and seizing the advantage. A couple said they felt like those Olympic athletes from obscure countries who had to sign up individually to compete, and then march into the stadium alone.

Historically, the bureaucracy viewed expatriation as an autonomous act, a kind of unilateral declaration of independence by those who wanted to cast their lot elsewhere. It was a view that seemed to miss, entirely, what was transpiring in the digital century. Countries with diaspora strategies had come to realize that as their citizens moved abroad they could stay more connected than ever, and join forces with more expats than ever, not only to build their own networks but to speak up for their country. Soft diplomacy,[29] some called it. I was told Ottawa had been studying such diaspora models since the 1990s, and came close to doing something significant during the brief tenure of the Paul Martin government, which came to power in December 2003. In the spring of 2004, the Privy Council Office received an in-depth diaspora study from Alison Loat, the former McKinsey consultant who went on to cofound the non-profit Samara Centre for Democracy with filmmaker and businessman Michael MacMillan. (In 2016, she became managing director of Focusing Capital on the Long Term, the Barton-Wiseman initiative.) Loat's 2004 study, "Canada Is Where Canadians Are," was part of graduate research she had started a year earlier at the Harvard Kennedy School, taking inspiration from some earlier work by Canada25, a small group of recent Queen's graduates that included her and future Calgary mayor Naheed Nenshi. In the paper, she explored options for a diaspora strategy, including the seemingly easy first step of an advisory council of global Canadians "to provide direct input into policy, trade or investment strategies, and be the bridge between Canadians at home and abroad."[30] We didn't need to start from scratch; we could have copied Greece's World Council of Hellenes Abroad, France's Le Conseil Supérieur des Français de l'Etranger, or the elected General Council of Italians Abroad, which was established in 1989 and chaired by the Minister of Foreign Affairs.[31] Frank McKenna, who moved to Washington as Canada's ambassador in 2005, liked the idea so much he launched a "Connect to Canada" portal for expats in the U.S. The Privy Council Office seemed interested enough to bring Loat to Ottawa to present her ideas to senior bureaucrats. And then, nothing. Ottawa's interest faded.

A decade into the new century, the Asia Pacific Foundation of Canada was so concerned about the lack of thinking around global Canadians that, led by researcher Kenny Zhang, it launched a series of reports arguing that a more outward-looking country needed more "outward-thinking Canadians."[32] One of the papers proposed a new strategy of "attachment"—a kind of social glue to keep our diaspora together. Another suggested a Ministry of Canadians Abroad. A third piece proposed an "imagined community of Canada" so governments could look beyond geography in their relationship with Canadians.[33] Yet another recommended we expand our definition of Canadians abroad, the way Ireland and Scotland had, and find ways to re-engage with descendants of one-time expats, even if it was just through "roots tourism." More ideas poured in: a concierge service for expats wanting to invest or work in Canada, enhanced university alumni networks, more support for overseas business networks, funding for groups like the C100. In 2010, the foundation funded a major survey of 2,093 Canadians, and found most (73 percent) agreed a central agency to work with overseas Canadians was a good idea.[34] Most agreed children born overseas to Canadians should be considered Canadian.

But Canadians seemed to draw the line at greater privileges, such as access to Canadian health and education, and had no desire to give out passports to those "imagined" Canadians whose closest relationship to citizenship might be a grandparent.

Beyond the general open-mindedness of Canadians on citizenship, 9/11 had set off a cultural earthquake that continues to reverberate through the collective conscience and hold government back from some of these ambitions. It's not just about the risk of terrorists coming and going from Canada. More broadly, Canadians remain suspicious of expats who use their citizenship, and passport, for personal gain—to minimize taxes, gain legal protections abroad or simply seek opportunity elsewhere while knowing a safe harbour, with cheap health care, education and comfortable retirement living, awaits them back in Canada. In the public mind, these are the expats known as "Convenience Store Canadians."

A big setback for any proposed Canadian diaspora strategy came in 2006, with the outbreak of civil war in Lebanon and a stampede of requests for consular support from a surprisingly large number of Lebanese Canadians. Through the 1980s and '90s, most of them had moved to Canada while keeping a foot (and often business presence) in their homeland. With Lebanon now at war, they had the right to be evacuated, as do all Canadians travelling abroad, provided such an operation could be reasonably launched. Only issue was, no one in Ottawa had budgeted for fifteen thousand passport holders showing up in the same war zone at the same time. Diplomats told me they had recommended a service charge for evacuation, which had been used in the past, but there wasn't a proper list of Canadians in the country, and with thousands at the departure gate, there was no time to lose. The minority Harper government, perhaps with an eye to the Lebanese vote in Montreal, also went against its instincts and waived the proposed service fee.

It grossly underestimated the eventual bill,[35] which came in at $94 million.

The episode drew a collective pause among Canadians who stopped to consider what this new jet-setting age meant for the country. John Chant,[36] an economist at Simon Fraser University, looked at our passport system, and concluded we had one of the best deals going. Most Canadians probably think of their passport as only a little blue book, but each one comes with a so-called passport package that includes the right to enter Canada freely; easier qualification for health care; consular services, including evacuation in war and strife; transfer to Canada to serve some sentences for offences committed in foreign countries; eligibility for resident tuition fees; and eligibility for descendants to become citizens.[37] Chant recommended[38] trimming benefits, eliminating dual citizenship and jacking up the price of a passport to $500, as well as adding requirements for the children of expats to demonstrate an association with Canada beyond their parents to get one. There was a ready group of listeners in the Harper government, not just for passport reform but for a rethink of our approach to citizenship.

While the Conservatives understood the importance of expats, they also recognized how different the world was from 1977, when Canada had last revised its citizenship laws. The internet, jihadism, electronic money laundering—the tools at any expat's disposal were powerful, and the Conservatives saw it as their duty to protect Canada and the integrity of our citizenship from those forces. Expats may be important, they felt, just not worth any cost. In 2009, while still a minority government, the Conservatives began to tighten rules for Canadians abroad, starting with changes to the very Citizenship Act that had modernized both immigration and emigration policies. Starting that year, citizenship in the diaspora would be limited to Canadians and those born outside Canada to a Canadian parent. The government made additional revisions in 2014, tightening eligibility requirements for citizenship and strengthening security provisions. For expats, the amendments required regular tax filings with the Canadian Revenue Agency, and prohibited citizenship for anyone charged abroad with an offence that would be indictable in Canada. The new law added a sort of "jihadi clause," allowing Ottawa to strip dual citizens of their Canadian citizenship should they be found to have acted against Canada's national interests.[39]

The Harper government moved next to limit voting rights for expats who were not eligible to vote after being out of the country for more than five years—a restriction that had been in place since 1993 but not actively enforced. No one had raised much of a fuss about the limitation, largely because Elections Canada allowed expats to reset the five-year clock simply by visiting home. For Liberals and Conservatives, it had been a kind of don't ask/don't tell policy. Then, in the May 2011 election, many expats discovered they were no longer eligible to vote. Two of them in the U.S, who were turned away from voting, filed a court challenge, claiming their rights had been violated because Section 3 of the Charter guarantees "every citizen of Canada has the right to vote in an election of members of the House of Commons or of a legislative assembly and to be qualified for membership therein."[40] Ontario Superior Court judge Michael Penny agreed with the complainants, taking note of the Asia Pacific Foundation's research that showed 94 percent of expats had visited Canada since establishing principal residence abroad.[41] He also noted Zhang's research, which showed far more expats paid Canadian taxes than voted: in 2008, 422,000 filed non-resident tax returns. In his view, the actions showed a collective attachment by our expats to home, which was one of the eligibility requirements for voting. He was equally impressed with how many expats contributed to public pension plans, and maintained investments, property and social ties—all grounds for the right to vote, no matter how long they had lived abroad, he reasoned. The federal government appealed the decision and saw the case to the Supreme Court where one of the complainants, Gillian Frank, who lectures in theology at Princeton, urged Canada to rejoin "progressive democracies around the world" by granting more generous voting rights to its citizens, regardless of soil.[42] In January 2019, the top court agreed.

In the Munk School survey of diaspora policies, no issue was more contentious than the right to vote. At the time, of the 144 countries that held elections,[43] voting rights in 115 of them were granted to overseas citizens. In five—Italy, France, Algeria, Haiti and Portugal—expats even enjoyed direct parliamentary representation. In my interviews with Canadian expats, voting came up more than any other issue, even though few ever voted, or even registered. Jean-Pierre Kingsley, Canada's former chief electoral officer, said that in each of the federal elections he oversaw between his appointment in 1990 and retirement in 2007,[44] only six thousand to nine thousand expats voted (not including Armed Forces members and diplomats). Why, then, the emotion? He felt the internet had transformed both voting and our notions of citizenship, making it possible for Canadians anywhere to be informed and engaged. Moreover, he pointed out, many expats had discovered they were the only Canadians to be officially disenfranchised. Prisoners, tax cheats, the mentally incapacitated—all are entitled to vote in Canada because, as Kingsley saw it, "death and voting are the two great equalizers."[45]

In 2016, after the Harper government's defeat, Alison Loat spoke again about diaspora diplomacy—this time at the World

Economic Forum, where she figured the idea might appeal to the Davos crowd. In the audience was Trudeau's new international trade minister, Chrystia Freeland, who had spent much of her career as a journalist working abroad. Five years earlier, when Freeland was with Reuters, she had written a piece that ran in the *New York Times* making the case for "seagulls"—international citizens who flock between global centres, as she had done over her career between Moscow, London and New York. National policies needed to catch up, she argued, because "in the age of the Internet, the jet airplane and the multinational company, the very concepts of immigration, citizenship and even statehood are changing." She went further to suggest "some countries are starting to imagine themselves more as social networks than as a physical place."[46] After Loat's talk, Freeland approached her and said she'd like to explore a diaspora strategy. But as was the case a decade earlier, there was no follow-up. As best Loat could figure, governments, Conservative or Liberal, were too set in their ways to think beyond hierarchies and services. Even as Facebook was changing the world, they could not see our diaspora for what it was: a vast, and valuable, social network.

In the minds of many global Canadians, the challenges are too pressing, and opportunities too great, to leave to Ottawa. Among them is Robert Greenhill, a former McKinsey consultant and Bombardier executive who ran the Canadian International Development Agency in the early 2000s and then moved to the World Economic Forum in Switzerland as chief business officer. When Greenhill returned to Montreal in 2014, after two decades in international business, he was struck by how much the country had changed on the home front, and how little we had changed abroad. Determined to do something about it, he formed a small group called Global Canada to essentially build a diaspora strategy for

Ottawa, whether it wanted one or not. He held gatherings with Canadian expats in New York, Geneva and Kigali, and he worked quietly with global executive recruitment firms to ensure that highly qualified Canadians were being considered for key positions in international organizations. From his time in Davos, working with leading CEOs and government leaders, Greenhill was acutely aware of how easy it would be for Canada's day in the sun to fade. It didn't really matter who was prime minister or which government wanted to do what. We had become too small in a world that was getting too big to keep doing things the same way. In an age of networks, Greenhill thought we should focus on connecting individuals, which in a way sounded like McKinsey's consulting model—a collection of committed people who, while never being the biggest, always strove to be the best.

Of course, plenty of countries can make the same claim, but only a few can offer the kind of multicultural expats—emigrants from an immigrant background—who have been surging in numbers since the late twentieth century. Many are children of Canadians who want to take on the world; others are new Canadians who prefer to stay out in the world, often enjoying the right to dual citizenship, which was created in 1977 and has since transformed the notion of an expat. Dual citizens can present plenty of policy challenges, as Canada discovered in Lebanon. But they're also part of a much bigger population of hyphenated Canadians who are quietly changing Canada's place in the world.

13

A Diaspora That Looks Like the World

HYPHENATED CANADIANS, DUAL CITIZENS AND A CHANGING GLOBAL FACE

The world had lost much of its enthusiasm for migration by the summer of 2018, when I met Ahmed Elnaiem in central London. Born in Khartoum, Ahmed had moved as a child to Canada, where he grew up in the suburbs of Toronto—first Scarborough, then Mississauga—learning the importance of, among other things, shovelling a neighbour's sidewalk in winter. He still remembers the day his father shared this about Canadians: "Winter teaches us to co-operate." The message stayed with young Ahmed as he pursued engineering at the University of Waterloo, studied for a term in Singapore and worked for tech companies in Silicon Valley and New York. When we met, he had just moved to Britain, at age twenty-seven, to join another Waterloo grad building a finance startup. They planned to use their "Canadianness" to transform how entrepreneurs raise money, by pooling funds and expertise with other entrepreneurs in a kind of online co-operative movement that echoed the ethos Ahmed had developed shovelling his neighbours' walks.

Ahmed struck me as someone who was everything Canada wanted be in the 2020s: mobile (in a world that was increasingly static), multicultural (in a world that was increasingly divided), digital (in a world that was increasingly tech-leery) and co-operative (in a world that was increasingly isolated). He was also the kind of expat—the hyphenated kind—who could take a new Canada back to the world. As I started to wrap up my research, I sat down with him and a small group of other Canadians in London, all in their twenties and almost all of them hyphenated, to compare notes and hear their views of where Canada's diaspora might head in the decade to come. We had borrowed an office near the banks of the Thames, which for centuries had welcomed the world's wanderers. Like the river before us, Ahmed and his friends had been part of the great human tides of the twentieth century. Their families had come to Canada from Sudan, France, Iran and India, and they—the settled generation—were now returning to the world as Canadians. One of Ahmed's friends, Yasmin Rafiei, was on a Rhodes Scholarship at Oxford, studying politics and preparing for med school. Yasmin's parents came from Iran to Canada in the 1990s, settling in Edmonton to raise their children. By leaving their chosen country, and seeking opportunities abroad, Rafiei felt she could shape her Canadian identity in ways her parents never could back in Edmonton. "I am the hyphen space," she told our group. "I exist somewhere between Iranian and Canadian." As a kid in Alberta, she had identified with the youthful characters of the British fiction she read in school—*Harry Potter*, *The Hobbit*, *The Lion, the Witch and the Wardrobe*—and their ability to solve complex problems that adults couldn't. "I was the kid who wanted to tackle world problems," she said. She credited the mix of arts and science for the integrative thinking she developed in Edmonton's public school system and at the University of Alberta's Peter Lougheed Leadership College.[1] She also credited snow, and tobogganing in Edmonton's valleys. It gave her resilience, and like her friend Ahmed, a sense of co-operation.

Hyphenated or not, the generation of Ahmed and Yasmin will shape the Canadian diaspora in profound ways in the 2020s. Simple math, if nothing else, will force it. A decade ago, when the Asia Pacific Foundation conducted its major surveys of expats, more than 40 percent said they were born outside Canada, and showed a much greater inclination to move abroad than Canadian-born citizens did. They had seen the world and were comfortable in it. From 1996 to 2006, exit rates for naturalized Canadians were more than three times higher than for the rest of the population, with immigrants from Hong Kong, Taiwan, the U.S. and France the most likely to leave. Among second-generation Canadians, the children of immigrants from Eastern Europe, South Asia and the Middle East had the highest exit rates.[2] In the past decade, another trend emerged, through the rise of millennials from immigrant families.[3] Roughly 2.5 million of Canada's seven million millennials were born abroad or have at least one foreign-born parent, due to the rapid increase in immigration levels in the 1990s and 2000s. Now that the bulk of them are in their early twenties, they're at the prime age for emigration, and their numbers will increase. According to Statistics Canada, the share of children with immigrant backgrounds will grow by close to 50 percent through the 2020s. That means in the decade ahead, there will be no country in the world quite like Canada, because no country will reflect the world quite as well.

Yasmin and Ahmed looked perplexed, though, when I asked them about the emerging identity of a hyphenated diaspora. They considered themselves to be as Canadian as Kraft Dinner, and didn't even think of, say, reaching out to a Sudanese or Iranian community in London. Why would they? As Ahmed said, "When I'm here, I'm Canadian. When I'm in Khartoum, I'm Canadian. When I'm in Canada, I'm Canadian." They eschewed clichés of every kind (especially those Facebook photos of expats and their Timbits at Heathrow), and were waiting for a new image of Canadians in the world, knowing it would be up to their generation to create it. Someone in a Raptors cap, Ahmed suggested. Or maybe carrying shawarma poutine. "Even without an obvious logo," he continued, "I think I can spot a group of Canadians in a crowd, something about how we stand by each other, and how we use the space we're in." For his generation, at least, people don't look Canadian; they act it.

Canada laid the foundation for this new kind of diaspora in the 1977 Citizenship Act, which reduced restrictions on dual citizens and allowed Canadians to build a competitive and compassionate immigration policy that told millions around the world they could come here and still keep a bit of themselves there. It was a new approach to citizenship for a new age of global citizens. Today, more than forty countries, including the U.S., Britain and France, allow their citizens to be citizens of other countries. In the Asia Pacific survey, more than a third (36 percent) of Canadian expats said they held dual citizenship. In the early years of Canada's experiment with dual citizenship, the hyphenated diasporas became a mantelpiece for multiculturalism, both here and there. It was not uncommon for communities to send their most celebrated youth—a Miss This or Junior That—back home to show just what their diaspora could accomplish in the new world. After her 1991 victory, the first winner of Miss India-Canada, Kamal Sidhu, moved to Mumbai and launched a successful TV career. Ruby Bhatia, who won the contest in 1993, followed her footsteps and became a VJ and instant celebrity on Star TV, a satellite channel that transformed mass entertainment in India. Both developed followings for their Western looks, unplaceable Canadian accents and clever command of Hinglish. Nisha Pahuja, a Toronto documentary maker who tracked the rise of Canadians in Bollywood, chalked up their celebrity to more than a knowledge of Hindi film and song. He found Canadians carried with them "a cultural confidence" and "a savvy to mix in Western and Indian milieus."[4]

If the idea of a hyphenated diaspora, so common in culture and commerce, had a political moment, it came on an otherwise placid, sunny day in February 2017, in central Mogadishu. Somalia was having a tough time electing a president, as most of the country was too dangerous for any kind of election-day effort. Determined to keep their struggling democracy alive, the Somalis had changed course in late 2016 and announced plans for an electoral-college system that would allow legislators to pick the new president from a field of twenty-four candidates. Ironies abounded as Donald Trump, in one of his first acts as president, tried to ban the lot—anyone from Somalia, for that matter, and six other Muslim countries—from entering the United States. Undaunted, on February 8, 2017, the lawmakers gathered in one of the country's only safe places, a hangar at Mogadishu's Aden Adde International Airport, named for its first president, to launch their own attempt at democracy. Protected by African Union peacekeeping forces, who surrounded the hangar, the legislators must have represented one of the most impressive gatherings of dual nationals since America's founders met in Philadelphia. Of the 275 Somali lawmakers present, one-third were foreign nationals, including twenty-eight from Britain, twenty-two from the United States, ten from Kenya and nine from Canada. Their ballot was just as diverse, with nine of the twenty-four names coming from the U.S., four from Britain and three from Canada. The international flavour of the election was not just a reflection of a diaspora's ability to uproot itself, move across the world and stick together; it reflected a new kind of transnationalism. The winning candidate, Mohamed Abdullahi Mohamed, had returned to Somalia after a decade working for the transportation department in Buffalo, New York. The new prime minister, Hassan Ali Khaire, was a dual citizen with Norway. His first cabinet included seven dual citizens from Canada, including foreign minister Ahmed Isse Awad, a graduate of Concordia University. Could this be the face of an increasingly hyphenated world?

Dual citizenship had become a norm in Somalia, which estimates 1.5 million Somalis live outside the country, including more than sixty thousand in Canada—among them the singer K'naan, supermodel Yasmin Warsame and Ahmed Hussen, whom Justin Trudeau appointed immigration minister in 2017 and minister of families, children and social development in 2019. Of those Canadian Somalis, one-quarter lived at least part of the year in Somalia, challenging and changing our notions of global citizenship. They had helped transform Canada, and were now helping transform Somalia. But as the hyphenated world grew, many Canadians—along with many Americans, Swedes and others—struggled with this morphing identity and with people who, in their view, couldn't seem to commit to one country. They saw too much temptation for duals to maximize their privileges in each country while minimizing their responsibilities.

While every day millions of hyphenated citizens travel back and forth between their chosen countries, the rise of digital networks and mobile video means they never have to. They can be an active part of their diaspora community wherever they are, whenever they want.[5] In 2012, the Paris-based Fondation Maison des Sciences de l'Homme funded an exhaustive series of research studies to better understand this idea of "virtual diasporas," by mapping thirty global groups and their use of digital and social media. The e-diaspora project concluded that the internet had scattered people more than it had brought them together. Indeed, most communities are much less organized than Western governments and media might think. They're no longer a monolith, largely because most immigrants and their children, at least in the West, have gained economic independence. Self-preservation—once the founding need of a diaspora—had given way to self-expression, which may be why so many of the duals I met in London had reversed their parents' tracks and gone back out into the world. Priya Kumar, a researcher at Ryerson University who studied South Asian groups for the project, observed most Sikhs in Canada and Britain had gained economic independence and developed nuclear family lives, and as a result abandoned group narratives for "their own interpretations of collective history and current affairs."[6] The research project found a similar scattering of narratives within the Lebanese Canadian community, which continued to grow rapidly after the end of the fifteen-year civil war in 1990 but never became the monolithic force once expected. According to the 2001 census, there were close to 144,000 people of Lebanese origin living in Canada, largely in Quebec. By 2006, it had grown to 165,000. But as it grew, the community fragmented, by religion, career, education and decade of arrival, giving it less and less reason to organize as a diaspora. Houda Asal, a McGill researcher who tracked the community for the project, detected an "absence of any common mobilization in the diaspora: not even basic demands such as voting rights for migrants abroad are shared."[7]

Despite a common image of diasporas being exiles from oppression—the huddled masses from central casting—those who have made it to Canada tended to come from economically prosperous homelands like Taiwan and Hong Kong, and frequently returned to them, keeping one foot in each world.[8] In the 2020s, that may well continue as Canada's dual citizens focus on trade and international business, a natural outcome of the increasing push for economic immigrants going back to the 1990s.

Similar patterns can be seen in the flow of remittances, which have exploded in the past two decades and formed their own kind of dollar diaspora that's shaping our place overseas as much as the comings and goings of Canadians ever did. According to the Mowat Centre, a think tank associated with the University of Toronto that was shut down by provincial funding cuts in 2019, one-quarter to one-third of all immigrants to Canada send remittances to their home countries, with those from the poorest places most likely to remit.[9] Immigrants from India, China and the Philippines—the biggest source countries over the past generation—send the most, accounting for about 40 percent of Canada's personal outflows.[10] The World Bank[11] estimated that in 2018, remittances globally reached $689 billion, up 60 percent from a decade earlier. Topping the list of destinations: India ($79 billion), China ($67 billion), Mexico ($36 billion), the Philippines ($34 billion), Egypt ($29 billion) and Nigeria ($24 billion). About 5 percent of that came from Canada, which policy researcher Timothy Yu concluded, in his work for the Asia Pacific Foundation, put us first among remitting nations. "No country, on a per capita basis, comes close," he found.[12] The rest of the world sees these financial flows as more than a simple cheque; they're part of a diaspora's social and economic adhesive. They make a statement, greater than aid projects and larger than trade initiatives. As the social demographer Michael Adams noted, when he studied these numbers, "they can help to enhance the positive effects of individual Canadians' connections to the global village—an effort that would fit nicely with Canadians' values and behaviours in the twenty-first century."[13]

This ideal of a global village, so promising in the 1990s, has been challenged by the rise of international terrorism and the fallout from 9/11. Governments everywhere have come to realize the free flow of passports in that earlier age helped foster a new kind of transnational traveller who could weaponize their international status and engage in asynchronous warfare—one against many—on a scale not seen before. Ahmed Khadr, the Egyptian who came to Canada as a student in the 1970s, was among the standard-bearers for this movement, using his Canadian and Egyptian status to move freely around the Muslim world as the terror movement grew. In 1995, he was detained by Pakistani authorities for his alleged role in a double bombing of the Egyptian embassy in Islamabad that killed fifteen people and two of the assailants. He might have faced a different fate from his interrogators had Jean Chrétien, during a visit to Islamabad in early 1996, not pressed his Pakistani counterpart, Benazir Bhutto, to ensure Khadr was given a fair and transparent trial. "The Canadian," as Khadr later became known in al-Qaeda, was released and disappeared into Afghanistan, where he was killed by Pakistani forces in 2003. His legacy endured, though, as the status that he and his family enjoyed in Pakistan and Afghanistan clashed with the principles that many Canadians thought were at stake in the aftermath of 9/11. As dual citizens, were they to have access to the same protections that every Canadian enjoyed? The answer was yes. As long-time overseas residents, did they have the right to return to Canada? Yes, again. And if they violated foreign or international laws, was Canada responsible for their fair treatment? Yes, again, as Canadians discovered.

To many, the treatment of the Khadrs was a litmus test of our approach to citizenship going back to the 1970s. The case of Ahmed's youngest son, Omar, would try Canada's expat policies in entirely new ways. At fifteen, Omar was badly wounded in a firefight with U.S. forces in Afghanistan in 2002, and, even though he was deemed to be a child, was sent by his American captors to

Guantanamo Bay with expectations from Ottawa that he would be treated as such. He was put on trial in a military court and in 2010 pleaded guilty to the murder of a U.S. army sergeant in the firefight. In 2012, he was transferred to Canada to serve out his sentence. But then, when he retracted the plea and claimed his Charter rights had been violated, the government was caught out. Ottawa issued an apology and paid a settlement of $10.5 million. It was the fifth multi-million-dollar settlement paid to a Canadian subjected to torture or mistreatment abroad during the U.S.-led War on Terror.

The rise of a different kind of global jihadism in the 2010s posed an even deeper crisis for Canada's approach to dual nationals and our hyphenated diasporas. IS had shocked the West with its gruesome brand of terror and also its ability to recruit thousands of young adherents to its promised caliphate, and to get them to Syria. In 2018, government sources told Global News's Stewart Bell[14] they believed about 190 Canadian extremists were active in terror groups overseas, mostly in Syria and Iraq, while another sixty had made their way back to Canada. They were largely of Middle Eastern origin, but it wasn't just a Middle East phenomenon. It was a home-grown problem, with home-grown consequences for our evolving approach to citizenship. In 2016, a Canadian was killed by Bangladeshi special forces after he allegedly masterminded the July 1 attack on a Dhaka café, killing nearly two dozen people. The assailant, Tamim Chowdhury, had grown up in Ontario and graduated from the University of Windsor in 2011 with a degree in chemistry before moving back, in 2013, to the country of his birth. On the surface, he came across as the sort of hyphenated expat to be celebrated—educated in Canada and ambitious enough to take on the world. Underneath, he was identified, posthumously, as ISIS's head of military and covert operations in Bangladesh.[15]

Chowdhury's fate spared Canada any debate over his legal rights, but the issue lived on as part of a greater and growing tension over the rights of citizens abroad, including dual citizens. The Trudeau government, in one of its first acts, had rescinded a Harper-era provision that allowed the government to strip duals of their Canadian citizenship—an act known as "denaturalization"—if they were convicted of terror offences by a Canadian court. Trudeau had made the idea a popular plank in his 2015 election campaign by saying, boldly, "a Canadian is a Canadian is a Canadian." But once in power, he discovered that this spirit was not universally shared. Well beyond the Chowdhury case, Canada and its allies—Britain, the U.S. and Australia, most notably—faced a wave of IS recruits, many of them captured as the terror group collapsed, who wanted to return home. In 2019, the British government, already buffeted by the Brexit crisis, took a startling hard line on its estimated nine hundred citizens who had gone to the Middle East to join IS. In one prominent case, it stripped the citizenship of Shamima Begum, a London schoolgirl who at age 15 had gone to Syria with two friends to join the caliphate movement. Once there, she married a Dutch IS recruit and had three children, who died of malnutrition and disease. After she was captured and moved to an internment camp in Syria, she was refused the right to return to Britain. The government in London declared her to be a public safety risk and said she should seek residence in Bangladesh, her family's ancestral country. The British applied the same arguments to the case of Jack Letts, a dual Canadian-British citizen who had gone to Syria in 2014. Even though Letts was born, raised and educated in Britain, where his Canadian father moved before Letts was born, the government deemed him to be a security risk like Begum and moved to strip him of his citizenship, which would make him Canada's legal problem should he be allowed to leave the Kurdish-run prison in northern Syria where he was held. The "Jihadi Jack" case, as it became known in Canadian media, sparked a public backlash over so-called terrorist travellers, with no more legal clarity. Under Canadian law, Letts was likely to have the right to move to Canada where, should the Crown be able to prove he had "knowingly" left to engage in terrorism, he could be placed under security surveillance. His intent as a Canadian, however, would be hard to prove as he had left Britain for Syria, and had little connection to Canada beyond the citizenship he enjoyed through his father. Recognizing the difficulty in giving Letts a fair trial in Canada, Christian Leuprecht and Todd Hataley,[16] both security experts at the Royal Military College in Kingston, Ontario, argued for an Australian-style law that would make it an offence to enter a declared terrorist area, which is easier to prove than intent. But for Canadians, a bigger challenge remains: Is someone like Letts, who was born abroad, raised abroad and lives abroad, a Canadian?

Ever since 9/11, this new strain of expat terrorism has stoked concerns across the West about our approach to citizenship and whether, going back to the 1970s, it's been too liberal. Such misgivings about dual citizenship are rooted in more than fears of jihadism; they can be traced as well to the financial crisis and its shattering of public confidence in the perceived deal between citizen and state, and the responsibility of each. The public now questions government and business more than ever, and we question each other, too, turning loyalty into a political issue. In Australia, in 2017, former Conservative prime minister Malcolm Turnbull lost his coalition majority when the High Court disqualified his deputy prime minister, Barnaby Joyce, and four senators, because they were citizens of another country. They had violated the constitution act passed in 1901, when Australia was still part of the British Empire.[17] Larissa Waters, who was the Green Party's deputy leader in the Senate, had to give up her seat when it was revealed she was born in Winnipeg, in 1977, to Australian parents who were at the time at school in Canada. With more than twenty dual citizens in Canadian parliament, our politicians were quick to distance themselves from the Australian controversy, knowing Canadian attitudes about citizenship can, at times, be just as unaccommodating. As the Harper government found in its campaign to overhaul the Citizenship Act, many Canadians wonder if citizenship in the age of globalization has become just another card in your wallet. Is it proof of membership or a vote of allegiance? A key to privilege or an act of patriotism?

If Canadians want our diaspora to help lead us through the 2020s, we will need to better define what it means to be Canadian out in the world. And we will need to determine how to make better use of the millions of new Canadians, and their children, who may be our greatest asset out in that world, even when there may be a number who abuse the rights and privileges of citizenship. We have the world's most ambitious approach to multiculturalism, and most successful. It's made Canada stronger economically, more sustainable demographically, more vibrant culturally and more relevant to the world politically. Our hyphenated diasporas have largely added to that success, taking Canada to places we'd otherwise not get, and gaining influence we might otherwise not merit. Over the next decade, we're likely to see a lot more of that diaspora, as the generation of Ahmed and Yasmin shows up with numbers and ambition that Canada has not seen. They've gotten there because of Canada's approach to public education and, increasingly, the ability of colleges and universities to bridge Canadians with the world. In recent years, Canada has drawn close to five hundred thousand international students a year. If we had anywhere near the same success in getting Canadian students abroad, we'd be among the world's most global nations.

Richard Liu has been trying to build those bridges for decades, since he went to UBC and then moved to China to work with students there. In many ways, he felt he was born into the challenge, as a grandson of Chinese immigrants who straddled the two countries through their own hyphenated diaspora of Chinese Canadians and Canadian Chinese. His grandfather's brother, Liu Shih-shun, was China's first representative to Canada, in the 1940s. In 1980, after Liu's family moved from Toronto to British Columbia, his father created the first sister-city program between the two countries, linking Suzhou and Victoria. In 1988, Richard went straight from high school to Peking University and spent the next two decades working with the Canadian embassy and other groups in Beijing to burnish Canada's image. At the time, he wondered how Canada, with our small expat population, could stand out in the world's most populous country, and decided to focus on our strengths. Our universities had bigger networks in countries like China than the Canadian government ever did, and if they pooled their alumni lists they could give Canada a leg up. Liu brought together twenty-six universities to create the Canadian Alumni Network, to connect the hundreds of thousands of Chinese who had studied in Canada as "they will be the future global leaders and we need to stay in touch with them."[18]

Liu knows that Canada has a rare set of advantages that can only grow as others build walls. He also knows our country can build its own invisible walls that keep us at home. Unfortunately, the very colleges and universities that attract so many students from around the world are struggling to convince Canadians to go the other way. In 2016, for example, only three out of every thousand Canadian university students went to China for a course. Liu looked around Beijing and saw what others—Australia, Britain, the United States, Germany—were doing to put students there, and saw how far Canada had slipped. As a Canadian student embracing the world, he had been the exception. If Canada is to regain our place in the world, a new generation of students going abroad will have to become the rule.

14

Our Stay-at-Home Students

THE STRUGGLE TO SEND YOUNG CANADIANS ABROAD

If you want a dispiriting picture of Canadian interest in the world, pop by any international university fair. You can find them in most major cities in the spring, and they're largely the same. Lots of schools from every corner of the world, and far fewer students. Take the one I visited in 2017, in the lower level of the Metro Toronto Convention Centre. To get to it, you had to pass the mining industry's biggest party of the year, at the annual convention of the Prospectors and Developers Association of Canada, which draws the craziest crowds, from every continent, to Toronto for a week of deal-making and drink-swilling. More than twenty thousand miners were packed into the downtown core, and enjoying the hospitality of mineral-rich countries from South Africa to Mongolia. At the centre of it, you could hear clutches of Canadians explaining what they were doing—drilling deep shafts, running community programs, building tailings ponds—in pretty much every corner of the world. And then there was the show downstairs. The university fair had plenty of flags, with sixty-three booths from Britain, nineteen more from continental Europe, six from Australia and New Zealand, and five from the Caribbean. But they were mostly schools you probably had never heard of, which perhaps wasn't surprising, because few students had shown up, either. The Americans had largely stayed away, bringing just seven colleges, as had the Chinese, who had brought only one. It was the Jiaotong University School of Software Engineering.

The deflating picture was all too familiar to Canadian educators. We may be good at sending our geologists to the far-flung corners of the globe, but our students? They were like an ore shaft that was largely left unmined. Pretty much every other advanced economy was finding novel ways to get their youth to study in other countries, knowing it was critical to expanding a nation's global population and influence. According to national estimates,[1] 32 percent of French students and 28 percent of Germans study abroad for at least part of their undergraduate programs. It's true that these students don't have to go nearly as far to be abroad, but isolation hadn't stopped Australia, which by the middle of the past decade was sending 18 percent of its undergrads abroad for at least part of their studies. Nor had insularity held back the United States, which sent 15 percent of its undergrads abroad. Canada? We were at about 11 percent, with the vast majority of those students going to countries that were culturally similar to us, like the United States, Britain, France, Germany and Australia. No wonder the Chinese sent only an obscure programming school to lure the current batch.

If Canada is to build an enduring global population, we will need to start young.[2] It's not just about broadening our students' education or opening their eyes to the world; it's about building Canadian networks in as many different places as we can, at an age when most people are connecting with as many people as they can. When David Johnston became governor general in 2010, he made it one of his goals to get more Canadians, especially students, to go abroad. He spoke from experience, having studied at Harvard and Cambridge and run two of Canada's most internationally minded universities, McGill and Waterloo. He knew what was at stake for Canada. "More Canadian students abroad will help to raise our profile and build global networks, which can only help us attract more international students and talent in what is known as a virtuous circle,"[3] Johnston said in November 2016, at the fiftieth anniversary of the Canadian Bureau for International Education, of which he was a patron. He considered international studies and their resulting global outlook "essential for navigating the complexities of today's world." In 2012, two years into his term at Rideau Hall, Johnston joined forces with former prime minister Jean Chrétien to create the Queen Elizabeth Scholars program, in honour of the Queen's diamond jubilee on the throne. Chrétien brought the idea to the governor general, who used his own network to help raise $80 million to send three thousand scholars abroad over the next decade. To Chrétien and Johnston, if the ambition did not not quite possess the scale of a Kennedyesque moon shot, it at least needed a moon shot's sense of urgency.[4] The rest of the world's students were already on the move, with an estimated three million studying outside their home countries at any given time, a number that according to UNESCO (the United Nations Educational, Scientific and Cultural Organization) had increased by 57 percent[5] between 1999 and 2009. Among Canadians, that number was stuck in the tens of thousands.

Despite his academic pedigree, Johnston still speaks in a folksy manner, exposing his roots as the son of a Sudbury hardware store owner.[6] In his mind, there are few problems that can't be fixed with some tools, a can of paint and a bit of elbow grease.[7] As if he's back in the shop, Johnston[8] enumerates the benefits of an international education by telling the story of his five daughters, who all studied abroad: "Four wonderful things happened to them when they went abroad to learn. First, their natural curiosity was stimulated. That simple question 'Why?'—which we're all born asking—was prompted by the exposure to new people, cultures and languages. Second, their tolerance for diversity was strengthened. Having no choice but to face the unfamiliar, they learned to appreciate and respect change and people who were different from them in custom and belief. Third, their judgment was improved. They became aware of the limitations of their knowledge, and thus grew hesitant to jump to conclusions. They grew in wisdom. And fourth, something very human: they became more empathetic. Not only were they better able to feel the pain of another's discomfort, but they also learned to place themselves in another person's shoes."

Inspired by Johnston, two of Canada's most seasoned global thinkers, Margaret Biggs and Roland Paris, led a study on international education to see how we stacked up against others. Not well was the answer. In 2017, their study group, which included leaders from across business and education, found, "Canada has no such strategy—and it shows. Not only do we send a smaller proportion of our students abroad than do most of our peer countries, but this gap has been growing." When they took on the project, Biggs was a veteran civil servant whose career included a term as president of the Canadian International Development Agency, from 2008 to 2013. Paris, who studied at Yale and Cambridge, taught international affairs at the University of Ottawa, after serving as Justin Trudeau's first foreign policy adviser. The two concluded that our ability to send Canadian students into the world was nothing like our ability to bring the world's students to Canada, and we would suffer as a result. "We are not preparing young Canadians to meet the challenges of a rapidly changing world," they wrote in their report. "The diversity of Canada's population does not automatically translate into worldliness, or into the skills that Canadians—and Canada—will require to succeed. These competencies and values are not given by nature; they have to be cultivated."[9]

In Canada's first quarter century, emigration outpaced immigration, as 820,000 people left the country between 1870 and 1900. The tide quickly shifted and our emigration rate, which peaked at 0.35 percent of our population in the 1920s, has not been above 0.15 percent since the Second World War.[10] The rapid decline in the need for physical labour in the U.S. meant only Canadians with special skills or an advanced education would be in great demand. A good number of those new knowledge workers and creative types—the coders in Silicon Valley or designers in Dubai, for instance—joined the global economy, but the vast majority of Canadians were left behind, which made the country more inward-looking when we needed to be more outward-facing. According to the KOF Globalisation Index, Canada peaked in terms of our openness in 2000 and has been in decline since the financial crisis. On a range of indicators—internet connections, newspaper readership, taxes and tariffs, embassies, UN participation, tourism and immigration—we're less global than we think.

To change that, Canada may want to look to what other countries have done, starting with their students. The European Union set the standard in 1987 with a new program called Erasmus that helped finance studies abroad. Erasmus (short for the European Community Action Scheme for the Mobility of University Students) financed part of the costs for students to complete study terms, lasting three to twelve months, as well as work placements in any of thirty-six European countries and a growing number of emerging markets it has since added. The EU found that graduates who had studied or worked abroad for at least one term faced a 23 percent lower unemployment rate than those who finished their undergrad degrees without leaving their country. In 2017, Germany's Academic Exchange Service,[11] known as DAAD, spent about $750 million to send seventy-eight thousand Germans abroad and to bring nearly sixty-two thousand foreigners to Germany, in a program known as "change by exchange." In the U.S., in 2009, the Obama administration upped its own ante with a "100,000-Strong" China initiative that was designed to get that number of Americans studying in China within five years. Working with large non-profits like the Ford Foundation and multinationals like Microsoft, the U.S. hit its goal in 2014. Encouraged by the results, the Obama administration in 2011 launched a similar initiative for the Americas, and in 2014 created another global effort, Generation Study Abroad, with the goal of doubling the number of American students abroad, from 283,000 to 600,000, by the end of the decade. Now that was a Kennedy kind of moment, for a new kind of space race.

Accepting the challenge, Australia launched the New Colombo Plan in 2014 to support ten thousand students going abroad every year for what it calls "learning experiences"—academic study, internships, mentorships, practicums or research—anywhere in Asia or the South Pacific. The plan's goal was to make study abroad terms "a rite of passage for Australian undergraduate students."[12] Canadian students would like to have the same opportunity. According to a 2016 *World of Learning* report by the Canadian Bureau for International Education, 85 percent of post-secondary students were interested in studying abroad, although only 25 percent said it was "very likely" they would.[13] According to the same survey, the vast majority of employers were on board and identified an extensive list of benefits, including an understanding by students of cultural differences inside and outside the workplace,[14] and an ability to adapt to unfamiliar environments and develop the sort of human skills Johnston found his daughters had gained.

While some industries were less concerned about international experience, roughly half the employers surveyed said they'd hire a graduate who had studied abroad over one who hadn't. In 2012, the federal Conservatives appointed an advisory committee to develop a new international education strategy for Canada. Led by Amit Chakma, who was then president of the University of Western Ontario, the group recommended Canada follow the U.S., Europe and Australia and establish fifty thousand study abroad scholarships over the next decade.[15] The group suggested a more targeted approach, too, with a focus on China, India, Brazil, Turkey, Vietnam and Mexico.[16] The response? Nothing.

Mika Saarinen, a Finnish education expert, has followed these trends for decades and heard most of the excuses. Governments can't afford such an elitist investment. Young people aren't clamouring for it anyway. They don't want to leave their friends and family. Or they can't afford to. Businesses don't really value foreign work terms, at least not nearly as much as local experience. Saarinen heard it all when he was an adviser to the Finnish government, wrestling with the same questions twenty years ago that Canada is struggling with today. In Finland, he said, there was reluctance in the beginning. But once an active study abroad program got going and became the norm, students, employers and educators couldn't get enough. Today, most university students and a majority of students in Finland's trades programs go abroad for at least one course credit or a work placement related to their studies. The key, Saarinen found, was to ensure students learn the same material as they would at home—except they're learning it in a foreign setting, where the context, references, perhaps even mindset is different. Don't make it a foreign frill, or worse, a party abroad term, he discovered. "It can't be an add-on," he stressed.[17] Today, a generation of young Finns has developed an international sensibility that's paying off for their country. Before the euro crisis put the brakes on growth, Finland's exports had tripled between 1992 and 2008,[18] as students followed trade—and trade followed students.

If only Canadians could get more Finnish. Yet when he tried, Guy Saint-Jacques felt helpless. As Canada's ambassador to China from 2012 to 2016, Saint-Jacques marvelled at what every other advanced economy was doing with their students, each upping their game while Canada stayed home. He found the biggest challenge to be students themselves. He toured Canadian campuses and found little interest. Everyone was in their Canadian comfort zone. His Chinese counterparts were more perplexed by our parochialism. Even though China had created scholarships and assigned seats at its best universities for Canadians, only a trickle came—fewer than four thousand a year, compared to thirty thousand Canadian students in the U.S. Even a Pacific-facing campus like UBC, which sent its first student to China in 1948, showed a limited appetite. According to a *Maclean's* special report[19] in 2016, only 47 of the campus's 1,072 exchange students went to China. The Chinese reminded Saint-Jacques they sent more than a hundred thousand students a year to Canada, and each was spending, on average, $37,500. That meant close to $4 billion for the Canadian economy, about double what we made selling computers and optical sensors to the world. Saint-Jacques recalled officials asking him, "Don't you like us? Do you think our schools aren't good enough?"[20] The Chinese reminded him that formal student exchanges with Canada went back to 1973 and the signing of a Scholars' Exchange Program by Zhou Enlai and Pierre Trudeau. It was groundbreaking for the two countries, and indeed the world. Since then, the exchange has been largely a one-way street. In 2017, more than 190,000 Chinese students studied in Canada, making us China's fourth most popular destination for education, while Canada sent only 3,817 students the other way, making us the thirty-third most active source for China.[21] (Of that cohort, 539 Canadians had received scholarship funding from the Chinese government.)

When Indira Samarasekera was president of the University of Alberta, she made it a strategic priority to get her students to spend at least one term abroad. She focused on five countries: China, India, the U.S., Mexico and Germany. Getting students interested was another matter. Even as she increased the international share of her own enrolment, from 3 percent of the student body to 14 percent, she saw barely a twitch in the number of Canadians wanting to go the other way. Upon her retirement, Samarasekera established a scholarship fund for overseas studies, but attracted little additional funding or student interest. She was also part of a group pushing Ottawa to do more.[22] The federal government responded in part in 2016, establishing the Canada Learning Initiative in China to help finance Canadians studying there and to ensure Canadian schools would recognize Chinese university courses as credits. The initiative was formally announced by Trudeau and Chinese Premier Li Keqiang, but for all the fanfare it ran into the same challenges that other efforts had faced. A year later, in the 2017–18 academic season, only 232 Canadian students went to China under the program—about half the original target.[23]

The academic Bessma Momani and diplomat Jillian Stirk studied the issue for the Pierre Elliott Trudeau Foundation, and concluded our relative lack of international studies was a key reason why we couldn't turn our own diversity into a greater economic dividend. In a 2017 paper, "The Diversity Dividend: Canada's Global Advantage," they concluded that many students wouldn't venture abroad because they felt it didn't help them get a job when they returned.[24] It was the very opposite of the Finnish attitude. In fact, many students felt they'd be less valued in the

Canadian job market if they didn't build their resumé on Canadian soil. "International experiences and connections can be one of Canada's greatest assets," Momani and Stirk wrote. "They set us apart from others and in theory set us up for success in a globalized economy. International connections need to be recognized and nurtured." Students often didn't see it that way. Many pointed to the cost of studying abroad, as well as barriers such as language and living conditions. The same concerns didn't pop up in Australia or Europe. In a survey of preferences by the New York–based Institute of International Education,[25] China was second as a preferred destination for Australians, fourth for Japanese, sixth for Germans and seventh for Americans. For Canadians, it was fourteenth, tied with Brazil and South Africa, based on a 2014 survey that asked students to name their top three choices for study-abroad programs. (Most preferred Australia, Britain, France, Germany and U.S.)[26]

An exception to the inwardness of Canadian campuses, the University of Waterloo came upon its international strategy almost by accident, and certainly by necessity. The university traces its ambitions to a *Globe and Mail* headline in 1956, "Wanted: 150,000 engineers." The accompanying article was based on a speech that year by Ira Needles, the first chair of Waterloo's board of governors, who advocated for a broader approach to education modelled on what the school's first faculty, the engineering department, had created through co-op education. During the postwar industrial boom, southern Ontario couldn't find enough engineers and so Waterloo, true to its Lutheran roots, took inspiration from the German model of work-integrated learning and required students to alternate their studies between the classroom and work placements. It prepared them for the workforce, and made employers happy, but the real breakthrough was in *how* they learned through co-op placements.[27] They learned practical applications, of course, but also learned to work in different environments. It's what the Finns discovered decades later with their foreign placements.

Even though blue-blooded schools like Queen's and Toronto sniffed at Waterloo's blue-collar approach, the co-op model took off, and the campus became both a nerve centre for innovation and a gusher of talent for tech firms. By the 1980s, Microsoft had made Waterloo one of its favourite feeder schools. By the 2000s, Google and Apple were flying Waterloo students to the Valley for co-op interviews, and then sending them around the world to help build the next big thing. Today, about one in eight Waterloo co-op students goes abroad, and although most land in the United States, they can be found learning as they work in sixty other countries, be they accounting students with Deloitte in Shanghai or actuary students with Manulife in Hong Kong. And although many stay abroad, most return home, bringing a world of experience with them. According to the university, only about 3 percent of its 150,000 engineering grads now live in Silicon Valley, while roughly 90 percent of the engineering school's alumni are in Canada.[28]

In early 2017, a small group of federal bureaucrats started to explore ideas to create more Waterloo-like experiences on more campuses. They knew campuses were really the jurisdiction of the provinces, but also recognized the national imperative to keep pace with the world. When I met with them, they had just visited the University of Toronto, where roughly a quarter of the sixty thousand undergraduate students come from abroad. The influx has transformed the Toronto campus, as has similar influxes on dozens of campuses across the country, mostly for the better, by bringing a variety of backgrounds, perspectives and networks of people from around the world. There was another reason for the surge in international students: colleges and universities needed the premium tuition rates for foreigners. By the end of 2018, Canada had attracted 572,000 international students to our universities, colleges, institutes, vocational and training centres, and high schools.[29] For colleges and universities, the number had tripled in one decade.[30] A quarter came from China; another quarter came from India. Rounding out the top ten were South Korea, France, the United States, Nigeria, Brazil, Saudi Arabia, Japan and Vietnam. In terms of inbound students, the Trudeau government made clear it wanted to increase the core number of full-time post-secondary students from 245,000 in 2016/17 to 450,000 by 2022. It also wanted to double the number of Canadian students heading into the world, albeit to a tiny fraction of that, at 25,000, and in its 2019 budget allocated $95 million over five years to see it happen.[31] The target, as modest as it seems, would be a stretch. In addition to the China initiative, Canada has established scholarships to places like Mexico and South Korea, only to see much of the money go unclaimed. The government has also tried to enlist businesses with foreign operations to send students abroad on work terms, but has met tepid interest there, too. It wasn't necessarily a foreign thing, the bureaucrats noted. Canadian students generally didn't like to move.[32] Forget about going to France for school; fewer than 10 percent of our post-secondary students had left their province to study.[33]

I once asked the head of Ford Canada what he considered to be the greatest difference between Canadians and his fellow Americans. "You don't move!" he replied. Even his rising stars at the company's Canadian headquarters in Oakville tended to shy away from transfers. In the U.S., where he had previously worked in half a dozen states, he said he would have been shown the door if he hadn't seized an opportunity. He wasn't wrong about his new home. In 2016, Statistics Canada asked Canadians if they'd move to another province for work.[34] More than two-thirds (68 percent) said no. Nearly as many (57 percent) said they wouldn't move within their own province, even if they were out of work. You might think financial concerns, such as the cost of housing, were a barrier, or other frictions like the recognition of credentials. Apparently not. The overwhelming reason, cited by half of respondents, was personal: not wanting to leave behind family and friends. Resistance from a spouse or children came next. Even unmarried individuals, presumably those best positioned to pull up stakes and move for a good opportunity, cited personal reasons more than any other. The result? According to the study, the percentage of working-age Canadians who migrated to another province dropped from 2 percent in the early 1970s to 1 percent in 2015. In an age of global mobility, we had become the stay-at-home nation, waiting for the world to come to us.

Living in India in the 1990s, I was struck by the number of deans and school presidents who began to show up on trade missions, signing deals to open campuses in places like Mumbai. We were told the Canadians would follow, expanding our country's reach through the intellectual canals of a thriving new world of emerging markets. A quarter century later, we don't have much to show for it, other than some storefront satellite campuses that are used more as an immigration channel back to Canada. On a 2018 trip to India and the Persian Gulf, the education writer and consultant Alex Usher was surprised to see the ambition of British schools next to the lacklustre presence of Canadians. In Dubai, the only Canadian presence he found among a hundred or so educational institutions was something called the Canadian University of Dubai, a locally owned, for-profit school that was originally connected to Toronto's Centennial College but apparently lost touch with its namesake country. Usher, who is the post-secondary system's sharpest critic as well as supporter, concluded "quite simply: Canadian universities just don't *need* to go abroad."[35] The money's too easy with so many international students coming here.

The Biggs-Paris study group argued that before Canadian imaginations turn outward, the federal government will have to do a lot more nudging, and put up a lot more money like it did in the 2019 budget. "Canada has stalled,"[36] was the group's assessment. They felt campuses could use the spirit of a Canadian moon shot, a bold declaration that by the end of this decade, one-quarter of all post-secondary students should spend part of their degree program abroad. Universities and colleges, and their provincial masters, will also need to better coordinate their efforts, to ensure there's a clear Canadian presence on the world's campuses, rather than just a Laval or Victoria presence. A group of leading research universities known as the U15 has started to do that, by jointly recognizing courses in various overseas schools. Universities Canada, which represents nearly one hundred schools and, along with Colleges and Institutes Canada, is administering the study abroad initiative, wants to build "a culture of mobility" among students—especially for those from families and communities that may not be apt to travel internationally.

We can learn from the exceptions. Even more than Waterloo has done for engineers, McGill has set a standard for outward-looking students for as long as Canada has been a country. It's by design. McGill's campus stares down a slope to the Saint Lawrence River, which once brought students here and sent Canadian alumni, ranging from William Osler to William Shatner, into the world. Marc Weinstein, McGill's vice-principal of university advancement, has a simple explanation: "Our students realize Canada is too small for them."[37] For generations, the university's purpose was to serve Montreal's anglophone community, but as that population dwindled, and as provincial support declined, the university had to seek more students from outside Quebec, and then from outside Canada. Now, close to 30 percent of its student body is foreign, similar to what you'd find at Cambridge. For a while, that was driven partly by a tuition deal that allowed students from France to pay in-province rates. Today, McGill stands on its own as a destination, pitching high academic standards surrounded by a cosmopolitan city that can be as attractive to a kid from Boston or Beijing as it is to a kid from Burlington. Its 275,000 alumni are just as widely distributed, with only about half in Quebec and another 30 percent elsewhere in Canada. That leaves McGill with about sixty thousand alumni living and working abroad—close to six thousand in the greater New York area and five thousand in California, and the rest in every region imaginable.

As in Waterloo's experience, the globalization of McGill was born by necessity as well as design. When David Johnston was principal, from 1979 to 1994, which were some of the most politically charged years in the province's history, he pointed the university outward, to get it to look well beyond Quebec and Canada. He started by raising money to deliver on those bigger dreams, and recruited the sort of faculty and students to make it happen. In the 1990s, McGill launched a building spree to overhaul its downtown campus. Then, between 2005 and 2015, it added a thousand staff, half of them from outside Canada. McGill's transformation took both time and resilience, a good message for those who want to see Canada take on the same ambitions. McGill required decades to reorient itself, and needed both the stick of political change and carrot of faculty, staff and students who aspired to something bigger. It also had to be willing to let some of its best move on, to leave the nest and fly to new homes, as Arthur Kerman, the late physicist, did in the 1940s when he left McGill for MIT. One difference today is that McGill is much better at staying connected to those who go, and at seeing them not as a loss so much as a new link to a growing global network of brains and ambition.

The tension between hometown loyalty and global aspirations can be found on many campuses, and in the thriving centres of innovation and entrepreneurship around them. This tension also cuts to the existential question for any expat: Should you have stayed home to build the country that got you going, or was it better to take some of that country into the world to build something Canada could not achieve on its own? In the age of digital communications and global networks, the question should be moot. Canadians have the opportunity to do both. And yet this country continues to show a boundless capacity for brain drain debates while much of the world focuses on brain circulation (the flow of people) and brain trusts (the building of coalitions). If Canada wants to do more with our diaspora, we will need to reset that conversation, to ditch the defensive view that our best and brightest are somehow disloyal when they leave—and adopt an offensive mindset around the opportunity that every expat creates when they leave. It's not just about the individual. Most are going to global centres of excellence—Tokyo, New York, London—that have concentrations of talent Canada will never have on our own. Those individuals can be our conduits to those centres, and for all the people in our own centres of excellence back to Canada.[38]

If there is one such centre above all others that challenges our sense of place in the world, it is Silicon Valley. With more Canadians per capita than anywhere else in the world, it seems to have a unique ability to generate doubts and anxieties in every Canadian community that aspires to be Valley North. I wanted to return to the Valley, to revisit a conversation that seemed to pop up every time I was there. It was linked to our perennial fear of a brain drain, that singular Canadian concern that shapes so much of our approach to the world and may yet limit what we can do in the 2020s.

15

A Global Brain Trust

HOW TO GET OVER "BRAIN DRAIN" AND BUILD A WORLDWIDE WEB OF CANADIANS

The centre of Berkeley campus projects a quiet air of supremacy. The Sather Tower, at 94 metres, is the third-tallest of its kind in the world, commanding a bird's-eye view of the campus town, and beyond it, the majestic sweep of San Francisco Bay. Beneath the bell-and-clock tower stands a row of private parking spaces, five in all, reserved for present-day Nobel winners. It's one of many blunt statements to a visitor that this is a global centre of brainpower. The most celebrated branch in the University of California system, it's a force in chemistry, business, history and, especially, physics, the source of seven Nobels for Berkeley since 1939. Striding across the sun-drenched square toward Birge Hall, where some of the world's leading physicists work, Bob Birgeneau could see the power of branding at every turn. He could hear it, too, from the faint sounds of "The Star-Spangled Banner" as it wafted from his building—a signal that another American athlete had won Olympic gold in Rio. He wondered, Could it be a Cal athlete? When he reached his office, Birgeneau handed me a printout of medal counts. The University of California system had already won more than Canada, and sat just behind Stanford, its Silicon

Valley rival. It was the outcome, he explained, of "a culture of excellence."[1]

A physicist himself, born and educated in Toronto, Birgeneau quit as president of the University of Toronto in 2004 to become chancellor of Berkeley, a position he held until 2013. He was quickly absorbed into that culture of excellence; it was the campus's greatest asset, he felt, and in many ways America's, too. Even as a professor, Birgeneau had come to see the same culture—in Europe and Asia, as well as the U.S.—as a primary reason for many Canadians to leave, and for many of them to stay abroad. They wanted to be with the world's best in their chosen field. As we settled into his modest professor's office, it was evident he hadn't left Canada behind. In one corner was a decorative Canadian moose, and along each wall was an impressive collection of First Nations, Inuit and Métis art, a reminder, he said, of his father's roots and the fact that only five thousand other Canadian Métis have post-secondary educations. As one of them, Birgeneau had led two of the world's great universities, and perhaps that was enough reason for him to let loose on this culture thing and why Canadians need to get over the departure of some of our best and brightest. We're missing the bigger picture of a diaspora. While many expats move back, many more like him stay in their new homes, hoping to play at the top of their game. They can still help Canada win gold. Canada can't lose, he stressed, as long as we stay connected to beehives like Berkeley, and encourage Canadian ideas and talent to come here.

After graduating from the University of Toronto, Birgeneau earned a PhD from Yale and went on to Oxford for further work as a Rutherford Fellow, an honour named for Ernest Rutherford, the New Zealand scientist who became the father of nuclear physics during his research career at Cambridge and McGill. Birgeneau noted that New Zealand never complained it had lost one of its best to England and Canada. That wasn't his experience when Canada lost him. In the 1960s, when he couldn't get a professorship at Toronto, Birgeneau joined Bell Labs in New Jersey and then taught for twenty-five years at MIT, including a term as dean of science, where he oversaw four Nobel prize winners. Finally, in 2000, Rob Prichard, the former U of T president and hyper-connected lawyer who keeps a log of talented Canadians abroad, tracked him down to pitch him on being the university's fourteenth president. He agreed.[2] But then, only a few years into his term, Berkeley called with an even better offer—to come to California and run a campus determined to stay among the world's best. Birgeneau shook his head at the experience. "I thought people would think, 'Isn't this wonderful for Canada? People in California will now look at U of T more positively.'" Instead, he was ambushed by the politics of brain drain. It started with a battery of media questions insinuating he was abandoning Canada for a bigger game down south. Then questions surfaced on campus, where his departure for Berkeley was seen as a knock on U of T, which is usually ranked first in Canada but near the bottom of the top twenty-five globally.[3] The scars were still evident in his voice as he paused to take a sip from a Diet Coke and leaned forward to share a reflection. When he finally got to Berkeley, and told the same story, one of his board members said, "Now we know why you're leaving Toronto."

When I mentioned "brain drain," it was enough to send Birgeneau into a tizzy that disrupted his otherwise calm, avuncular manner. No other country seems to see the migration of superstar professionals as a loss—be they academics, surgeons, executives or researchers—quite like Canada does. When Ron Daniels, who was the dean of law at Toronto during Birgeneau's time, moved to the University of Pennsylvania to become provost, he got the same blowback. At U of T, he had pioneered the transition to market-based tuitions, paving the way for other Canadian professional schools to offset a decline in government funding. Without more philanthropic giving, which is always a struggle in Canada, he had no other way to raise enough money to compete with U.S. and British schools for star faculty and students. Daniels had always been struck by the "drive for excellence" and "derring-do" he saw at U.S. schools. But when he left for Penn, and went on to become head of Johns Hopkins University in Baltimore, he was called a sell-out to that culture. That parochial mindset, which he thought fed Canada's brain drain obsession, was why he kept a copy of a 2002 *Globe and Mail* column by Jeffrey Simpson, which lambasted the complacent management style on many Canadian campuses. The headline: "U of T's gold medal goals in a bronze medal country." Birgeneau cited the same column. "This is a distinctly Canadian problem," he said, recalling a conversation he had with Michael Ignatieff when he was hoping to lure Ignatieff back from Harvard to U of T. "The U.S. has a culture of excellence," Birgeneau thought. "Canada has a culture of very good."

Birgeneau conceded it's an elitist argument. Expats are an elite. They're among the best in the world—or aspire to the best—at what they do. Criticizing them for leaving would be like criticizing Steve Nash for going to the U.S. to play basketball, or Céline Dion for moving to Las Vegas to sing. It's the Show. James Gosling, a self-described Alberta geek who fell in love with coding as a teenager, moved from the University of Calgary to Pittsburgh's Carnegie Mellon University because that's where the best in his field were.[4] He was following in the footsteps of another Albertan, Kenneth Iverson, who went to Harvard and then joined IBM, where he won the 1979 Turing Award for creating the programming language known as APL. Iverson gave Silicon Valley its Rosetta stone. Gosling built on it, crafting the language now known as Java, which made the internet visually dynamic and interactive. Would Canada be better off had Iverson and Gosling stayed home? Or is Canada stronger for being in a world they made better? If it's the latter, Birgeneau wondered, what have we done to take advantage of all those Canadian brains at the heart of America's culture of excellence? The answer, he knew, was not enough.

The brain drain debate is as unique and existential to Canada as fresh water, hockey and equalization payments, and it almost always refers to the U.S. You rarely hear such anxieties in India or Singapore, but then again those countries don't have the world's richest, most scientifically advanced and commercially ambitious country sitting next to them, with a border that's still largely open for elite professionals. Our anxieties seem to fluctuate with the Canadian dollar, which more than any other signal can whisper uncertainty in the mirror. Every few decades—the 1950s, the 1990s, again in late 2010s—you can hear those whispers grow to murmurs, and sometimes shouts, as political pressure mounts on governments to do more to keep the stars at home. What rarely gets mentioned is that across the professions, Canada gains a lot more talent through immigration than we lose, including a lot of academics and other professionals who go to the U.S. for a period and then come back with a knowledge, pedigree and networks they may not have developed at home. One federal survey of forty-three hundred Canadians who had studied in the U.S. found that about a fifth had come home within five years.[5] Those who stayed tended to pursue further education, but only those who gained PhDs were more likely to stay, the study found.[6] They were the reason Birgeneau preferred to view migration through the ambitions of the knowledge economy, in which people come and go, advancing their skills and networks along the way. In this new economy, brain circulation had become the new rocket fuel.

The causes and consequences of the so-called brain drain are as old as the outflow of Canadian scientists and engineers. In a 2006 paper, "What Happened to the Canada-United States Brain Drain of the 1990s?" Richard Mueller from the University of Lethbridge found the exodus to be driven mostly by economic opportunity in the U.S., rather than perceived push factors such as Canadian tax rates or health care standards.[7] About 55 percent of those who left for the U.S. in recent decades held professional or management jobs, and reported a median family income of $85,000.[8] Another study[9] around the same time found Canadian expats with a post-secondary education could earn, on average, 24 percent more than their classmates simply by moving to the U.S. In a 2000 paper, "Putting the Brain Drain in Context," the C.D. Howe Institute's Daniel Schwanen highlighted another related push factor: a lack of jobs for all the skilled professionals our schools were producing. In the 1990s, Canadian scientists and engineers faced a 3.2 percent unemployment rate; in the U.S., it was 1.6 percent.[10]

During the 1990s brain drain debate, Peter Kuhn, a Kitchener-born economist at the University of California, Santa Barbara, was asked, "What's it like to be brain drained?" He responded with a provocative essay in *Policy Options*, published on November 1, 2000, that laid out his concerns over Canada's approach to equality versus merit. We're not willing to pay for merit, he argued. We're too cheap.[11] "The relative reluctance of Canadian universities to tolerate merit- and market-based pay differentials, both within and across departments, makes a U.S. destination even more attractive for precisely those individuals Canada presumably most wants to keep."[12] The same complaint can be heard from hospitals clinging to their star surgeons, or oil companies trying to hold on to their best geologists, or banks hoping to retain their top data scientists.

It's more than salaries, though, especially in academia, where the best researchers are also drawn to the vast reservoir of research money that leading U.S. schools enjoy thanks to a surge in endowment funding over the past quarter century that coincided with steady cuts to Canadian spending. Although the Trudeau government tried to reverse that decline in its 2018 budget, the gap for researchers is now overwhelming. In an alarming 2018 report, the Council of Canadian Academies warned that after nearly two decades of research cuts by business, government and universities, Canada was so far behind we'd need to double spending just to catch up to our science allies. In terms of research papers published, between 2009 and 2014 we fell from seventh to ninth place, ceding ground to India and Italy. Moreover, we had focused our research on fields like visual arts, psychology and public health, while cutting funding for mathematics, engineering and chemistry.[13]

The disparity in spending was one of the first things Daniels noticed when he arrived at Johns Hopkins, which is among the world's leading research universities. In 2017, the Baltimore school[14] spent $2.56 billion on research, equivalent to one-quarter of what the entire Canadian post-secondary system[15] spent. Like many elite U.S. universities, and this goes back to the 1800s, his school benefits from far greater spending on research and development by the private sector, a more ambitious approach to research by government, and a willingness on the part of wealthy Americans to give money to universities. In Canada, Daniels struggled to get philanthropists to donate to their alma mater; they assumed tuition and taxes took care of that. In the U.S., he could count on benefactors like the business magnate and former New York mayor Michael Bloomberg, who in November 2018 donated $1.8 billion to the school, the largest philanthropic gift ever to an American academic institution. The proceeds will go entirely to financial aid for low- and middle-income students, ensuring the university can forever guarantee admissions regardless of a student's financial state.[16]

While lavish research budgets are a draw in any field, many scientists, like entrepreneurs, also can't resist the lure of American moxie, and a willingness in the U.S. to test boundaries, to experiment and to fail. America's celebration of success doesn't hurt, either. For the physicist Bob Dynes, fifty years in the U.S. did not diminish his fascination for the differences that both attracted him to America and keep him Canadian. "Americans act like they know everything," he told me, taking a break in his San Diego lab. "To be more aggressive with your assertions, that's American. That's what attracted me to the U.S. American physicists are much more willing to take risks. If you read a Canadian paper, you can generally believe it. An American paper might have a bit more hyperbole. Canadians are rather conservative in the way they do physics. They won't speculate as much. It's an advantage and a disadvantage. Speculation leads to discovery."[17] And discovery draws talent.

Jim Stone found this when he moved to Princeton,[18] where Canadians had been going since George Mackay landed in the 1860s to train for his overseas mission work. The Ivy League college has had two Canadian presidents, and with an endowment from Montreal's Molson family administers a Canadian studies program that features Canadian speakers and visiting professors. Stone arrived on campus in 2003, nearly twenty years after he first went to the U.S. to complete a PhD in astrophysics, at the University of Illinois. The decades notwithstanding, he and his wife still consider themselves Canadian; their two grown American children carry Canadian passports, too. He also recognizes that in America opportunities exist that are harder to find in Canada or anywhere else. Elite U.S. schools have far more resources because of their alumni and research spending by their federal government. "If you can be around good students, great colleagues, and a place with the resources you need to do your work, it's a big attraction," Stone noted. "Canada is wonderful. But for me, I found more opportunities for my career in America. Maybe that makes me part of the brain drain I always heard about when I was a kid."

In the 1990s, Exhibit A in the brain drain debate was the field of medicine.[19] Canada was losing nineteen doctors to the U.S. for every American physician who moved here. For nurses, the ratio was fifteen to one, whereas for engineers,[20] it was only seven to one. A decline in health care spending in Canada and falling levels of private-sector R&D were well-documented push factors, while America's health care boom created boundless opportunities at the other end.[21] It was the same across most professions. By 2007, according to the *Canadian Medical Association Journal*, one in nine Canadian-trained physicians was going stateside.[22] When the Canadian Medical Association tried to dig deeper, surveying roughly fifteen hundred Canadian-educated physicians in the U.S. that year, it found the most common reasons cited for leaving were compensation, availability of medical facilities and services, and availability of jobs. Only 13 percent said they had any intention of returning. Most felt they had laid down new roots.[23]

Birgeneau offers an example of how expats help Canada just as much, if not more, from abroad. From Berkeley, he continued to engage with his old school, the University of Toronto, advising his successors in the president's office on educational and financial matters. He also served on the Trudeau government's Fundamental Science Review Panel, which was commissioned by the science minister at the time, Kirsty Duncan, and chaired by another former U of T president, David Naylor. The Naylor Report led to one of the most significant federal budget commitments to basic research in decades, in part because of Birgeneau's push for the panel to be globally ambitious. "Canadians like me never really leave," he said.

The American author Dan Senor has spent decades studying the movement of people and ideas, and how countries are now building economies on this mobility of knowledge. His bestselling book, *Start-up Nation*, tracked Israel's success in innovation, largely through what it does with its people. While Senor grew up in the U.S., he attended the University of Western Ontario in the late 1980s and worked summers selling beer in the stands at Toronto Blue Jays games.[24] Whenever he met Canadians abroad, he wondered why we weren't able to do more with our emigration, the way we had with our immigration. He pointed to Israel, which seems to think of its diaspora in the same way a winning sports team or successful theatre company would. It sets out to attract and retain the best people it can get, regardless of where they come from. And it develops its own people by sending them away, through the military or academic exchanges, to learn from others, so they can bring back the best of their thinking. Here's what's key: when any of those people stay away, they're not seen as a loss. They're not traitors. They're instant ambassadors, serving their country as agents for its progress. Israelis don't agonize over a brain drain. Instead, they see migration as what Senor calls "an asset to the soul of the country,"[21] as existential as anything in a constitution.

Entering the 2020s, when global demand will surely grow for the sort of talent Canada is so good at developing, we need to ask ourselves, Should we try to stop the outflow? Should we block any perceived brain drain? Or should we focus on developing more brains, perhaps by creating more Waterloos and recruiting people from around the world? And what can our diaspora do to help recruit and develop talent for Canada's benefit?[25]

The tension is likely to grow, as the Western world comes to grips with a demographic decline that will see baby boomers retiring in greater numbers and fewer and fewer millennials entering the work force to replace them. The resulting war for talent will be a pitched battle whose outcome will shape the fortunes of countries in a rapidly growing knowledge economy, with Canada both well-positioned and vulnerable, thanks to our expats. On the home front, we're already short about two hundred thousand tech workers, and can't seem to keep up with demand.[26] In terms of engineers as a share of post-secondary graduates, we're ranked eleventh globally, well behind Israel and the U.S.,[27] and many are leaving as soon as they graduate. In 2017, two students from the University of Waterloo, Atef Chaudhury and Joey Loi, surveyed eighty-two classmates from their Systems Design Engineering program, and found 60 percent were either working or looking for work in the U.S., largely in the Bay Area and Seattle. The math was simple. Those with jobs in the U.S. made, on average, $143,000 a year; in Canada, their classmates earned, on average, C$65,000.[28 29] To resist this so-called techsodus, Canada is developing the right social conditions to keep more of our talent at home, at least if you believe Richard Florida's theory on creative clusters. We also have a well-functioning immigration system that seems to fill gaps when they emerge; by the C.D. Howe Institute's count, Canada gets twice as many educated immigrants as the numbers we lose to emigration. But the bigger picture is this: if we continue to see departures as a loss, we'll miss the very nature of the emerging knowledge economy and its blindness to borders. Even if we could force Canadians to stay home—something most Canadians would oppose—we'd lose the chance to see them on another stage where they could be Canada's best allies, connecting us with more business opportunities, more research dollars and more potential immigrants. Their success could even inspire a new generation back home.

Cecil Green was one of the first to try to make this happen for Canada. An immigrant kid, Green's family had come from England to Nova Scotia and then to San Francisco, before settling in Vancouver. He studied applied economics (before it was called engineering) at the University of British Columbia, and made his fortune in the 1930s oil fields of Oklahoma where he developed the world's first big geo-mapping business.[30] After the war, Green and his business partner Eric Jonsson, who later became mayor of Dallas, bought an electronics firm that they renamed Texas Instruments (TI), and used it to create the world's first pocket transistor radio, the first mass-selling pocket calculator and the first mass circuit boards. Green's only disappointment in Canada was our ability to connect with him in the decades after the war, when Canadian emigration shifted from brawn to brains and young Canadians like Art Kerman, Bob Birgeneau and Bob Dynes headed south. Seeing the need for talent networks rather than talent pipelines, Green invested his fortune in universities, giving away $200 million to Green College at UBC, Green Templeton College at Oxford and the Green Building for earth sciences that towers over the MIT campus where Birgeneau once taught. He had come to appreciate the increasingly global nature of research and the need for brain circulation before anyone called it that. Perhaps it was because he understood the power of standard deviation, to go away from the norm. He had designed TI devices, after all, to calculate it and financed universities to harness it.

Several years ago, at a meeting of the Association of American Universities, which represents North America's top research schools, Ron Daniels looked around the table and noticed two others Canadians—Birgeneau from Berkeley and Shirley Tilghman, a molecular biologist who was then president of Princeton. Chatting about their careers, they discovered they were each products of the Toronto public school system and agreed it had instilled in them a sense of equity. That equity, Birgeneau argued, can make the "culture of excellence" a little harder to achieve. Excellence, he said, requires a greater standard deviation than you typically get in a home market. Expats are willing to deviate. They do that the moment they decide to leave home, giving up their established social network for a world of unknowns.

In the 2020s, the global race for talent will be about more than a deviation in ambition. It will be about more than an amassing of educated people, as important as that will be. More than ever it will require a new vector of principles, to help humanity find its course in an age of cognitive machines that will simultaneously take up the old work of humans and create new opportunities no one can quite foresee. Even as these new technologies replace routine tasks, on assembly lines and in call centres, they're creating more new jobs than most forecasts anticipated. These new jobs demand a tech-savviness that was unknown a generation ago, but require more than techies to succeed. They require people with human skills—complex problem solving, critical thinking, communications, collaboration, creativity—and an ability to work with those ever-smarter machines. Those are the skills that Canadian colleges and universities can be excellent at developing. In 2018, a Royal Bank of Canada research report, *Humans Wanted*,[31] showed through data analysis the skills increasingly in demand were those that had been around the longest. The study also found a growing demand for global skills and the sort of cultural quotient that help people—be they nurses, engineers or bus drivers—navigate an ever-more crowded and complex planet. We had entered an economic period in which demand was surging for IQ+EQ+CQ.

Bob McClure might even have called it the new Canadian formula for adventure.

It's a formula that can be found on many Canadian campuses, and speaks to the makeup of the Canadian diaspora, of those expats who went abroad to challenge themselves and challenge the world, wanting to make both better along the way. But as our collective IQ increasingly is being hardcoded by machines, the premium for EQ and CQ will be greater than ever. In her 2019 book, *The Big Nine*, the digital futurist Amy Webb dissected how the world's most influential tech companies—six of them American, three Chinese—were using artificial intelligence to rewire the planet and perhaps warp humanity. She argued the root of any evil was actually us, as we programmed computers to solve all our problems and take all the blame when things went wrong. "This is the optimization effect, where unintended outcomes are already affecting everyday people around the world," Webb wrote. A professor at New York University's Stern School of Business, she posits one of the most critical questions for Canadians working anywhere, but especially in the Valley: "How are humanity's billions of nuanced differences in culture, politics, religion, sexuality and morality being optimized? In the absence of codified humanistic values, what happens when AI is optimized for someone who isn't anything like you?"[32] In this new machine age, the very idea of brain drain will need to be rethought.

After seeing Birgeneau, I left the calm of Berkeley, crossed the Bay Bridge to San Francisco and headed south to Silicon Valley, into the belly of the Big Nine beast. I had arranged to meet one of those rare Canadians who had opted to study abroad, where she had discovered the premium value of her Canadian upbringing. Shivon Zilis was now at the forefront of the new machine age, helping another Canadian, Elon Musk, deploy artificial intelligence while trying to carve out a better place for humanity in it. Artificial or not, she feared that intelligence without empathy was leading us to a dark place.

In a world that was transcending geography, with machines that could transcend humanity, Zilis thought there was no better way for her, a Canadian, to help than to code a bit more of the world's future with a few more Canadian values. In the age of disruption, it may be the greatest role Canadians can play in the world, and the greatest way they can shape Canada's place in the twenty-first century.

Conclusion | The Everywhere People

BEING CANADIAN IN THE AGE OF IDENTITY

Shivon Zilis feels like she's been shaping the new Canadian identity her entire life. She grew up in Markham, just outside Toronto, the child of Indian and American immigrants who came to Canada during the early years of multiculturalism and raised their daughter to be more Canadian than hockey. She obliged, playing the nation's sport, as a goaltender, and eventually winning a varsity scholarship to Yale, where she felt she was selling her country short by leaving it for school. She was so convinced of Canada's superiority that she had thought of turning down the Ivy League for a Canadian university, but knew she wouldn't find Yale's combination of academics and athletics anywhere close to home. She had seen America's culture of excellence, the kind Bob Birgeneau described, and even before she got to New Haven she knew what it said about Canada. After graduation, she accepted a position at IBM, the bluest of American blue chips, and then, a few years later, took a bold leap to Bloomberg, a more entrepreneurial firm that hired her to help build Bloomberg Beta, its relatively new arm that invests in cutting-edge technology efforts. Bloomberg wasn't a tech player like the rest of Silicon Valley, and she wasn't a true techie, but Zilis fancied herself a data geek and had a special interest in artificial intelligence. Growing up, she was consumed by science fiction, and saw the potential for machines and humanity to take the world in new directions. She wanted to be part of it, convinced there was a special role for Canadians. As marginalized as Canada had become in some fields, she felt there was a greater place than ever for Canadians in a world riven by identity.[1]

I had met Zilis a few times at technology conferences and liked her Twitter tag, "Made in Canada." I wanted to get her thoughts on the idea of Canadian values, and whether they could be applied to the world stage, especially in Silicon Valley, which thinks it can engineer a new world stage. On the topic of AI, Zilis had talked with Elon Musk, Michael Bloomberg and Justin Trudeau about how to ensure AI remains a force for good. It struck me as very Canadian. When I met up with Zilis, the *Economist* had just put Canada on its cover, under the headline "Liberty Moves North," and urged Canada to be a model nation by resisting the riptide of nationalism that had pulled Europe into its undertow and now had America in its grip. I wanted to know if she thought there was such a thing as northern liberty, and could it be applied to the machine age, to create a new kind of digital liberty? Could Silicon Valley be open to a different value set than the one that had become its source code? And could our emerging diaspora—the two million Canadians like her—make it happen?[2]

"Only if we have a national purpose," she told me when we met. "That's our only hope."

Zilis was a natural convener of Canadians. In her job, she met about fifty new people a week. Usually, after some time had passed, she would ask the good listeners if they were Canadian. About three-quarters of the time they'd say yes. It's not hard to stand out as a listener in a Valley of egos, where most people—men, especially—see themselves atop the Mount Olympus of technology, casting their lightning bolts of brilliance, Zeus-like, at the never-ending problems the rest of the species send their way. But Zilis found enough listeners, and people who could reflect on the greater challenges facing the world, to keep her perspective. When in doubt, she'd fall back on her motto: "Carte blanche for helping women and Canadians."[3]

Perhaps because I was in the latter category, she invited me to a dinner at Eric Schmidt's escape pod for entrepreneurs. Schmidt, who at the time was still executive chairman of Google, was the one who told Patrick Pichette that if Google were a country, it would be Canada: curious, inclusive and free. In 2010, he had used some of his fortune to launch Innovation Endeavors, an investment fund and incubator for tech companies that aimed to change the world. As part of that, Schmidt had teamed up with an Israeli entrepreneur, Dror Berman, to create a platform for people wanting to "radically collapse time." They called the project "super evolution," which they felt they had achieved with early investments in Uber and SoFi, the lending company created to disrupt America's massive student loans business. Schmidt and Berman parked Innovation Endeavors in the Loft, the name for their escape pod, which was spread out across the top floor of a small office building opposite Stanford's palm-lined avenues.

When Zilis and I arrived at the Loft, some of the Valley's more radical thinkers were already there. In addition to Berman, there was Barney Pell, an early entrepreneur in AI who had teamed up with a Canadian, Bob Richards, for his latest venture, Moon Express, to send commercial missions to the moon. There was George Babu, a Canadian co-founder of Kindred, an AI company dedicated to building, in its own words, "machines with human-like intelligence."[4] And there were some the engineers who coded

Siri, Alexa and Google Now. As is often the case in the Valley, everyone was either Canadian or worked directly with Canadians, the country that was apparently trying to move liberty north even as the tech platforms represented here were disrupting liberty pretty much everywhere else.

Our timing was auspicious. Donald Trump was settling in as president, and the rest of the world was coming to grips with his brand of politics and the upheaval it was causing through social media. Facebook algorithms were steering us to things it thought we might like. Google was rank-ordering history on the fly. Siri and Alexa were answering our questions according to monolithic codes, and even making powerful choices based on our answers. The people gathered for dinner in the Loft had written some of that code as if they were writing a new operating system for humanity. Once dinner was served, the techies began to talk about their latest advances in coding and their progress in getting machines to think like us, only better. Driverless cars. Robotic nurses. Unmanned space missions. In their minds, the future could be very bright with very few humans. I could see Zilis across the table, losing her goaltender's cool, as the exchange became more deterministic and less humanistic. She finally seized the conversation, and turned it back to human issues, specifically elder care and loneliness. She wanted to know why all the brainpower around this table, and across the way at Stanford, could not solve the growing challenges of an aging society. "Why not create a drug?" one of the Israelis at the table asked. An American piped up, "Why don't we accept loneliness as a motivator for the elderly?" Zilis pushed back, politely, questioning why the group saw technology as the only, and inevitable, solution to our social ills. She kept probing them until people started to open up about their own parents and concern for their isolation, wherever they were that evening.

Zilis resolved to make elder care one of her AI projects, not least because she was concerned about her own relatives back in Canada, and her time away from them. In the Valley, she doubted she could get the puck out of her own end without a good team in front of her. She would need to work with Canada, and a network of Canadians, if she could find one, to build a twenty-first-century bridge between technology and humanity. Unfortunately, "I feel ignored by my government and so do all my friends here," she said frankly. Berman, our host, shook his head in disbelief. He was as active with the Israeli government as he was with Schmidt and the world of Google. His government was all over him, when he needed it to be.

I started this project out of concern that, as a country, we were spiting ourselves by not engaging more with our emerging diaspora. As I spent time with expats like Zilis, I began to realize they were essential in defining Canada beyond our geography and habits—as a people more than a place. Expats like Zilis and Ellen Quigley and Tookie Graham had not left Canada because of a lack of opportunity. They'd left to take on the world, and yet still contributed to Canada in ways most Canadians did not see, or perhaps appreciate. Our challenge as a country is not whether we can keep them down on the farm or bring them home, but whether we can support them and connect them with the rest of our diaspora, to shape the 2020s and Canada's place in it.

The coming decade will see more human dependence on machines than we've ever known, and with that a growing challenge to identity, for people, communities and nations. We already rely on technology to select our news, pick our next vacation spot and guide us home. None of those choices are made objectively; they're the result of algorithms that are biased by their coders, like the ones I met at the Loft. Those engineers insert preferences and judgments the way our parents coded most of us as children with commands like "Look both ways before crossing the street." In the future, machines may decide which way we should look, and there may just be a Canadian way to ensure humanity gets across the street safely.

Consider two examples from the frontiers of artificial intelligence to see why:

Al Lindsay is an Ottawa-born engineer who helped create Alexa, the voice technology of Amazon's Echo devices. Lindsay initially worked on voice technology for his former employer, Nortel, and one of its predecessor companies, Bell-Northern Research, in the days when Ottawa really was Silicon Valley North. When those firms imploded, he made his way to the U.S., to join Amazon and its ambitious mission to remake voice technology, becoming employee number three on the Alexa project. As the Alexa platform grew, Lindsay realized[5] he'd need more Canadians, not just for their coding aptitude but for our appreciation of different cultures and how they present themselves verbally. He quickly expanded his Toronto team with hundreds of programmers who could appreciate the intonations and expressions of Quebec French, South Indian Hindi and North Indian English, as they coded a machine to converse with humanity and even understand some of humanity's humour. Who other than a Canadian could connect Franglais and Hinglish?

Peter Szulczewski is a Waterloo-trained engineer who built Wish.com into one of the world's most popular e-commerce platforms. Szulczewski, whose family brought him to Canada as a child, joined Google in the early 2000s—part of the Shona Brown era—and helped transform its business by coding its search algorithms to understand colloquialisms such as "sneaker," for people who were actually searching for a running shoe. Before setting off on his own, he helped transform Google again, in South Korea, by ditching the company's preferred minimalist home page and replacing it with the local preference of busy, noisy sites that look more like nighttime Myeong-dong than daytime Mountain View. He left Google to build his own method to predict people's interests as a way of improving their online shopping experience, by allowing for more local diversity—more choice, in other words—at a time when the Valley was giving us less. As *Forbes* wrote of the Canadian in 2019, after he had become a billionaire, "he learned to focus on something people wanted rather than what Silicon Valley thought they should want."[6]

That struggle, between efficiency and choice, will likely deepen as this new machine age takes humanity to frontiers we can't imagine. We should not be surprised if all this technology coincides with a surge in nationalism. Our human need for identity, to be both solo and tribal, will surely collide with a dependence on smart machines that increasingly, and subtly, are shaping that identity. Quite possibly, such a collision could diminish the place of Canadians in the world. Those generations of aid workers and corporate diplomats, of storytellers and justice hunters, may no longer be needed by those who can find a balance between hyper-local and hyper-global. It's an existential challenge for any middle power, and its global citizens. But as the world struggles for balance, between individuals, communities, tribes and nations, it surely will need people to moderate and mediate the transition, to keep the whole thing from tipping over. Those intermediaries will need a cultural fluency that machines don't yet have. They will rely on an emotional intelligence that machines may never have. And they will require a humility of which many nations seem incapable. These global go-betweens will need to be a lot like the Canadians out in the world right now, thriving in this age of identity. They're thriving because they don't foist their identity on others or deny the identity of others. For those global Canadians, like Karina Vold, the question is not whether they'll be needed in a more tumultuous world, but whether they can take enough of Canada with them to be relevant to that world.

I met Vold, almost accidentally, when I was wrapping up my research, and she was back in Toronto from her new home in Britain, where she had moved to join the vanguard of global AI research at Cambridge University's Centre for the Future of Intelligence. Born in Victoria, she had studied philosophy at the University of Toronto and completed her PhD at McGill. At Cambridge, she was exploring how machines impact our short-term memory by making redundant those parts of our brains that are hard-wired to do certain tasks, such as protecting us from dangers. Over the eons, we have come to call this "instinct," but really it's just coding for how to get home or when to duck for cover. In one generation, we have surrendered these basic instincts to Google.

Vold wanted to know if our innate survival skills would be automated, too, as we turn to augmented intelligence to wire our brains with machine brains. From a philosopher's point of view, she saw the shift as fundamental to our sense of agency—to having control over our daily navigation of life. She wondered if we humans were aware of how much of ourselves we might be surrendering to the new imperial powers of data, the ones that tell us what to watch, where to stay and how much to eat? How long might it be before these autonomous systems became the GPS of humanity, telling us who to marry, how long to work or perhaps even when to die? Vold worried that by reducing every decision to a function of data optimization, we were stripping ourselves of our instincts, and consigning the journey of our lives to the algorithms of our machines. In Canadian fashion, she was neither a techno-optimist (that would be American) nor a techno-cynic (that would be British). She was a techno-realist, hoping to help steer the world back to what she calls a "human-centred" path of progress that can keep us in the grey space between utopia and dystopia. How very Canadian: the middle ground.

To continue our conversation, we slipped away from the AI conference we were both attending at U of T's Munk School. It was a cool, wet autumn day and the campus was shrouded in a mist that seemed to reflect the ethical debates raging inside. Vold had come back to Toronto to explore how machine learning—essentially algorithms that learn on their own—might solve some of humanity's challenges, be they disease, climate change or democracy. Ethical AI was a field in which Canada had earned international respect, thanks to a new generation of academic centres like Toronto's Vector Institute and the Montreal Institute of Learning Algorithms. Vold said her British colleagues considered Canada "an ethical superpower." Trouble was, Canada was doing little to harness the growing number of Canadian scientists around the world, in universities and corporations, who could become powerful nodes in an ever-growing Canadian global network. She pointed to the number of prominent figures in British AI who had come to Toronto, at the invitation of the Canada-UK Council, to connect with Canadians. Despite all the chaos over Brexit, the British are managing to develop an ambitious and thoughtful approach to artificial intelligence through the government's Office for AI, which is led by a Canadian, Sana Khareghani, a computer science graduate from Simon Fraser University and former management consultant who joined Britain's cabinet office in 2013. The country also enjoys a Centre for Data Ethics and Innovation, which serves as an independent advisory group to the government on AI matters. As Britain established itself as a leading middle power on artificial intelligence, along with France and Germany, it was looking across the ocean for stronger academic, scientific and commercial ties, and maybe a bridge to the U.S. But as Vold noted, watching the crowd mill about as the conference broke up, Canada had no one like Khareghani—a Canadian, no less—who had also flown over from London for the session. For all of our advisory groups, and the good research underway, there was no one leading Canada's AI charge on the world stage.

As we move into a new stage of cyberpower, dominated by the U.S. and China, with the likes of Russia, Israel and India orbiting around them, many in the global AI community are hoping a new constellation of middle powers will emerge and provide a balance, not unlike what the middle powers did in the Cold War. Canada was a key player then, using our military skills and diplomatic strength to connect with Americans and Europeans as well as a host of non-aligned countries. With artificial intelligence, we have the same opportunity, to use the scientific strength that's been developed in schools like U of T, along with our strategic influence in the world, to ensure AI does not lead to catastrophe. We can do that with allies like Britain, France and Singapore; we can do it with our expats, too, who are in universities and companies in each of those countries. It would need the kind of diaspora strategy Canada has never had.

If Canada is to maintain or even build our relevance in a technology-driven world in the decades ahead, we may have no greater tool at our disposal than those expats. We can start by recognizing them, and acknowledging that after centuries of attracting diasporas, we have one of our own—formed not out of hardship or misery but on the shoulders of opportunity. The energy and enthusiasm that took those Canadians abroad can be harnessed for the whole country, to enhance our interests, promote our values and connect us in a more networked world. They may even help us understand what it means to be Canadian, no matter where you live.

In a way, that's what a diaspora does. It defines a people beyond a common geography, language or culture. Denise Helly, a scholar at L'Université du Québec's Institut national de la recherche scientifique, came to grips with this when she studied the origin of the term *diaspora* and found it was interpreted differently in different parts of the world, especially in the anglosphere, where it's no longer equated simply with forced displacement. She found diasporas are characterized by four motivations: a shared history; a shared narrative; a network of centres to share that narrative; and the economic and cultural means to maintain that network around the world.[7] Wherever I went in that world, I encountered such networks and an impressive range of Canadians doing extraordinary things in this ephemeral eleventh province that was as significant to Canada as any of the other ten. Just as striking, though, was the breadth of people from everywhere else also doing extraordinary things, often with the help of their home countries. Whether from India or Ireland, those diasporas were showing Canada what a truly global people could be, by competing locally and co-operating globally.

There's plenty Canada can do to catch up. The federal government could start by creating a dedicated unit, perhaps through the governor general and Rideau Hall, to stay connected with Canada's global population, and even use our expats to help the country. Inspired by the approaches of France and India to their diasporas, Rideau Hall could host an annual or biennial summit of leading expats, and honour the best among them with a special Order of Canada for overseas Canadians. A diaspora group could work with key federal departments (Global Affairs and Innovation, Science and Economic Development) as well as private sector groups (the Business Council of Canada, for instance) and academic associations (Universities Canada and Colleges and Institutes Canada) to ensure such an expat strategy is more than an exercise in patriotism. Properly funded, the group could help develop a database of our diaspora, while respecting privacy rights, and invest in twenty-first century ways to communicate with its members. This group could help governments develop a more thoughtful approach to expat rights, to help Canada move beyond the reactive policies that emerge every time overseas Canadians land in trouble. We might even consider giving our diaspora some sort of voice in Parliament, while clearly laying out the rights and privileges for Canadians living and working outside Canada. Beyond government, our colleges, universities and polytechnics can do more—much more—to convince students to study abroad, and to activate their alumni networks on behalf of the country and not just for fundraising. For their part, Canadian businesses can also find new ways to invest in these networks, for their own competitive sake. If our companies are to compete globally, they need more global competitors on their side. No matter the steps, we will have to be more outward-looking as a people at home and more ambitious with Canadians abroad, knowing that if we support them, those expats can help shape and secure our collective identity in a world that is rapidly changing.

For the better part of a century, Canada was the poster child of middle powers, one of those few that was muscular enough—economically, militarily, diplomatically—to defend our interests abroad yet too small to impose those interests on others. All along, we were acting from self-interest, knowing our economy rested on a global trading system just as our borders depended on international security and our ability to attract people relied on a confidence in global prosperity. Peace, order and good government has always been our best export because it's what secures every other export. But as the international order frays, and as the rest of the world grows, we should realize our middle power status cannot survive solely on the back of government anymore. It will need the stealth force of a global population that seems to show up anyway in every corridor that matters.

It's not beyond reach. Canadians often leave Canada because they don't want to conform to a perceived Canadian way. Some of them are cultural rebels and social misfits. But once they're gone, they tend to discover their Canadian self, amidst others. Even when they've set down roots in another country, they discover a Canadian identity. Among the most celebrated, and at times derided, of our international wanderers is Michael Ignatieff, the writer and academic who gained international renown and domestic praise when he left Canada for a bigger stage in the late 1970s. When he returned in 2006 to enter federal politics, and in 2009 became Liberal leader, he was portrayed as a carpetbagger. The Conservatives' 2011 election barb, "Just visiting," rang a little too true in the minds of many Canadians. In Ignatieff's own mind, only after he had left and come back did he realize his basic need for belonging, that soft kindling of any expatriate movement. He spoke frankly of those instincts in a 2009 *New Yorker* interview, when he admitted, "I love cosmopolitans, some of my best friends are cosmopolitans. But not when they look down on the longings for identity that captive nations may have. I discovered in myself a much stronger need for belonging than I suspected."[8]

Ignatieff's antagonist, Stephen Harper, may come to a similar conclusion, but from a very different direction. In his 2018 book, *Right Here, Right Now*, Harper explained the rise of populism as the outcome of a struggle between those from Anywhere and those from Somewhere.[9] The Anywheres were Ignatieff's cosmopolitan friends, who could live in New York or London or Hong Kong and feel quite at home, wherever their individual ambitions were nourished. The Somewheres were community folk, those people who valued neighbours and tradition more than global ambitions. While Ignatieff and Harper were both thoughtful in different ways about Canadians and the world, they each missed something fundamental about the age of social media and digital citizenry: as we enter the 2020s, we're from neither Anywhere nor Somewhere. Increasingly, we're a little bit from Everywhere.

The struggle between Anywhere, Somewhere and Everywhere is tearing the world apart in ways that are familiar to those who have studied the preludes to conflict. On all continents, people are being locked down, or pushed out, or turned off those who live on the other side of a line. The need for Canadians, and people like Canadians, to be out there, helping to build bridges instead of walls, is greater than ever. And it will continue to be in Canada's interest to support them. Our economic and social well-being depends on a peaceful and prosperous world, with the free flow of people, capital and ideas. No longer can we rely solely on institutions like the United Nations to protect those interests. We need Canadians demonstrating for our interests—the very interests that have made Canada a rare model of openness and bridge between North and South, East and West, the one the *Economist* celebrated as a northern beacon of liberty. That openness is not only a model for other countries; it could be a model for our relationship with a diaspora that is growing with each passing year, and with each wave of Canadians who take to the world. At a time when citizen action is filling the void left by government inaction, and when entrepreneurs are changing the world as much as large companies ever did, Canadians abroad may be the voice we need.

That diaspora—creative, driven, connected—can help position Canada for the rest of the twenty-first century. It can be a megaphone for our small voice, a connector for our small numbers and a lever for our big ambitions. For generations, Canadians have lived in fear of being the fifty-first state. But as the world challenges Canadians to take on a greater role, we need to think beyond our borders, and beyond our geography, to the possibilities of an eleventh province and where it can lead the rest of Canada in the decades ahead. Our place in the world will depend on it.

Acknowledgements

A bit like our country, the creation of this book relied on a community of communities, and I'm grateful to each of them.

The first were the journalists of the *Globe and Mail*, especially the foreign correspondents who for decades have told the stories of Canadians, good and bad, in every corner of the world. When I was a foreign correspondent for the paper in the 1990s, I was struck by the number of expats I encountered, and range of their interests, and grateful to the *Globe* for allowing me to explore their stories. That tradition continued with the reporting of Geoffrey York, Stephanie Nolen, Mark MacKinnon, Eric Reguly and Nathan VanderKlippe. Their work inspired me, as did that of other writers, including Doug Saunders, Marina Jimenez, Sonia Verma and John Geiger, who have added immeasurably to our collective understanding of Canada's diaspora. I'm also grateful for the work of Joe Friesen, whose 2011 article on our diaspora explored some of the issues that launched me into this project.

The second community to acknowledge is the faculty, staff and students of the Munk School of Global Affairs at the University of Toronto, which I joined in 2014 as a senior fellow. I'm indebted to its former directors, Janice Stein and Stephen Toope, who welcomed and encouraged me to take on this project. Ron Levi and Randall Hansen were generous in helping me navigate the university, and establish a research project through the Masters of Global

Affairs program. My research team—Malek Chouikh, Allison McHugh, Neil Peet, Caroline Senini and Sahl Syed—produced the intellectual spine for this book and inspired me with their curiosity and worldview. Two other Munk graduates—Trinh Theresa Do and Meghan King—added greatly to the research and connected me with a fascinating range of Canadians abroad. Special thanks to Mark Manger, director of the MGA program, for supporting their work, and Gillian Mathurin, who heads strategic communications, for promoting it.

Thirdly, I'm grateful to a broader community of researchers whose work was critical to my own thinking. Among Munk faculty, Deanna Horton was generous in sharing her knowledge of issues surrounding our diaspora. The Pierre Elliott Trudeau Foundation was another important ally, particularly under former president Morris Rosenberg and former content director Jennifer Petrela. I'm grateful to them for organizing a 2015 conference in London on the topic of diasporas and for supporting the Pluralism Project led by Bessma Momani of the University of Waterloo and former diplomat Jillian Stirk. The project's research director, Anna Klimbovskaia, who later worked with me at RBC, was superb in bringing together disparate ideas and people, and helping shape our work. Historians Alvyn Austin and Karen Minden helped me understand important periods of Canadians abroad. Jordan Banks, who later joined Rogers Media, and his former team at Facebook Canada kindly agreed to help map Canada's global population. And the Montreal-based demographer Jack Jedwab was extraordinarily generous in sharing his analysis of data from Canadian and U.S. censuses, along with his broader knowledge of expatriate movements.

A fourth community consisted of self-styled global Canadians who shaped my view of expats and their contributions to Canada. Atop that group is Robert Greenhill, the former senior public servant who continues to work tirelessly to push Canadians to be more outward looking. A long telephone conversation with him in 2014 convinced me to take on this topic. The inimitable Dominic Barton was an endless font of wisdom and insight from the outset, as was Allison Loat, whose own work on the Canadian diaspora laid the foundation for much of my research and that of others. I'm equally grateful to Canada's academic community for giving me access to colleges and universities, including alumni networks. And while the faculty and administrators are too many to mention here, I would single out Paul Davidson and his team at Universities Canada for their unwavering confidence in this project in the name of a more global Canada.

A fifth community of supporters was Canada's diplomats, at home and abroad, who showed both patience for my limited knowledge of their files and a generosity with their time and spirit. Among them, I'm especially grateful to Janice Charette, Gordon Campbell, Rana Sarkar, Chris Cooter, James Villeneuve and Zaib Shaikh. This book should not be seen necessarily as a reflection of their views; it is, I hope, a reflection of their determination to strengthen Canada's place in the world.

Sixth, I relied heavily on a community of non-government organizations, in Canada and overseas, who helped me identify and navigate clusters of Canadians. Khalil Sharif of the Aga Khan Foundation of Canada provided invaluable counsel to my understanding of issues and forces shaping our place in the world. The foundation's director of public affairs, Jennifer Pepall, was gracious in connecting me with many people around the world. The Asia Pacific Foundation of Canada, and its president Stewart Beck, was another key ally. Jasmine Gill and the Century Initiative, Kasi Rao and the Canada India Business Council, and Sarah Kutulakos of the Canada China Business Council were faithful supporters throughout, providing direction and insights that always helped improve my work. In Britain, the Ditchley Foundation provided a welcome home and invaluable network of Canadians in Britain and beyond. I'm grateful to Ditchley director James Arroyo, and his predecessor John Holmes, as well as their Canadian chief of staff Emerson Csorba and conference coordinator Sandra Ricks.

Seventh, I'm indebted to the Canadian techies of Silicon Valley, and notably those behind the C100 who took me under their wing in 2014 when I embarked on this project and never lost patience with my requests for introductions, guidance and feedback. From them I learned the unique Valley culture of paying it forward, as clichéd as that sounds. The group's former executive director Joanne Fedeyko was among the early champions of the project, bringing together a mix of expats who helped me see the unique qualities of our diaspora. Her successors Terry Doyle and Laura Buhler, and their teams, were unfailingly supportive with contact names and historical insights. I'm additionally grateful to dozens of C100 members, notably Scott Bonham, Angela Strange, Anthony Lee, Chris Albinson, Lars Leckie, Katherine Barr, Rob Burgess and Jennifer Holmstrom. If there's a positive spirit to this book, it was imbued by them.

The same must be said for the broader community of Canadians around the world who spent countless hours with me—to share their stories, of course, but equally to help me understand the value of our shared homeland. To those who took my calls, opened their doors and pointed me in the right direction, thank you. I hope I have effectively captured your experiences and your outlook. None of this, of course, would be possible without the commitment of those who have been with me from the outset of this project. My agents, Bruce Westwood and Michael Levine, were among the first to believe that the story of Canada is always worth telling and worth reading. I'm grateful to the team at Random House Canada, led by CEOs Kristin Cochrane and Brad Martin (now retired), and publisher Anne Collins, for embracing the idea and pushing me to stick with it through a marathon of research. No one deserves more credit than my editor, Craig Pyette, who managed both the heavy lifting in the book's construction and light touches in its finishing stages. His intellectual rigour, gracious manner and gift with language were indispensable. Our copy editor, Linda Pruessen, carried out additionally heroic work, chasing down errors in fact, logic and style.

Finally, I'm grateful to my family, friends and coworkers whose support through his project was never in question. To those who read different versions of the manuscript, I'm grateful for your comments and guidance. To my friend and former colleague, Richard Siklos, thank you for welcoming me on my research trips, and for never letting up with your valuable, and endlessly positive, guidance. You represent the best Canada has to offer. To my colleagues at Royal Bank of Canada, I don't have sufficient words to acknowledge my appreciation for both welcoming and challenging me. President and CEO Dave McKay has been unwavering in his support for my work, just as he is determined to see Canadians take on an ever-more challenging world. Most importantly, to my family, to Cindy, Matthew and Lauren, and my sisters Mary, Elizabeth and Ruth: thank you for your grace and generosity. You never ask for anything in return, which fittingly seems very Canadian.

Notes

Introduction: The Eleventh Province

1 Sean Mannion, author interview, 2019.

2 The size of Canada's overseas population is widely debated. Good historical reviews can be found in "Canadians Abroad: Canada's Global Asset" (Vancouver: Asia Pacific Foundation of Canada, 2011); "Where in the World Is Canada?" (Ottawa: Action Canada, 2011); and Malek Chouikh, Allison McHugh, Neil Peet, Caroline Senini and Sahl Syed, "Canada's Expatriates" (Toronto: Munk School of Global Affairs, 2015). Other figures are taken from "Estimated 2.8 Million Canadians Live Abroad," CBC News, October 29, 2009.

3 Jean-Christophe Dumont and Georges Lemaitre, "Counting Immigrants and Expatriates in OECD Countries: A New Perspective," Working Paper No. 25, Organization for Economic Co-operation and Development (Paris: OECD, 2005).

4 Joe Friesen, "As Nation of Immigrants, Canada Must Now Confront Its Emigrants," *Globe and Mail,* June 26, 2011.

5 Steven Vertovec, *The Political Importance of Diasporas*, Working Paper No. 13, Centre on Migration, Policy and Society (Oxford: University of Oxford, 2005).

6 Mark Boyle and Rob Kitchin, "A Diaspora Strategy for Canada? Enriching Debate through Heightening Awareness of International Practice" (Vancouver: Asia Pacific Foundation of Canada, 2011).

7 Jennifer Welsh, *At Home in the World: Canada's Global Vision for the 21st Century* (Toronto: HarperCollins, 2004), 239.

8 Doug Saunders, *Maximum Canada: Why 35 Million Canadians Are Not Enough* (Toronto: Knopf Canada, 2017), 123-27.

9 Jim Coyle, "A Canadian is Poised to Shake Up Cambridge University—the First Non-Briton in 800 Years," *Toronto Star,* September 10, 2017
10 In the 2020 Times Higher Education ranking of the world's top universities, which is widely considered the most prestigious league table, Cambridge placed third after Oxford and Caltech. Rounding out the top ten were Stanford, MIT, Princeton, Harvard, Yale, Chicago and Imperial College (Times Higher Education, *World University Rankings 2020,* London, September 11, 2019).
11 Stephen Toope, author interview, 2019.
12 In 2019, *Forbes* magazine listed Edwin Leong as the world's 478th richest person, with an estimated net worth of $4.1 billion. Born in Hong Kong, Leong studied in Canada in the 1970s and then returned to the territory, making his fortune there in real estate. In addition to his gifts to the Universities of Toronto and British Columbia, and Cambridge University, he endowed five professorships, each named in honour of his father. He also created the Edwin S.H. Leong Scholarship to support international students in financial need ("New $25-Million Gift to U of T Creates Leong Centre for Healthy Children," University of Toronto Faculty of Medicine, March 8, 2019; Paul Waldie, "Edwin Leong's Foundation Funds Health-Care Programs for Seniors and Children," *Globe and Mail,* May 31, 2019; and "#478: Edwin Leong," *Forbes*, December 10, 2019.)

Chapter 1: Outliers

1 Chris Cooter, author interview, 2016. In September 2019, Cooter moved to Brussels to serve as head of mission in the Canadian embassy to the European Union.
2 United Nations Department of Economic and Social Affairs, "International migrant stock: By destination and origin," New York, 2015.
3 Alison Loat, "Canada is Where Canadians Are: The Canadian Expatriate as an Element of International Policy," working paper, Privy Council Office, Ottawa, April 2004.
4 Chouikh et al., 19-33.

5 "Canadians Abroad: Canada's Global Asset," (Vancouver: Asia Pacific Foundation of Canada, May 2011), 3-4.
6 Chouikh et al., 5. In the Munk School study, Facebook's data showed a greater geographic dispersion than appeared to be the case in other studies. Among its Canadian-identified users in 2015, roughly 33 percent were in the U.S; 5 percent were in France and the United Kingdom; and 4 percent were in Mexico. After that: India, the Philippines, Australia, Italy, Hong Kong, Algeria and Brazil.
7 Tyler Brûlé, author interviews, 2017, 2019.
8 Colin Nagy, "What's behind Air Canada's New Look and New Branding," *Skift*, February 13, 2017.
9 "Spaz: American Graffiti," Vimeo interview, 2:42, posted by Scott Leberecht, 2017.
10 Steve Williams, author interview, 2019.
11 Marc Tessier-Lavigne, author interview, 2017.
12 Lylan Masterman, author interview, 2017.
13 "Global Canadians: A Survey of the Views of Canadians Abroad" (Vancouver: Asia Pacific Foundation of Canada, 2007).
14 HSBC conducts an annual survey of expats that seeks opinions about quality of life, career prospects, incomes and family environment. In the 2019 survey, the top three destinations were Switzerland, Singapore and Canada ("Expat Explorer Survey," HSBC, 2019.)
15 Angelique Mannella, author interview, 2019. Mannella has been a quiet champion of Canadian innovation during her stints at home, serving as a mentor to entrepreneurs and adviser to startup programs such as Techstars and Next AI. She hoped to continue that from Munich, where she moved in September 2019, although told me she has found Canadian companies and their advisers don't instinctively reach out to expats.
16 In 1997, National Public Radio's *This American Life* produced a series entitled "Who's Canadian?" in which host Ira Glass explored "the Canadians among us." David Rakoff explained his own journey in Act One: White Like Me (*This American Life*, NPR, May 30, 1997.)
17 Drake Bennett, "Social+Capital, the League of Extraordinarily Rich Gentlemen," Bloomberg, July 26, 2012.

18 Chamath Palihapitiya, author interview, 2016.

19 Lionel Gelber, "What is a Canadian?" *Free World,* January 1946, 62–65, and "A Marriage of Inconvenience," *Foreign Affairs* 41, January 1963, 310–22. Gelber was one of Canada's most significant mid-century voices on foreign policy, articulating the ideals of a middle power that was trying to find itself in the power shifts between the United States, Europe and the Soviet Union following the Second World War. After his death in 1989, his family endowed the Gelber Prize to annually recognize the best English-language book on foreign policy published in the previous year. The prize is now administered by the University of Toronto's Munk School of Global Affairs and *Foreign Policy* magazine. Two of Gelber's essays, in particular, articulated the emerging role of Canada, and Canadians, in the post-colonial, new world order. "What is a Canadian?" appeared in one of the final issues of *Free World*, a short-lived monthly magazine published during the war to spread ideas about a new global architecture. (Article retrieved from www.unz.org on December 3, 2014.) "A Marriage of Inconvenience," in the January 1963 edition of *Foreign Affairs*, explored the uncomfortable alliance between Western Europe and the United States, with Canada caught in between.

20 Palihapitiya stirred up controversy in 2017 when he criticized Facebook for not doing enough to prevent abuse of its platform and tools. He said he kept his children from social media, although later said he was still a supporter of Facebook (James Vincent, "Former Facebook Exec Says Social Media Is Ripping Apart Society," The Verge, December 11, 2017.)

21 Hajo Adam, Otilia Obodaru, Jackson G. Lu, William Maddux and Adam Galinsky, "How Living Abroad Helps You Develop a Clearer Sense of Self," *Harvard Business Review*, May 22, 2018.

22 Graeme Hamilton, "Lavish Life of Dead Canadian Multimillionaire—and Accused Cybercriminal—Revealed," *National Post*, July 20, 2017; Andrea Bellemare, "The Secret Life of Alexandre Cazes, Alleged Dark Web Mastermind," CBC News, July 23, 2017.

23 Emily Steele, "At Vice, Cutting-Edge Media and Allegations of Old-School Sexual Harassment," *New York Times*, December 23, 2017.

24 Keach Hagey, "Vice Media Names A+E's Nancy Dubuc as CEO; Shane Smith Steps Down," *Wall Street Journal*, March 13, 2018. With his business partners Suroosh Alvi and Gavin McInnes, Shane Smith founded the company in 1994 by acquiring *Voice of Montreal*, which they renamed Vice. Smith stepped down as CEO in 2018.

25 Jack Jedwab, author interview, 2017; Siddharth Bannerjee, Tieja Thomas and Stuart Soroka, "Cultural Intelligence and Identity Development: Concepts, Measures and Relationship to Canadian Forces Professional Development" (Canadian Forces Leadership Institute, Department of National Defence, Ottawa, August 2011).

26 Mike Myers, *Canada* (Toronto: Doubleday, 2016), 247–49.

27 U.S. Census Bureau, "Statistical Abstract of the United States, Section 31: 20th Century Statistics," December 9, 1999, 272.

28 Yearbook of Immigration Statistics, 2016, "Table 21: Persons Naturalized by Region and Country of Birth: Fiscal Years 2013 to 2015," (Washington: Department of Homeland Security, 2015.)

29 George Woodcock, *The Canadians* (London: Faber & Faber, 1970), 293.

30 Barbara Ward quoted in Joe Clark, *How We Lead: Canada in a Century of Change* (Toronto: Random House Canada, 2013), 8.

31 Woodcock, 294.

32 Ron Daniels, author interview, 2017.

33 "Applied Research: How a University Tries to Take on the Social Problems That Surround It," *The Economist*, September 1, 2016.

34 Rob Daniels, "'Ominous Path': Johns Hopkins President on Trump's Refugee Travel Ban," *Washington Post*, February 2, 2017.

35 The full letter, entitled "In this historic moment, we cannot stand by," was published on the Johns Hopkins University website on February 1, 2017.

36 Peter Baker, "Trump Assails Elijah Cummings, Calling His Congressional District a Rat-Infested 'Mess,'" *New York Times*, July 28, 2019. Cummings passed away in October 2019, at age 68. His body lay in state in the U.S. Capitol, the first African American granted the honour.

37 Ronald J. Daniels and Kevin Plank, "Baltimore Leaders: 'Proud Not Only to be in Baltimore, but of Baltimore,'" *Baltimore Sun*, July 29, 2019.

38 Adam Gopnik, "We Could All Have Been Canadians," *New Yorker*, May 15, 2017. The magazine's online headline was "We Could Have Been Canada." For a critique of Gopnik's work, the media writer James Wolcott authored a scathing review of his 2007 book, *Through the Children's Gate*, that begins, "I sometimes wonder if Adam Gopnik was put on this earth to annoy. If so, mission accomplished" (James Wolcott, "Smugged By Reality," *New Republic*, February 11, 2007).

Chapter 2: Missionaries, Mathematicians and Misfits

1 Arthur Herman, *How the Scots Invented the Modern World* (New York: Random House, 2001).
2 Ibid., 268.
3 Ibid., 368.
4 Ibid., 345.
5 Ibid., 243.
6 A 2007 study from the University of Chicago looked at the impact of migration on national identity, and included an analysis of the massive outmigration from Canada in the late 1800s and early 1900s and how it shaped the young country's early social and economic policies. See Bruno Ramirez, "Migration and National Consciousness: The Canadian Case" in *Citizenship and Those Who Leave: The Politics of Emigration and Expatriation*, ed. Nancy L. Green and Francois Weil (Chicago: University of Illinois Press, 2007), 211–23.
7 Byron Lew and Bruce Cater of Trent University documented the significant increase in migration in the late nineteenth century to the U.S., and found the larger and more diverse American economy was irresistible to many post-Confederation Canadians who chose to head south rather than west. See Lew and Cater, "The Language of Opportunity: Canadian Interregional and International Migration, 1911–1951," Working Paper, Department of Economics, Trent University, 2013.
8 Damien-Claude Belanger and Claude Belanger, "French Canadian Emigration to the United States, 1840–1930," Marianopolis College, Montreal, August 23, 2000.

9 Susan Mann, *The Dream of Nation: A Social and Intellectual History of* Quebec, 2nd ed. (Montreal: McGill-Queen's University Press, 2002.)
10 Belanger and Belanger, 10.
11 The American Community Survey provides county-level projections of the place of birth for the U.S. foreign-born population.
12 Jack Jedwab, "Don't Expect Americans to Rush the Border if Donald Trump Wins," *Huffington Post*, August 15, 2016.
13 Terence J. Fay, "Catholics," in *The Religions of Canadians*, ed. Jamie S. Scott (Toronto: University of Toronto Press, 2012), 68.
14 Alyvn Austin and Jamie S. Scott, eds., *Canadian Missionaries, Indigenous Peoples: Representing Religion at Home and Abroad* (Toronto: University of Toronto Press, 2005); Wilbert R. Shenk, ed., *North American Foreign Missions, 1810–1914: Theology, Theory and Policy* (Grand Rapids, MI: Eerdmans Publishing, 2004).
15 George Leslie Mackay, *From Far Formosa: The Island, Its People and Missions* (New York: Fleming H. Revell Co., 1896), 12.
16 "The sent ones" were young missionaries, although not necessarily associated with the schools where they studied.
17 Mackay, 24.
18 Ibid., 23.
19 Ibid., 292.
20 Ibid., 307.
21 Ibid., 322.
22 Ibid., 25.
23 Jonathan Spence, *To Change China: Western Advisers in China, 1620–1960* (New York: Little Brown, 1969).
24 Alvyn Austin, *China's Millions: The China Inland Mission and Late Qing Society, 1832–1905* (Grand Rapids, MI: Eerdmans Publishing, 2007).
25 Karen Minden, *Bamboo Stone: The Evolution of a Chinese Medical Elite* (Toronto: University of Toronto Press, 1994), 16.
26 Omar Kilborn, *Heal the Sick: An Appeal for Medical Missions in* China (Toronto: Missionary Society of the Methodist Church, 1910), 52.
27 Ibid., 48.
28 Minden, 57.

29 Alvyn Austin, "Wallace of West China: Edward Wilson Wallace and the Canadian Educational Systems of China, 1906–1927," in *Canadian Missionaries, Indigenous Peoples*, ed. Austin and Scott, 124–5.
30 A compelling history of the Laurier era and how Canada emerged as an independent-thinking nation can be found in Robert Craig Brown and Ramsay Cook, *Canada: A Nation Transformed, 1896–1921* (Toronto: McClelland and Stewart, Toronto, 1974).
31 Bill Trent, "Dr. Robert McClure: Missionary-Surgeon Extraordinaire," *Canadian Medical Association Journal* 132 (February 15, 1985): 431–41.
32 Robert Farquharson, *For Your Tomorrow: Canadians and the Burma Campaign, 1941–45* (Victoria, BC: Trafford Publishing, 2004).
33 Munroe Scott, *McClure: The China Years of Dr. Bob McClure* (Toronto: Canec Publishing and Supply House, 1977), 344.
34 Ibid., 89.
35 Ibid., 206–7.
36 Sheng-Ping Guo, "Ideology, Identity, and a New Role in World War Two: A Case Study of the Canadian Missionary Dr. Richard Brown in China, 1938–1939," Historical Papers 2015: Canadian Society of Church History, Emanuel College, University of Toronto.
37 Hochschild, Adam; *Spain in Our Hearts: Americans in the Spanish Civil War, 1936-1939* (Houghton Mifflin Harcourt, Boston, 2016); Kaarina Mikalson, "Spain's Democracy Talks to Canada: Pamphlets and Tours During the Spanish Civil War," as part of Dalhousie University's digital media project, *Canada and the Spanish Civil War.*
38 Victor Howard, *Mackenzie-Papineau Battalion: The Canadian Contingent in the Spanish Civil War* (Montreal: McGill-Queen's Press, 1987).
39 Scott, *McClure*, 230.
40 Roderick Stewart and Sharon Stewart, *Phoenix: The Life of Norman Bethune* (Montreal: McGill-Queen's University Press, 2011); Larry Hannant, ed., *The Politics of Passion: Norman Bethune's Writing and Art* (Toronto: University of Toronto Press, 1998).
41 Scott, 81.

42 Ibid., 232.
43 W.H. Auden and Christopher Isherwood, *Journey to a War* (London: Faber & Faber, 1939).
44 Scott, 304.
45 Ibid., 369.
46 The *New York Times* writer Nicholas Kristof once estimated Jim Grant "probably saved more lives than were destroyed by Hitler, Mao, and Stalin combined." Adam Fifield, *A Mighty Purpose: How Jim Grant Sold the World on Saving Its Children* (New York: Other Press, 2015.)
47 Gelber captured Canada's postwar opportunity in his essay, "Canada's New Stature," (*Foreign Affairs* 24, Council on Foreign Relations, January 1946, 277–89. Retrieved from jstor.org on Dec., 3, 2014.)
48 Arthur Kerman, author interview, 2016.
49 Christina McCall Newman, "The Canadian Americans," *Maclean's*, July 27, 1963, 9.
50 Antoine van Agtmael and Fred Bakker, *The Smartest Places on Earth: Why Rustbelts are the Emerging Hotspots of Global Innovation* (New York: PublicAffairs, 2016), 57–58.

Chapter 3: The Optimization Game

1 Rob Burgess, author interview, 2016; Karen Mazurkewich, "Who's Who: The CGI Kingpins," *Playbook*, January 11, 1999.
2 Mazurkewich, "Who's Who."
3 Ibid.
4 Amid Midi, *The Art of Pixar Short Films* (San Francisco: Chronicle Books, 2009).
5 In 2018, The Logic, a Canadian digital media outlet, published a story refuting the high number of Canadians in the Valley. Using American census data, which does not capture every Canadian living or working in the U.S., it suggested the number was fewer than one hundred thousand (Sean Craig, "No, There Aren't 300,000 Canadians in Silicon Valley," The Logic, August 7, 2018).
6 Jennifer Holmstrom, author interview, 2016.
7 Doug Bergeron, author interview, 2016.
8 Donna Morris, author interview, 2016.

9 Ryan Estis, "Blowing up the Performance Review: Interview with Adobe's Donna Morris," Ryan Estis & Associates, blog, June 17, 2013.
10 Anne Fisher, "How Adobe Keeps Employees from Quitting," *Fortune*, June 16, 2015.
11 As of November 12, 2019, the value of all outstanding shares of Google's parent company, Alphabet Inc., was $894 billion.
12 Patrick Pichette, author interview, 2018; Eric Schmidt, email correspondence with author, 2019.
13 Shona Brown, author interview, 2018.
14 Angus Birchall, author interview, 2017.
15 Shuman Ghosemajumder, author interview, 2019.
16 Pichette, author interview, 2018.
17 Chris O'Neill, author interview, 2017.
18 Tamsin McMahon, "Former Google CFO Patrick Pichette Sets His Sights on Keeping Canadian Tech Talent at Home," *Globe and Mail*, May 13, 2018.
19 Cade Metz, "Google Is 2 Billion Lines of Code—and It's All in One Place," *Wired*, September 16, 2015.
20 Rachel Potvin, author interview, 2017.

Chapter 4: Putting the Crazy Back in Canuck

1 The story of the C100 origins is based on interviews with Chris Albinson, Anthony Lee, Lars Leckie, Katherine Barr, Atlee Clark and Stewart Beck. The author is grateful to Albinson and Lee for providing records of the group's early meetings.
2 Lars Leckie, author interview, 2016.
3 Katherine Barr, author interviews, 2016, 2019.
4 Shaan Pruden, author interview, 2019.
5 Anthony Lee, author interviews, 2016, 2019.
6 Shawn Price was another driving force behind the C100. A software executive from Ottawa, he built several companies and also helped lead Oracle from his base in San Francisco before he died from cancer in 2016, at age fifty three. The son of a Canadian diplomat, Price grew up in Europe, Australia, Africa and the Caribbean, and appreciated the value of Canadians abroad (Mai Nguyen, "Oracle VP Shawn

Price Showed Drive in Every Sense of the Word," *Canadian Business*, October 28, 2016).

7 Stewart Beck, author interview, 2017.

8 Atlee Clark, author interview, 2016.

9 "Crazy Canucks" was the nickname for a group of Canadian downhill ski racers whose aggressive style and World Cup successes in the 1970s and '80s captured the public imagination.

10 Anthony Lee, author interviews, 2016, 2019.

11 Chris Albinson, author interviews, 2016, 2019.

12 Ajay Royan, author interviews, 2017–2019.

13 Joshua Cooper Ramo, *The Seventh Sense: Power, Fortune and Survival in the Age of Networks* (New York: Little Brown & Co, 2016).

14 Ibid., 220–21.

15 Caroline Wagner, *The New Invisible College: Science for Development* (Washington, DC: Brookings Institution Press, 2008), 4.

16 Ibid., 72.

17 Ibid., 25.

18 Richard Florida, *The Rise of the Creative Class:* Revisited (New York: Basic Books, 2012), viii.

19 Ibid., 268.

20 Ibid., 234.

21 Ibid., 201.

22 Sandra Martin, "Doctor Had a Raging Curiosity Matched with Intellect," *Globe and Mail*, November 28, 2011.

Chapter 5: Pragmatic Dreamers

1 Dana Goodyear, "Man of Extremes," *New Yorker*, October 26, 2009.

2 Peter Bogdanovich, *Who the Devil Made It* (New York: Random House, 1999).

3 Andrew Clark, *Stand and Deliver: Inside Canadian Comedy* (Toronto: Doubleday Canada, 1997), 20.

4 Ibid., 58–9.

5 Ibid., 199.

6 Ibid., 209.

7 Myers, 186.

8 Nick Patch, "Grammys 2012: Toronto Promoter Elliott Lefko Hits It Big in L.A," Canadian Press, February 9, 2012.
9 Elliott Lefko, author interview, 2016.
10 Alan Cross, Chouikh et al. interview, 2015.
11 Bob Ezrin, author interview, 2015.
12 Richard Florida and Scott Jackson, "Sonic City: The Evolving Economic Geography of the Music Industry," Martin Prosperity Institute, University of Toronto, January 2008, 192.
13 Eddie Schwartz, author interviews, 2017, 2019.
14 For a more complete look at Canadians in the United States, and Americans in Canada, the demographers Jack Jedwab and Susan Hardwick prepared a data analysis, "Ameri-can-adians: Demography and Identity of Borderline Canadians and Americans," which documents the cross-border flow of people. Douglas Todd wrote a good analysis of their findings in the *Ottawa Citizen,* drawing on his own American heritage ("Ameri-Canadians Point Fury at Uncle Sam," *Ottawa Citizen*, May 9, 2014).

Chapter 6: Humour, Humility and Chutzpah

1 Simon and Martina Stawski, author interview, 2018.
2 Clark, *Stand and Deliver*, 165.
3 Mark Rowswell, "Why Do So Many Chinese Learners Seem to Hate Dashan (Mark Rowswell)?" Quora (blog post), April 20, 2015.
4 Government of Canada, "PM Names Mark Rowswell 'Dashan' as Canada's Goodwill Ambassador to China," news release, February 7, 2012.

Chapter 7: Architects of Change

1 Raefer Wallis, author interviews, 2017-19.
2 Ellen Himelfarb, "Inside Sherry Poon's Eco-Chic Shanghai Home," *Globe and Mail*, January 15, 2011.
3 Wallis, author interview.
4 Nathan VanderKlippe, "Canadian Architect Living in China Hailed as 'Guiding Light' in the Pursuit of Healthier Buildings," *Globe and Mail*, April 22, 2019.

5 Aric Chen, "36 Hours in Shanghai," *New York Times*, March 10, 2009.
6 "The Red Hot List, 2009," *Conde Nast Traveller*, May 2009.
7 Jeffrey Cody, *Building in China: Henry K. Murphy's Adaptive Architecture, 1914–1935* (Hong Kong: Chinese University Press, 2001).
8 Harry Hussey, *My Pleasures and Palaces* (New York: Doubleday, 1968), 47–8.
9 Ibid., 230.
10 Ibid., 92
11 Ibid., 68.
12 Ibid., 237–38.
13 Ibid., 225.
14 Ibid., 230.
15 Ibid., 275.
16 Will C. Van Den Hoonaard, "Baha'is," in *The Religions of Canadians*, ed. Jamie S. Scott (Toronto: University of Toronto Press, 2012), 380.
17 Witold Rybczynski, "The Green Case for Cities," *The Atlantic*, October 2009.
18 Jordan Bishop, "A Conversation with Allan Zeman: The Father of Lan Kwai Fong," *Forbes*, October 30, 2016.
19 Ibid.
20 Like Dubai and Singapore, Hong Kong is a destination for expatriates, and for generations was known as one of the most accommodating centres for global professionals. Its low tax rates, diverse culture, dependable rule of law and proximity to strong economies, led by mainland China, were part of the draw. Britain, its former colonial power, tried to secure that foundation when it handed over control of the territory in 1997 to China, which committed to a policy of "one country, two systems." But confidence in that model was rocked in 2019 when the mainland tried to push an extradition law on the territory—jeopardizing its judicial independence—sparking street protests that led to the imposition of emergency rule.
21 Hong Kong is home to an estimated three hundred thousand Canadian citizens, although the vast majority of them hold dual citizenship, using Canada as a secondary residence or station for family members. The local government says there are only about

sixteen thousand Canadians in the territory, as it counts people of Chinese origin as its own, regardless of shared nationality. (Christopher DeWolf, "In Hong Kong, Just Who Is an Expat, Anyway?" *Wall Street Journal*, December 29, 2014.

22 Lisa Bate, author interview, 2017.

23 Geoffrey York, "China Saps Maple Town of Canadian Style," *Globe and Mail*, January 10, 2007.

24 "After Years in Shanghai, Lisa Bate Returns to Canada as B+H's Regional Managing Principal North America," Cision, February 2, 2016.

25 Wallis, author interview.

26 Kerry Allen, "Formaldehyde Emerges as New Risk in China's Housing Boom," BBC Monitoring, September 6, 2018.

27 Dominic Barton, author interview, 2017.

Chapter 8: Lindsay of Arabia

1 J. Keeler Johnson, "The Global Racing Empire of Sheikh Mohammed bin Rashid al Maktoum," *The Sport*, September 11, 2017.

2 Rory Miller, *Desert Kingdoms to Global Powers: The Rise of the Arab* Gulf (New Haven, CT: Yale University Press, 2016), 134.

3 Mohammed bin Rashid al-Maktoum, *My Vision: Challenges in the Race for Excellence* (Dubai: Motivate Publishing, 2012), 38.

4 Johnson.

5 Marc Montgomery, "History: November 6, 1991: Canadians Cap the Last Oil Fire in the Gulf," Radio Canada International, November 6, 2015.

6 David Finch, "Petroleum Industry Oral History Project: Mike Miller," Glenbow Museum, Calgary, April 2004.

7 Lindsay Miller, author interviews, 2018-19.

8 Sujata Burman, "UAE's Thriving Creative Scene Catapults Dubai Design Week onto a Global Stage," *Wallpaper**, November 16, 2018.

9 Emma Graham-Harrison, "Missing Emirati Princess 'Planned Escape for Seven Years,'" *The Guardian*, December 4, 2018.

10 BBC News, "Princess Haya Bint al-Hussein: The Dubai Royal 'Hiding in London,'" July 30, 2019.

11 In 2019, Beth Hirshfeld stepped down from the Canadian Business Council of Dubai and Northern Emirates to open a Dubai office for the Toronto-based firm, Heirloom Investment Management.
12 Hirshfeld, author interview, 2019.
13 Deborah Beatty, Joel Finlayson, author interviews, 2018-19.
14 Carly Weeks, "More Than 1,100 Saudi Medical Residents Get Extended Deadline to Leave Canada," *Globe and Mail*, August 22, 2018.
15 Abdulellah Alaboudi, Anthony Atkins and Bernadette Sharp, "A Holistic Framework for Assisting Decision Makers of Healthcare Facilities to Assess Telemedicine Applications in Saudi Arabia," eTELEMED 2015: The Seventh International Conference on eHealth, Telemedicine, and Social Medicine, 2015.
16 Andrew Padmos, author interviews, 2016, 2019.
17 Mohammad Alharbi, "An Analysis of the Saudi Health-Care System's Readiness to Change in the Context of the Saudi National Health-Care Plan in Vision 2030," *International Journal of Health Sciences* 12, no. 3 (May-June 2018): 83–87.

Chapter 9: Justice Hunters

1 James Orbinski, "Nobel Peace Prize speech," Médecins Sans Frontières, December 10, 1999.
2 Catherine Tsalikis, "IWD 2017: MSF's Joanne Liu on a World in Denial," Open Canada, March 8, 2017.
3 Joanne Liu, "European Governments Are Feeding the Business of Suffering," open letter, Médecins Sans Frontières, September 7, 2017.
4 Before the turn of the nineteenth century, Canadians could be found from South Asia to West Africa, running schools and hospitals. They were considered highly competent, culturally sensitive and loyal to the colonial mission. Perhaps none was more determined than Rowland Bingham, a young missionary who arrived in Lagos, Nigeria, in December 1893, with American Tom Kent and fellow Canadian Walter Gowans. Their goal was to build a health system for sixty million people across the Soudan, a malaria-stricken region that was known as the "White Man's Grave." Kent and Gowans both died within a year, from malaria. Bingham, suffering from fever, returned

to Canada, but didn't give up. He reorganized his team as the Soudan Interior Mission, and in 1901 established an inland base in Nigeria, which eventually became the American-based group, SIM, or Service in Mission, that continues to operate around the world. (Peter Pigott, *Canada in Sudan: War Without Borders,* Toronto, Dundurn Press, 2009, 172.)

5 K.V. Ram, *History in Africa*, Vol. 7 (New York: Cambridge University Press, 1980).

6 Bob Jones. Chouikh et al. interview, 2015.

7 John Evans and Fraser Mustard developed the McMaster model for health care education with David Sackett, who was known as "the father of evidence based medicine." A British clinical epidemiologist, Sackett taught at McMaster from 1967 to 1994. In 2001, he was awarded the Order of Canada (Richard Smith, "David Sackett; Obituary," *British Medical Journal* [May 14, 2015]).

8 Ibid.

9 "Expert Panel on Canada's Strategic Role in Global Health," Canadian Academy of Health Sciences, 2011.

10 In September 2019, Tim Evans returned to Canada as McGill University's inaugural director and associate dean of the School of Population and Global Health in the Faculty of Medicine, and associate vice-principal (global policy and innovation). His wife, Alayne Adams, also joined McGill as an associate professor in the Department of Family Medicine.

11 Lyse Doucet, author interview, 2017.

12 Jeffrey Kofman, author interview, 2017.

13 Jeff Grey, "James Stewart: Canada's Man in The Hague," *Globe and Mail*, January 18, 2013.

14 Marlise Simons, "South Africa Should Have Arrested Sudan's President, I.C.C. Rules," *New York Times*, July 6, 2017.

15 Jina Moore, "Burundi Quits International Criminal Court," *New York Times*, October 27, 2017.

16 David Bosco, "Is the International Criminal Court Crumbling Before Our Eyes?" *Foreign Policy*, October 26, 2016.

Chapter 10: The Opposable Minds of Globalization

1 Gwyn Topham, "Moya Greene to Step Down as Royal Mail's Chief Executive," *Guardian*, April 20, 2018.
2 J.C. Curleigh, author interview, 2016.
3 Dominic Barton, author interview, 2016.
4 Roger Martin, *The Opposable Mind: Winning through Integrative Thinking* (Boston: Harvard Business Press, 2009).
5 Ibid., 114.
6 Brenda Trenowden, author interview, 2017.
7 Adam Boyes, author interview, 2018.
8 Brad Katsuyama, author interview, 2016. Katsuyama felt the New York Stock Exchange's dominant market share had led to a phenomenon known as "concentrated benefit and diffuse harm" that often is the result of an oligopoly. In this case, every participant in the market is required to pay a small extra charge—not enough to hurt—while the market operator collects a big windfall, which creates the concentrated benefit. The loser? Market efficiency, as money in this case may be directed from millions of investors and listed companies to a smaller number of NYSE shareholders.
9 Matt Levine, "Beyond Flash Boys," *Bloomberg Markets* (November 2016), 72.
10 John Stackhouse, "Flash Forward from Flash Boys: How a Canadian is Shaking Up Wall Street," Royal Bank of Canada blog, November 25, 2016.
11 There are more than sixteen thousand registered Canadians living in Manhattan, although likely many more who don't declare themselves. In 2008, one of them, Leigh Kamping-Carder, now with the *Wall Street Journal*, wrote in the *Observer*, "Most Canadians don't move to New York for love. We come to steal your jobs, mostly in the fields of finance, law and, to a lesser extent, the arts and media. (We call this migration "brain drain.") Canadian New Yorkers are generally in their 20s to 40s. They are more highly skilled and wealthier than the general population in the U.S.—and in Canada. As Mahmood Iqbal noted in a report for the Center for Comparative Immigration Studies, these emigrants 'are the best and brightest

of the Canadian human resource pool'" (Leigh Kamping-Carder, "Canadians Among Us!" *Observer*, July 31, 2008).

12 Dominic Barton, "Capitalism for the Long Term," *Harvard Business Review*, March 2011.

13 CPPIB had assets of about $250 billion in 2014. In 2019, that had grown to roughly $400 billion (CPP Investment Board, "Investing for Generations," 2019 Annual Report, April, 2019).

14 Dominic Barton and Mark Wiseman, "Focusing Capital on the Long Term," *Harvard Business Review*, January-February 2014.

15 In 2016, Mark Wiseman left CPPIB to join BlackRock, the world's biggest investment manager, and moved to New York as its senior managing director. He left in December 2019 after violating company policy by not disclosing a relationship with another employee.

Chapter 11: How Very Canadian

1 Cecil John Rhodes was a British businessman and prime minister of the Cape Colony from 1890 to 1896, and an architect of some of its most racially divisive policies, including laws that pushed blacks off their lands to make way for industrial development. He also was a proponent of settler colonialism as a means of advancing the Anglo-Saxon race, which he considered superior.

2 Laurence Brockliss, *The University of Oxford: A History* (Oxford: Oxford University Press, 2016).

3 Gelber, "A Marriage of Inconvenience," 289.

4 Attracta Mooney, "Pressure Grows on £6.3b Cambridge University Fund to Drop Fossil Fuels," *Financial Times*, October 8, 2017.

5 Rosie Bradbury, Stephanie Stacey and Noella Chye, "What Toope Said—and Didn't Say—at Yesterday's Meeting," *Varsity* (Cambridge), March 17, 2018.

6 Tookie Graham, author interview, 2017.

7 Logan Graham, author interviews, 2017-18.

8 The British government's Office for National Statistics measures foreign populations in every county (Office for National Statistics, "Population of the UK by country of birth and nationality). In 2011, *The Guardian* analyzed foreign populations by region and, among other

discoveries, found that Canadians were not clustered anywhere in great numbers ("The UK's Foreign-Born Population," *The Guardian*, 2011).

9 An Asia Pacific Foundation project analyzed major trends among the estimated seventy thousand Canadian expats in Britain, and profiled some of the better-known ones, including the singer Nicole Appleton, boxer Lennox Lewis, royal family member Autumn Phillips and tech pioneer Terry Matthews (Diane Coulombe and Don DeVoretz, *Portrait of Canadians Abroad: United Kingdom* [Vancouver: Asia Pacific Foundation of Canada, 2009]).

Chapter 12: Diaspora Diplomacy

1 Tara Zahra, *The Great Departure: Mass Migration from Eastern Europe and the Making of the Free World* (New York: W.W. Norton & Co., 2016), 71.
2 Ibid., 260.
3 Ibid., 257.
4 Ajay Parasram, "Us and Them: The Plumbing and Poetry of Citizenship Policy and the Canadians Abroad," Canadians Abroad Project, Asia Pacific Foundation of Canada, Vancouver, June 2010, 6.
5 *Maquiladoras* are industrial zones in Mexico that offer duty-free status, and certain regulatory exemptions, to attract foreign investment and export capacity. The government promoted *maquilas* in the 1980s as a way of attracting investment following the 1980 debt crisis and collapse of the peso. Their popularity grew rapidly with the 1994 introduction of the North American Free Trade Agreement, as American companies shifted operations to Mexico to take advantage of trade concessions, lower labour costs and a cheaper currency.
6 Loat, "Canada Is Where Canadians Are," 31.
7 Jeremy Eves, Chouikh et al. interview, 2015.
8 Jeffrey Simpson's 2000 book *Star-Spangled Canadians* (Toronto: HarperCollins, 2001) remains one of the most authoritative looks at Canadians in the United States. A good survey can be found in Diane Coulombe and Don DeVoretz's *Portrait of Canadians Abroad: United States* (Vancouver: Asia Pacific Foundation of Canada, 2008).

9 Rob Hain and Derek Linfield, author interviews, 2018-19.
10 Boyle and Kitchin, 15.
11 Chouikh et al., 32.
12 Ibid., 32.
13 Ibid., 26.
14 Ibid., 26.
15 Boyle and Kitchin, 7.
16 Ibid., 31.
17 Ibid., 15–17.
18 Ibid., 44.
19 World Bank, "Data on Outward Remittance Flows," Migration and Development Brief 31, Washington, DC, April 2019.
20 Chouikh, et al., 29.
21 Ibid., 19.
22 Ibid., 25.
23 Ibid., 28.
24 Ibid., 27.
25 Boyle and Kitchin, 38.
26 In 2008, Vietnam received $7.4 billion in remittances from overseas residents, five hundred thousand or more of whom return every year. (Trang Nguyen and Vu Thi Hai Anh, "Portrait of Canadians Abroad: Vietnam," Asia Pacific Foundation of Canada, January 2010.) The country moved to allow expats to reclaim their lapsed citizenship and gain special investment rights. Remittances rose to $15.9 billion in 2018, according to the World Bank. ("Personal remittances received," World Bank Data, 2019.) Entering the twenty-first century, Nigeria saw a similar economic opportunity. While the internet had made the country synonymous with money laundering and financial scams, the Nigerian government realized it had to do more to legitimize financial flows from its overseas residents, who were sending home so much money they appeared to need their own banking channel. At $12 billion a year, remittances were worth more than the economies of twenty-four of the country's thirty-six states. In response, the government created expatriate identity cards to enable easier, and legal, money transfers. (Chouikh et al., 22.)
27 Boyle and Kitchin, 26.

28 Loat, 52.
29 Boyles and Kitchin, 32.
30 Loat, 6.
31 Ibid., 18.
32 Kenny Zhang, "Canadians Abroad: Policy Challenges for Canada," *Korean Review of Canadian Studies* 15, no. 1 (2009): 75–99.
33 Parasram, 25.
34 Asia Pacific Foundation, "Global Canadians."
35 Consiglio Di Nino (Chair), "The Evacuation of Canadians from Lebanon in July 2006: Implications for the Government of Canada." Senate Committee on Foreign Affairs and International Trade, Ottawa, May 2007.
36 John Chant, "The Passport Package: Rethinking the Citizenship Benefits of Non-Resident Canadians," Backgrounder No. 99, C.D. Howe Institute, December 2006.
37 Ibid., 2.
38 Ibid., 4-5.
39 Chouikh, et al., 10.
40 Ibid., 14.
41 Ibid., 15
42 Gillian Frank, "If Canada is back, let's restore expats' right to vote," *Globe and Mail*, November 17, 2015.
43 Boyle and Kitchin, *Diaspora Strategy*, 38.
44 Chouikh, et al., 15-16.
45 One of the more peculiar disputes over citizenship involves "lost Canadians"—the estimated two hundred thousand people born overseas to at least one Canadian parent. Until recently, they had only a tenuous claim on citizenship. Before 1997, the overseas-born children of Canadians had no Canadian rights at all, until a court accepted the Charter provisions on equality and recognized the rights of a child born to a Canadian expat mother. But that excluded those with Canadian fathers and non-Canadian mothers, particularly the large number of children of "war brides" in the Second World War. The issue was finally tested in court by Joe Taylor, a British citizen who was born in 1944 to an English mother and Canadian father stationed with the

military overseas. Taylor had never pushed his claim for Canadian citizenship, as his parents didn't stay together long. But after 9/11, as border security tightened everywhere, he felt the need, and right, to be Canadian. He applied for citizenship, and although twice denied, finally won on appeal and, in 2008, was granted citizenship. He was sixty-four. The Taylor case affirmed that anyone born to a Canadian father or mother was entitled to Canadian citizenship.

46 Chrystia Freeland, "Global Seagulls and the New Reality of Immigration," *New York Times*, October 6, 2011.

Chapter 13: A Diaspora That Looks Like the World

1 Jennifer Pascoe, "The Protagonist," *folio* (University of Alberta), November 29, 2016.

2 Asia Pacific Foundation, "Canadians Abroad," 4.

3 Statistics Canada, "Children with an Immigrant Background: Bridging Cultures," October 25, 2017.

4 Nisha Pahuja, Chouikh, et al. interview, 2015.

5 Sherry Yu, *Mapping Canadian Diasporic Media: The Existence and Significance of Communicative Spaces for Overseas Canadians,* Research Report, Canadians Abroad Project (Vancouver: Asia Pacific Foundation of Canada, March 2010).

6 Priya Kumar, "Sikh Narratives: An Analysis of Virtual Diaspora Networks," April 2012, e-Diasposa, Foundation Maison des Sciences de l'Homme, 20. Kumar also mapped the digital networking of the Tamil diaspora, in "Transnational Tamil Networks: Mapping Engagement Opportunities on the Web," April 2012, e-Diasposa, Foundation Maison des Sciences de l'Homme.

7 Houda Asal, "Community Sector Dynamics and the Lebanese Diaspora: Internal Fragmentation and Transnationalism on the Web," April 2012, e-Diasposa, Foundation Maison des Sciences de l'Homme, 16.

8 Asia Pacific Foundation, "Canadians Abroad."

9 The administrative cost of remittances remains a public policy concern but is rarely considered in the spirit of building global networks for Canada. Provincial governments tend to look at the issue as one of

consumer protection, and focus on fees, rather than also looking at technologies like blockchain that could be developed to make Canada a pioneer in digital remittances. The opportunities are presented in Don and Alex Tapscott's *Blockchain Revolution: How the Technology Behind Bitcoin Is Changing Money, Business, and the World* (Toronto: Penguin Random House, 2016). See also Jon Medow, "Regulating remittance fees makes sense for Ontario," iPolitics, June 8, 2012.

10 Maurice Bitran and Serene Tran, "Diaspora Nation: An Inquiry into the Economic Potential of Diaspora Networks in Canada," Mowat Centre, University of Toronto, September 2013, 13-14.

11 World Bank, "Data on Outward Remittance Flows," Migration and Development Brief 31, Washington, DC, April 2019.

12 Timothy Yu, "A Fairer Form of Money Migration," Asia-Pacific Foundation of Canada, March 31, 2014.

13 Michael Adams, "Canada's Do-it-Yourself Foreign Aid," *Globe and Mail*, March 28, 2014.

14 Stewart Bell, "Canada's Plan for Managing the Return of ISIS Fighters Revealed in Documents," Global News, May 14, 2018.

15 Tamara Khandaker, "ISIS Just Identified a Dead Leader by Name—and That's Unusual," Vice News, October 6, 2016.

16 Christian Leuprecht and Todd Hataley, "If Jihadi Jack Comes Home, Canada Has Only Itself to Blame," *Globe and Mail*, August 20, 2019.

17 Rod McGuirk, "Australian Court Disqualifies Deputy PM Due to Dual Citizenship," Associated Press, October 27, 2017.

18 Richard Liu, author interview, 2016.

Chapter 14: Our Stay-at-Home Students

1 Margaret Biggs and Roland Paris (co-chairs), "Global Education for Canadians: Equipping Young Canadians to Succeed at Home & Abroad," Report of the Study Group on Global Education, Centre for International Policy Studies, University of Ottawa and Munk School of Global Affairs, University of Toronto, November 2017.

2 Tim Johnson, "Why Do So Many Canadian Students Refuse to Study Abroad?" *University Affairs*, May 25, 2016.

3 David Johnston, "50th Anniversary of the Canadian Bureau for International Education," speech to the Canadian Bureau for International Education, November 14, 2016.
4 David Johnston, author interview, 2017.
5 Government of Canada, International Education, "Recent Trends in International Student Mobility and Economic Impact," 2016.
6 Tim Wharnsby, "Why Did Governor General David Johnston Pass Up a Tryout with the Boston Bruins?" CBC News, March 20, 2015.
7 David Johnston, *Trust: Twenty Ways to Build a Better Country* (Toronto: Penguin Random House Canada, 2018).
8 David Johnston, *The Idea of Canada: Letters to a Nation* (Toronto: Penguin Random House, 2016), 186-7.
9 Biggs and Paris.
10 Statistics Canada, "Population and Growth Components, 1851-2001 Censuses." The author is grateful for additional research and tabulations of census data provided by Jack Jedwab.
11 German Academic Exchange Service, *Annual Report, 2017*, Berlin, 12.
12 Australian Government, "About the New Colombo Plan," Department of Foreign Affairs and Trade website, Canberra.
13 Canadian Bureau for International Education, "A World of Learning," Ottawa, 2016, 43.
14 Ibid., 35.
15 Amit Chakma (chair), "International Education a Key Driver of Canada's Future Prosperity," Advisory Panel on Canada's International Education, Ottawa, August 2012.
16 According to United Nations data, 2.0 percent of Canadians of college and university age were studying abroad for their entire degree in 2014. This placed Canada behind Norway (5.3 percent), Germany (2.6 percent) and France (2.1 percent), but ahead of the United Kingdom (0.7 percent) and United States (0.3 percent). (Source: data.uis.unesco.org.)
17 Mika Saarinen, author interview, 2018.
18 Bank of Finland Bulletin, "A Brief History of Finnish Foreign Trade," December 18, 2015.
19 Josh Dehaas, "Canadian Students Need to Go to China, but They Need Some Help," *Maclean's*, November 15, 2016.

20 Guy Saint-Jacques, author interview, 2019.

21 Zheng Xintao, "Education Key in Nurturing Canada-China Relationship," *Vancouver Province*, August 11, 2018.

22 Indira Samarasekera, author interview, 2017.

23 Dehaas, "Canadian students Need to Go to China."

24 Bessma Momani and Jillian Stirk, "The Diversity Dividend: Canada's Global Advantage," Centre for International Governance Innovation, Waterloo, ON, April 2017.

25 Project Atlas, Institute of International Education, 2019.

26 Canadian Bureau for International Education, "World of Learning," 24. In 2016, the CBIE conducted an Education Abroad Student Survey across thirty-five member institutions, asking 7,028 post-secondary students for their views on a range of issues related to studying abroad. Among the questions, the students were asked, "If you were considering an education abroad program, which THREE countries would be of interest to you?" According to the findings, "Top choices tended to be in highly developed countries, primarily in Europe, where Canada's official languages are widely spoken."

27 Kenneth McLaughlin, *Out of the Shadow of Orthodoxy: Waterloo @ 50* (Waterloo, ON: University of Waterloo, 2007).

28 Since its founding in 1957, the University of Waterloo has graduated more than 200,000 students. Based on their preferred addresses, more than 159,000 live in Canada and 9,600 more in the United States, including 2,500 in California. (Email communications in 2019 between the author and the university administration.)

29 Moira MacDonald, "International student enrolment continues to soar in Canada," University Affairs, May 6, 2019.

30 Statistics Canada, "Canadian postsecondary enrolments and graduates, 2016/17," The Daily, November 18, 2018.

31 Joe Friesen, "Trudeau government outlines five-year, $148-million plan to attract more foreign students to Canadian universities," *Globe and Mail*, August 25, 2019.

32 Canadian Bureau for International Education, "World of Learning," 36. CBIE's 2016 Education Abroad Student Survey found 2.3 percent of university students (undergraduate and graduate) went abroad for a credit or not-for-credit experience in the 2014-15 academic year.

It found that at most of the schools, the rate of outbound mobility ranged from 0.4 percent to 6 percent.

33 Jill Lawrance, "Inter-Provincial Post-Secondary Student Mobility: A review of data sources from a British Columbia perspective," 28-9. The study for the British Columbia Council on Admissions and Transfer found that only about 6.2 percent of B.C.'s high school graduates enrolled in post-secondary programs outside the province. Close to 40 percent of them went to Alberta or Ontario, and close to half of those went to just nine well-known Canadian universities. Only 1.4 percent enrolled in schools outside Canada. This fits with general mobility patterns for the Canadian population. According to Statistics Canada, in the second quarter of 2018, international arrivals accounted for the vast majority of provincial population growth. In Ontario, for instance, inter-provincial migration accounted for net growth of 3,274, while international migration added 28,329 people. (Statistics Canada, Quarterly Demographic Estimates, April to June 2018, September 27, 2018.)

34 Peter Shawn Taylor, "Frozen in Place," *Report on Business*, March 2018, 5–6.

35 Alex Usher, "Notes on Canada's International Advantages (and Disadvantages)," Higher Education Strategy Associates blog, November 2018.

36 Biggs and Paris.

37 Marc Weinstein, author interview, 2016.

38 John Zhao, Doug Drew and Scott Murray, "Brain Drain and Brain Gain: The Migration of Knowledge Workers from and to Canada." *Education Quarterly Review* 6, no. 3 (2000).

Chapter 15: A Global Brain Trust

1 Bob Birgeneau, author interview, 2016

2 Rob Prichard, author interview, 2019. Prichard served as president of the University of Toronto from 1990-2000, and recalled trying to lure Birgeneau from MIT, where he was dean of science, to be dean of arts and science at U of T, but Birgeneau declined to be considered. When Prichard stepped down as president, he recommended Birgeneau to the search committee, which made the final hiring decision.

3 In the 2019 Times Higher Education World University Rankings, Toronto placed twenty-first, while Berkeley ranked fifteenth ("World University Rankings 2019").

4 Shane Dingman, "Canada Java Code Guru James Gosling Is an International Star in Computing," *Globe and Mail,* June 11, 2017.

5 In 2017, the Trudeau government's Advisory Panel on Federal Support for Fundamental Science, chaired by David Naylor, recommended a massive increase in funding for basic research, including for foreign researchers to study in Canada. The panel urged the government to see the attraction of international researchers—and their networks—as a critical step in making Canada a bigger force in global science. It noted international graduates from Canadian universities rose from 16,101 students in 2006 to 33,003 in 2014, while international students completing doctorate degrees reached 21.1 per cent. Those numbers still trailed other advanced research nations. (Naylor, 44.)

6 The launch of NAFTA in 1994 opened more doors for "brain circulation," with the introduction of a new visa class that made it easier for professionals, entrepreneurs and scientists to move north and south. The movement tended to be cyclical. Between 1986–91 and 1991–96, as NAFTA came into effect, the number of Canadian emigrants counted by the U.S. rose from 125,300 to 170,400, and then peaked in 1996–2001 at 241,200. In the half-decade after 9/11, the flow of Canadians south ebbed to 167,300. According to the American Community Survey, which is run by the U.S. Census Bureau, the U.S. saw a one-third decline in the number of Canadians moving south on a temporary or permanent basis—from 113,000 in 2000 to 73,000 in 2006. In 2014, net migration to the U.S. fell below 10,000 for the first time this century, and many of those were retirees and students (Patrice Dion and Mireille Vezina, "Emigration from Canada to the United States from 2000 to 2006," Canadian Social Trends, Statistics Canada, Catalogue 11-008).

7 Richard Mueller, "What Happened to the Canada-United States Brain Drain of the 1990s? New Evidence from the 2000 US Census," *Journal of International Migration and Integration* 7, no. 2 (2006): 167–94.

8 Dion and Vezina, "Emigration from Canada to the United States from 2000 to 2006," 24.
9 David Zarifa and David Walters, "Revisiting Canada's Brain Drain: Evidence from the 2000 Cohort of Canadian University Graduates," *Canadian Public Policy* 34, no. 3 (2008): 305–19.
10 Among the studies of the flight of Canadian-educated professionals in the 1990s, two are worth comparing. Daniel Schwanen of the C.D. Howe Institute looked at the push and pull factors in "Putting the Brain Drain in Context: Canada and the Global Competition for Scientists and Engineers," and found lack of jobs for specific professionals to be the biggest driver of emigration (Toronto: C.D. Howe Institute, 2000). In 2001, Don DeVoretz and Chona Iturralde wrote in *Policy Options* about the income gap and how it tends to be overcome by an "extraordinary" desire among Canadians to stay, regardless of income level. ("Why Do Highly Skilled Canadians Stay in Canada?" *Policy Options*, March 1, 2001.)
11 Many people in the tech sector believe Canada loses global talent to other markets, notably the U.S., because Canadian employers won't match international pay scales (Craig Daniels, "The Talent War," Communitech News, April 2019).
12 Peter Kuhn, "The Brain Drain: A View from Stateside," *Policy Options* 22, no. 9 (2001): 69–73.
13 Max Blouw (chair), Expert Panel on the State of Science and Technology and Industrial Research and Development in Canada, "Competing in a Global Innovation Economy: Current State of R&D in Canada," Council of Canadian Academies, Ottawa, xvii.
14 Johns Hopkins University, "Johns Hopkins Tops U.S. Universities in Research Spending for 39th Consecutive Year," Baltimore, December 17, 2018.
15 Statistics Canada, "Spending on Research and Development in the Higher Education Sector, 2015," Ottawa, 2017.
16 Johns Hopkins University, "Michael Bloomberg Makes Largest Ever Contribution to Any Education Institution in the United States," Baltimore, November 18, 2018.
17 Bob Dynes, author interview, 2016.

18 Jim Stone, author interview, 2017.

19 In a 2001 paper for the Institute for Research on Public Policy, Ross Finnie asked "Brain Drain: Myth and Reality?" and answered, more the former than the latter. Even at the height of public concern in the 1990s, Canada recorded an annual loss of only 450 physicians and 825 nurses, which Finnie concluded "is certainly not a question of great hordes of Canadians leaving en masse." Canada had managed down our physician population as part of an overall reduction in health care spending. When it came time to add more doctors, to cope with an aging population, Finnie argued we could turn to immigration from just about every corner of the world. (Ross Finnie, "Brain Drain: Myth and Reality?" Institute for Research on Public Policy, November 27, 2001).

20 In 2014, the Harper government appointed a panel led by David Naylor, the physician, medical researcher and former president of the University of Toronto, to explore healthcare innovation. The subsequent report, "Unleashing Innovation: Excellence for Healthcare in Canada," concluded "Canada has been spending relatively more money for thoroughly middling performance." The panel criticized a "visionary incrementalism" that was the result of an onerous approach to healthcare by the federal and provincial governments, a lack of scale and the sector's inability to develop long-term working capital. Among other recommendations, it called for a healthcare innovation agency with a ten-year commitment to an innovation fund.

21 Mamoru Watanabe, Melanie Comeau and Lynda Buske, "Analysis of International Migration Patterns Affecting Physician Supply in Canada," *Healthcare Policy Journal* 3, no. 4 (May 2008).

22 Robert Phillips Jr., Stephen Petterson, George E, Fryer Jr. and Walter Rosser, "The Canadian Contribution to the U.S. Physician Workforce," *Canadian Medical Association Journal* (April 10, 2007): 1083–87.

23 More perspective on the historic inflow and outflow of medical professionals is included in: Hugh Grant and Ronald, "Supply and Migration of Canadian Physicians, 1970–1995: Why We Should Learn to Love an Immigrant Doctor," *Canadian Journal of Regional Science* (Spring/Summer 1997): 157–68.

24 Dan Senor, author interview, 2017.

25 Canadian policy and attitudes are not the only factors in promoting emigration. The rise of nationalist policies, particularly in the United States and Britain, could make it more difficult for Canadians to gain work and even study visas. Donald Trump's "America First" campaign targeted tech workers under the H1B visa program. But even before Trump came to office, the federal government had cast an eye on northern migrants, including snowbirds who spend several months of the year in Florida, Arizona, California and other sunshine states. The introduction of electronic passport scanning, in 2012, made it easier for American tax authorities to track the days a Canadian is in the U.S., making them more susceptible to U.S. tax enforcement (Reuters, "Why Canadian Snowbirds Are Under US Scrutiny," February 11, 2013.)

26 Nestor E. Arellano, "Canada needs 182,000 people to fill those IT positions by 2019," *IT World Canada*, December 12, 2015.

27 Florida, *The Rise of the Creative Class*, 272.

28 Atef Chaudhury and Joey Loi, "Systems Design Engineering 2017 Class Profile," July 2017.

29 Max Greenwood, "Study from Waterloo Grads Details Canadian Brain Drain," Techvibes, August 21, 2017.

30 Robert R. Shrock, *Cecil and Ida Green: Philanthropists Extraordinaire* (Cambridge, MA: MIT Press, 1989), 16–18.

31 Royal Bank of Canada, "Humans Wanted: How Canadian Youth Can Thrive in the Age of Disruption," Toronto, March 27, 2018.

32 Amy Webb, *The Big Nine: How the Tech Titans and Their Thinking Machines Could Warp Humanity* (New York: PublicAffairs, 2019), 113.

Conclusion: The Everywhere People

1 Shivon Zilis, author interviews, 2016-19.

2 Sue Gardner, a Canadian journalist and media executive, tried to alter Silicon Valley's culture during her time running the Wikipedia Foundation from 2007 to 2014. As former head of cbc.ca, she was startled to see how little concern there was among technologists for the social consequences of their coding. As she told the *Globe and Mail* in 2017, "The first four months here, I went to major fundraising

meetings and there was never another woman—I asked myself is this 1922? It's hard when you're in the middle of whatever you're doing to get a sense of big shifts. Around 2010, I started to feel increasingly uncomfortable with what we were building. And it was becoming clear that targeted advertising was going to be pretty much the only business model that powered the industry." In 2018, she cofounded the Markup, a digital media venture funded by Craig Newmark, the creator of Craigslist, to shine a critical light on Big Tech (Cynthia Martin, "Sue Gardner: Hubris Is the Engine of Silicon Valley," *Globe and Mail*, April 14, 2017).

3 For a critical look at the Valley's diversity crisis, see Liza Mundy, "Why Is Silicon Valley So Awful to Women?" *The Atlantic*, April 2017.

4 Kindred boasts on its website of creating "machines with human-like intelligence." Its main customers are warehouses, for what it calls "AI-enhanced, piece-picking robots designed for ecommerce order fulfillment."

5 "Hey Alexa, What's Next for Voice Tech?" RBC Disruptors (podcast), March 28, 2019.

6 Parmy Olson, "Meet the Billionaire Who Defied Amazon and Built Wish, the World's Most-Downloaded E-commerce app," *Forbes*, March 13, 2019.

7 Denise Helly, "Diaspora: History of an Idea," in *Muslim Diaspora: Gender, Culture and Identity*, ed Haideh Moghissi (London: Routledge, 2006).

8 Adam Gopnik, "The Return of the Native," *New Yorker*, September 7, 2009.

9 Stephen Harper, *Right Here, Right Now: Politics and Leadership in the Age of Disruption* (Toronto: McClelland and Stewart, 2018).

Bibliography

BOOKS

Agtmael, Antoine van, and Fred Bakker. *The Smartest Places on Earth: Why Rustbelts are the Emerging Hotspots of Global Innovation.* New York: PublicAffairs, 2016.

Austin, Alvyn. *China's Millions: The China Inland Mission and Late Qing Society, 1832–1905*. Grand Rapids, MI: Eerdmans Publishing, 2007.

Austin, Alvyn and Jamie Scott, eds. *Canadian Missionaries, Indigenous Peoples: Representing Religion at Home and Abroad*. Toronto: University of Toronto Press, 2005.

Auden, W.H. and Christopher Isherwood. *Journey to a War*. London: Faber and Faber, 1939.

Bogdanovich, Peter. *Who the Devil Made It*. New York: Random House, 1999.

Brown, Robert Craig and Ramsay Cook. *Canada: A Nation Transformed, 1896–1921*. Toronto: McClelland and Stewart, 1974.

Clark, Andrew. *Stand and Deliver: Inside Canadian Comedy*. Toronto: Doubleday, 1997.

Clark, Joe. *How We Lead: Canada in a Century of Change*. Toronto: Random House Canada, 2013.

Farquharson, Robert. *For Your Tomorrow: Canadians and the Burma Campaign, 1941–45*. Victoria, BC: Trafford Publishing, 2004.

Fifield, Adam. *A Mighty Purpose: How Jim Grant Sold the World on Saving Its Children*. New York: Other Press, 2015.

Florida, Richard. *The Rise of the Creative Class:* Revisited. New York: Basic Books, 2012.

Hannant, Larry, ed. *The Politics of Passion: Norman Bethune's Writing and Art*. Toronto: University of Toronto Press, 1998.

Harper, Stephen. *Right Here, Right Now: Politics and Leadership in the Age of Disruption*. Toronto: McClelland and Stewart, 2018.

Helly, Denise. "Diaspora: History of an Idea." In *Muslim Diaspora: Gender, Culture and Identity*, edited by Haideh Moghissi, 3-22. London: Routledge, 2006.

Hochschild, Adam. *Spain in Our Hearts: Americans in the Spanish Civil War, 1936–1939*. Boston: Houghton Mifflin Harcourt, 2016.

Howard, Victor. *Mackenzie-Papineau Battalion: The Canadian Contingent in the Spanish Civil War*. Montreal & Kingston: McGill-Queen's University Press, 1987.

Hussey, Harry. *My Pleasures and Palaces*. New York: Doubleday, 1968.

Ignatieff, Michael. *Fire and Ashes: Success and Failure in Politics*. Cambridge, MA: Harvard University Press, 2013.

Jedwab, Jack, ed. *The Multiculturalism Question: Debating Identity in 21st Century Canada*. Montreal & Kingston: McGill-Queen's University Press, 2014.

Johnston, David. *The Idea of Canada: Letters to a Nation*. Toronto: Penguin Random House, 2016.

Johnston, David. *Trust: Twenty Ways to Build a Better Country*. Toronto: Penguin Random House, 2018.

Kilborn, Omar. *Heal the Sick: An Appeal for Medical Missions in China*. Toronto: Missionary Society of the Methodist Church, 1910.

MacKay, George Leslie. *From Far Formosa: The Island, its People and Missions*. New York: Fleming H. Revell Co., 1896.

al-Maktoum, Mohammed bin Rashid. *My Vision: Challenges in the Race for Excellence*. Dubai: Motivate Publishing, 2012.

Mann, Susan. *The Dream of Nation: A Social and Intellectual History of Quebec*, 2nd ed. Montreal & Kingston: McGill-Queen's University Press, 2002.

Martin, Roger. *The Opposable Mind: Winning through Integrative Thinking*. Boston: Harvard Business Press, 2009.

McLaughlin, Kenneth. *Out of the Shadow of Orthodoxy: Waterloo @ 50*. Waterloo, ON: University of Waterloo, 2007.

Midi, Amid. *The Art of Pixar Short Films*. San Francisco: Chronicle Books, 2009.

Miller, Rory. *Desert Kingdoms to Global Powers: The Rise of the Arab Gulf.* New Haven, CT: Yale University Press, 2016

Minden, Karen. *Bamboo Stone: The Evolution of a Chinese Medical Elite*. Toronto: University of Toronto Press, 1994.

Pigott, Peter. *Canada in Sudan: War Without Borders*. Toronto: Dundurn Press, 2009.

Ramirez, Bruno. "Migration and National Consciousness: The Canadian Case." In *Citizenship and Those Who Leave: The Politics of Emigration and Expatriation*, edited by Nancy L. Green and Francois Weil, 211-23. Chicago: University of Illinois Press, 2007.

Ramo, Joshua Cooper. *The Seventh Sense: Power, Fortune and Survival in the Age of Networks*. New York: Little Brown & Co., 2016.

Saunders, Doug. *Maximum Canada: Why 35 Million Canadians Are Not Enough*. Toronto: Knopf, 2017.

Scott, Jamie S., ed. *The Religions of Canadians*. Toronto: University of Toronto Press, 2011.

Scott, Munroe. *McClure: The China Years of Dr. Bob McClure*. Toronto: Canec Publishing and Supply House, 1977.

Shrock, Robert R. *Cecil and Ida Green: Philanthropists Extraordinaire*. Cambridge, MA: MIT Press, 1989.

Simpson, Jeffrey. *Star-Spangled Canadians: Canadians Living the American Dream*. Toronto: HarperCollins, 2000.

Spence, Jonathan. *To Change China: Western Advisers in China, 1620–1960*. New York: Little Brown, 1969.

Stewart, Roderick and Sharon Stewart. *Phoenix: The Life of Norman Bethune*. Montreal & Kingston: McGill-Queen's University Press, 2011.

Tapscott, Don and Alex Tapscott. *Blockchain Revolution: How the Technology Behind Bitcoin Is Changing Money, Business, and the World.* Toronto: Penguin Random House, 2016.

Wagner, Caroline. *The New Invisible College: Science for Development*. Washington, DC: Brookings Institution Press, 2008.

Webb, Amy. *The Big Nine: How the Tech Titans and Their Thinking Machines Could Warp Humanity*. New York: PublicAffairs, 2019.

Welsh, Jennifer. *At Home in the World: Canada's Global Vision for the 21st Century*. Toronto: HarperCollins, 2004.
Woodcock, George. *The Canadians*. London: Faber & Faber, 1970.
Zahra, Tara. *The Great Departure: Mass Migration from Eastern Europe and the Making of the Free World*. New York: W.W. Norton, 2016.

REPORTS AND PAPERS

Action Canada. "Where in the World Is Canada? Building a Global Network of Canadians Abroad." Ottawa, February 2011.
Asal, Houda. "Community Sector Dynamics and the Lebanese Diaspora: Internal Fragmentation and Transnationalism on the Web." e-Diasposa Project, Foundation Maison des Sciences de l'Homme, Paris, April 2012.
Asia Pacific Foundation of Canada. "Canadians Abroad: Canada's Global Asset." Vancouver, May 2011.
Barton, Dominic (chair). "The Path to Prosperity: Resetting Canada's Growth Trajectory." Advisory Council on Economic Growth, Ottawa, December 2017.
Belanger, Damien-Claude and Claude Belanger. "French Canadian Emigration to the United States, 1840–1930." Marianopolis College, Montreal, August 2000.
Biggs, Margaret and Roland Paris (co-chairs). "Global Education for Canadians: Equipping Young Canadians to Succeed at Home & Abroad." Report of the Study Group on Global Education. Centre for International Policy Studies, University of Ottawa and Munk School of Global Affairs, University of Toronto, November 2017.
Bitran, Maurice and Serene Tran. "Diaspora Nation: An Inquiry into the Economic Potential of Diaspora Networks in Canada." Mowat Centre, University of Toronto, September 2013.
Blouw, Max (chair). "Competing in a Global Innovation Economy: The Current State of R&D in Canada: Expert Panel on the State of Science and Technology and Industrial Research and Development in Canada." Council of Canadian Academies. Ottawa, April 2018.
Boyle, Mark and Rob Kitchin. "A Diaspora Strategy for Canada? Enriching Debate through Heightening Awareness of International

Practice." Asia Pacific Foundation of Canada, Vancouver, May 2011.

Canadian Bureau for International Education. "A World of Learning: Canada's Performance and Potential in International Education." Ottawa, November 2016.

Chakma, Amit (chair). "International Education a Key Driver of Canada's Future Prosperity." Advisory Panel on Canada's International Education, Ottawa, August 2012.

Chant, John. "The Passport Package: Rethinking the Citizenship Benefits of Non-Resident Canadians." Backgrounder No. 99, C.D. Howe Institute, Toronto, December 2006.

Chouikh, Malek and Allison McHugh, Neil Peet, Caroline Senini and Sahl Syed. "Canada's Expatriates." Munk School of Global Affairs, University of Toronto, March 2015.

Cooper, Laura. "Attracting International Talent." RBC Economics, Toronto, May 2017.

DeVoretz, Don and Ajay Parasram. "Crises and Canadians Abroad: A Case for a Ministry of Canadians Abroad?" Asia Pacific Foundation of Canada, Vancouver, March 2010.

Di Nino, Consiglio (chair). "The Evacuation of Canadians from Lebanon in July 2006: Implications for the Government of Canada." Senate Committee on Foreign Affairs and International Trade, Ottawa, May 2007.

Dion, Patrice and Mireille Vezina. "Emigration from Canada to the United States from 2000 to 2006." Canadian Social Trends, Statistics Canada, Ottawa, April 2014.

Dumont, Jean-Christophe, and Georges Lemaître. "Counting Immigrants and Expatriates in OECD Countries: A New Perspective." Organization for Economic Co-operation and Development Social, Migration and Employment Working Papers, Paris, June 2005.

Finch, David. "Petroleum Industry Oral History Project: Mike Miller." Glenbow Museum, Calgary, April 2004.

Finnie, Ross. "The Brain Drain: Myth and Reality—What It Is and What Should Be Done." Institute for Research on Public Policy, Ottawa, January 2001.

Florida, Richard and Scott Jackson. "Sonic City: The Evolving Economic Geography of the Music Industry." Martin Prosperity Institute, Toronto, January 2008.

Fullilove, Michael. "World Wide Webs: Diasporas and the International System." Lowy Institute for International Policy, Sydney, February 2008.

Guo, Sheng-Ping. "Ideology, Identity, and a New Role in World War Two: A Case Study of the Canadian Missionary Dr. Richard Brown in China, 1938–1939." In Historical Papers 2015: Canadian Society of Church History, Emanuel College, University of Toronto, 2016.

Lawrance, Jill. "Inter-Provincial Post-Secondary Student Mobility: A review of data sources from a British Columbia perspective." British Columbia Council on Admissions and Transfer. Vancouver, November 2009.

Lew, Byron, and Bruce Cater. "The Language of Opportunity: Canadian Interregional and International Migration, 1911–1951." Working Paper, Department of Economics, Trent University, Peterborough, ON, February 2013.

Loat, Alison. "Canada is Where Canadians Are: The Canadian Expatriate as an Element of International Policy." Working paper. Priorities and Planning Secretariat, Privy Council Office, Ottawa, April 2004.

Mikalson, Kaarina. "Spain's Democracy Talks to Canada: Pamphlets and Tours During the Spanish Civil War." As part of "Canada and the Spanish Civil War," multimedia project, Dalhousie University, Halifax, February 2013.

Momani, Bessma and Jillian Stirk. "The Diversity Dividend: Canada's Global Advantage." Centre for International Governance Innovation, Waterloo, ON, April 2017.

Naylor, David (chair). "Investing in Canada's Future: Strengthening the Foundations of Canadian Research." Advisory Panel on Federal Support for Fundamental Science, Ottawa, April 2017.

Naylor, David (chair). "Unleashing Innovation: Excellent Healthcare for Canada: Report of the Advisory Panel on Healthcare Innovation." Ottawa, July 2015.

Parasram, Ajay. "Us and Them: The Plumbing and Poetry of Citizenship Policy and the Canadians Abroad." Canadians Abroad Project, Asia Pacific Foundation of Canada, Vancouver, June 2010.

Royal Bank of Canada. "Humans Wanted: How Canadian Youth Can Thrive in the Age of Disruption." Toronto, July 2018.

Schwanen, Daniel. “Putting the Brain Drain in Context: Canada and the Global Competition for Scientists and Engineers.” C.D. Howe Institute, Toronto, April 2000.

Singer, Peter (chair). “Canadians Making a Difference: The Expert Panel on Canada’s Strategic Role in Global Health.” Canadian Academy of Health Sciences, Ottawa, November 2011.

United Nations Department of Economic and Social Affairs. “International migrant stock: By destination and origin.” New York, 2015.

Vertovec, Steven. “The Political Importance of Diasporas.” Centre on Migration, Policy and Society, University of Oxford, January 2005.

World Bank, “Data on Outward Remittance Flows,” Migration and Development Brief 31, Washington, DC, April 2019.

Yu, Sherry. “Mapping Canadian Diasporic Media: The Existence and Significance of Communicative Spaces for Overseas Canadians.” Canadians Abroad Project, Asia Pacific Foundation of Canada, Vancouver, March 2010.

Zhang, Kenny. “Global Canadians: A Survey of the Views of Canadians Abroad.” Asia Pacific Foundation of Canada, Vancouver, September 2007.

ARTICLES

Adam, Hajo, Otilia Obodaru, Jackson G. Lu, William Maddux and Adam Galinsky. “How Living Abroad Helps You Develop a Clearer Sense of Self.” *Harvard Business Review*, May 22, 2018.

Adams, Michael. “Canada’s Do-it-Yourself Foreign Aid: Let’s Make It Easier to Send Money Abroad.” *Globe and Mail*, March 28, 2014.

Barton, Dominic. “Capitalism for the Long Term.” *Harvard Business Review*, March 2011.

Barton, Dominic, and Mark Wiseman. “Focussing Capital on the Long Term.” *Harvard Business Review*, January–February 2014.

Daniels, Craig. “The Talent War.” Communitech News, Waterloo, April 2019.

Dehaas, Josh. “Canadian Students Need to Go to China, but They Need Some Help.” *Maclean’s*, November 15, 2016.

DeVoretz, Don, and Chona Iturralde. "Why Do Highly Skilled Canadians Stay in Canada?" *Policy Options*, March 1, 2001.

Frank, Gillian. "If Canada Is Back, Let's Restore Expats' Right to Vote." *Globe and Mail*, November 17, 2015.

Gelber, Lionel. "Canada's New Stature." *Foreign Affairs*, January 1946.

———. "What Is a Canadian?" *Free World*, January 1946.

———. "A Marriage of Inconvenience." *Foreign Affairs*, January 1963.

Goodyear, Dana. "Man of Extremes." *New Yorker*, October 26, 2009.

Gopnik, Adam. "The Return of the Native." *New Yorker*, September 7, 2009.

———. "We Could All Have Been Canadians." *The New Yorker*, May 15, 2017.

Johnson, J. Keeler, "The Global Racing Empire of Sheikh Mohammed bin Rashid al Maktoum." *The Sport*, September 11, 2017.

Johnson, Tim. "Why Do So Many Canadian Students Refuse to Study Abroad?" *University Affairs*, May 25, 2016.

Kamping-Carder, Leigh. "Canadians Among Us!" *Observer*, July 31, 2008.

Kuhn, Peter. "The Brain Drain: A View from Stateside." *Policy Options*, November 1, 2001.

Mazurkewich, Karen. "Who's Who: The CGI Kingpins." *Playbook*, January 11, 1999.

Mueller, Richard. "What Happened to the Canada-United States Brain Drain of the 1990s? New Evidence from the 2000 US Census." *Journal of International Migration and Integration*, June 2006.

VanderKlippe, Nathan. "Canadian Architect Living in China Hailed as 'Guiding Light' in the Pursuit of Healthier Buildings." *Globe and Mail*, April 22, 2019.

Ward, Barbara. "The First International Nation." *Canadian Forum*, October 1968.

Zarifa, David and David Walters. "Revisiting Canada's Brain Drain: Evidence from the 2000 Cohort of Canadian University Graduates." *Canadian Public Policy* 34, no. 3 (September 2008): 305-19.

Zhao, John, Doug Drew and Scott Murray. "Brain Drain and Brain Gain: The Migration of Knowledge Workers from and to Canada." *Education Quarterly Review*, May 24, 2000.

Zhang, Kenny. "Canadians Abroad: Policy Challenges for Canada." *Korean Review of Canadian Studies*, November 2009.

Index

JOHN STACKHOUSE is a nationally bestselling author and one of Canada's leading voices on innovation and economic disruption. Since 2014, he has served as senior vice-president in the Office of the CEO at Royal Bank of Canada, leading the organization's research and thought leadership on economic, technological and social change. Previously, he was editor-in-chief of the *Globe and Mail* and editor of *Report on Business,* and for most of the 1990s a foreign correspondent for the newspaper in Asia. He is a senior fellow at the C.D. Howe Institute and University of Toronto's Munk School of Global Affairs, and author of the books *Out of Poverty: And Into Something More Comfortable*; *Timbit Nation: A Hitchhiker's View of Canada*; and *Mass Disruption: Thirty Years on the Front Lines of a Media Revolution.*